# THE WAITING LAND

# THE WAITING LAND
## *A Spell in Nepal*

### Dervla Murphy

**THE OVERLOOK PRESS**
Woodstock, New York

First published in 1987 by
The Overlook Press
Lewis Hollow Road
Woodstock, New York 12498

Library of Congress Cataloging-in-Publication Data
Murphy, Dervla, 1931-
    The waiting land.

    Reprint. Originally published: London : Murray, 1967.
    Nepal—Description and travel. 2. Murphy, Dervla,
1931-    —Journeys—Nepal. I. Title.
DS493.53.M87 1987 915.49′6 87-5736
ISBN 0-87951-251-2 (cloth)
ISBN 0-87951-305-5 (paper)

Printed in the United States of America

To Brian,
Daphne, Robin and Peter
with love

# Contents

# *Prologue*

My six months among the Tibetans in 1963 had shown me that many refugees do not deserve the haloes with which they have been presented by sentimental fund-raisers in Europe or America. But by the time one has been disillusioned by Tibetans one has also been captivated by them; though unpleasant individuals and events may demolish the idealised version there remains an indestructible respect for the courage, humour and good manners that mark most Tibetan communities.

Before leaving India, early in 1964, I had determined to come back to the Tibetans as soon as possible. However, refugee situations can change quickly and by the spring of 1965 conditions in India had improved so much that nothing really useful remained to be done by an untrained volunteer, and I felt that it would be wrong to inflict on the Tibetans yet another aimless 'Tib-worshipper'. But then came an item of news from Nepal concerning a recently-formed refugee camp in the Pokhara Valley, where 500 Tibetans were living as family units in 120 tents with only one Western volunteer to help them. It was considered that here I would at least not be in the way, even if my limitations prevented me from achieving much, so on 5 April 1965 I flew from Dublin to London to prepare for the journey to Nepal.

In contrast with my January 1963 departure from Ireland that flight seemed sadly drained of adventure; but my wanderlust revived next day when I went to the Royal Nepalese Embassy to apply for a visa. There I was presented with a leaflet headed 'A Guide to those who intend to visit Kathmandu, capital of Nepal', and with a booklet—poorly printed in Kathmandu for the Department of Tourism—entitled *Nepal in a Nutshell*. The leaflet announced with rather touching inaccuracy that, 'The best months to visit the valley are February–April and September–November. The rest of the months are either very wet or too cold'; but the booklet truthfully claimed that 'The cold season is pleasant throughout Nepal with bright sun-

shine and blue skies'—and at once I warmed to this bewildered
country which couldn't make up its mind how best to sell itself
to fussy tourists. Then, reading on, I found a still more endear-
ing statement to the effect that 'The fascination of Biratnagar
lies in its picturesque spots and industrial areas. Biratnagar has
some of the largest industrial undertakings in Nepal'. Somehow
it is difficult to believe that those travellers who are fascinated
by 'industrial undertakings' would ever go to Nepal to gratify
this particular passion.

On the booklet's first page Tibet was referred to as 'the Tibet
Region of China'—a politic 'siding with the boss' which would
have infuriated me were I not so aware of Nepal's terror lest she
should herself soon become 'the Nepal Region of China'. Merely
to glance at a map of Asia reveals the uncertainty of the kingdom's future; it is a slender strip of land squeezed between
Chinese-controlled Tibet and a decreasingly neutral India, and
already a mysteriously-motivated Communist army is arrayed
along its northern frontier. Some experts argue that the Central
Himalayas are themselves defence enough against any army and
that a south-bound Chinese invasion force would always have
the good sense to skirt Nepal; but the Nepalese Government has
not forgotten how cunningly Tibet was subdued within a decade
and at present Nepal's diplomats and politicians are almost
dizzy from their efforts to placate simultaneously both East and
West.

On 13 April I spent two very interesting and instructive hours
at the Nepalese Embassy's New Year party. *Nepal in a Nutshell*
had informed me that 'The State was integrated by King
Prithvi Narayan Shah the Great in 1769', but now I began to
realise that Nepal's nationhood is a very artificial thing. For all
the tempering influence of a London social function it was soon
clear that the various groups to whom I talked represented a
basically tribal society which has only recently acquired the
ill-fitting political garments of a modern state. The mistrust,
jealousy and dislike of one ethnic and religious group for another
showed through repeatedly, and it was interesting to compare
the suave, astute Ranas and the ambitious, slightly arrogant
Chetris with the inarticulate but gay little Gurungs and the
poised, cheerful Sherpas of Tibetan descent. One wonders if

there will be time to weld all these dissimilar tribes into a truly united nation before either the Chinese or the Americans annihilate every ancient Nepalese tradition. It seems regrettable that any such welding process should be considered necessary, but perhaps only thus can Nepal hope to preserve her independence.

The flight to Delhi was a mixed experience. We left London Airport at 4.15 p.m. on 21 April and, as always, I resented the slickness of flying and felt too nervous to sleep. As we flew over Erzurum and Tabriz I remembered 'the old days', when I had cycled on Roz through that region, and inevitably I experienced an acute sense of anti-climax.

Then came an uncannily beautiful descent to Teheran. At a height of five miles the engines were suddenly switched off and we began to glide soundlessly down, down, down through the darkness; to look out then and feel the silence and see the gigantic length of wing in a faint shimmer of moonlight gave me the fairy-story illusion of being carried along by some monstrous, softly sailing moth.

Here I disembarked—for Auld Lang Syne—and unmistakably I was back in Asia, where air hostesses mix their passenger lists and then fly off their nests in a delightfully unprofessional way. At European airports hostesses are trim machines who rarely muddle anything and scarcely register on a passenger's mind as fellow-beings: but here they are girls who flush with anxiety and snap angrily at each other because all the passengers bound for New York were very nearly sent to Hong Kong.

When we emerged on to the tarmac two hours later the sky was paling above the mountains and, as we climbed, the stark symmetry of Demavand soared high and proud above hundreds of lesser peaks—a flawless blue cone against a backdrop of orange cloud; and immediately beyond stretched the Caspian, its metallic flatness oddly surprising at the base of the mountains.

One has to admit that just occasionally flying provides beauty of a quality otherwise unattainable. Below us now a scattered school of porpoise-shaped cloudlets lay motionless and colourless in the void; and down on that plain which Roz and I had traversed en route to Meshed several tiny lakes were looking weirdly like pools of blood as they reflected the pre-sunrise flare. We had regained our normal cruising altitude when a crimson ball appeared so suddenly above the horizon that it seemed to have been flung over the earth's rim by an invisible hand—and momentarily I was too taken aback to recognise this object as the sun. Then it climbed—so rapidly that one could *see* it moving —until the sky above the horizon was pale blue, shading off, because of our altitude, to an extraordinary navy blue at the zenith.

We soon turned south, and now the Great Desert below us was covered in cloud so that one looked down on a limitless expanse of grotesque white softness, in which were visible broad 'valleys' and narrow 'gorges' and 'mountains' that threw shadows as real mountains would in early sunshine—the whole 'landscape' exquisitely distorted and eerily immobile, as though all that vapour were frozen solid.

At 5.45 a.m. we touched down at Palam Airport. In a desperate effort to retain some grip on reality I had kept my watch at Greenwich Mean Time, but now I put it on to 10.15 a.m., before staggering out into the dusty glare. Luckily the day was 'cool' (only eighty-five degrees Fahrenheit in the shade) though coming from forty-four degrees in London I can't say it felt particularly cool to me.

As the rickety old airport bus rattled and blared its way along the narrow road to New Delhi I was conscious of an extraordinary sense of peace. When we were approaching Connaught Circus, through the usual tangle of loaded cyclists, ambling buffaloes, sleek cars, lean pedestrians and bouncing, Sikh-driven 'chuff-chuffs', I tried to define what I was feeling— but could only think of it as the peace of poverty. People may jeer at this phrase as romantic nonsense, yet to arrive suddenly in India after a fortnight's immersion in an affluent society does induce a strong sense of liberation from some intangible but threatening power. One is aware of man being free here, at the deepest level, as he cannot possibly be in societies where elaborately contrived pressures daily create new, false 'needs', and wither his delight in small and simple joys.

At Dharamsala, where I had previously worked in the Tibetan Refugee Nursery, it was a joy to see how enormously conditions had improved since my departure. Pema Janzum, the younger sister of His Holiness the Dalai Lama, is now running the camp, and her intelligence, common sense and flair for leadership have transformed the place from a squalid, disease-ridden inferno to a model nursery full of bouncing, rosy-cheeked Tiblets.

Since 1961 the Dalai Lama himself has been living in a heavily guarded bungalow quite close to the Nursery. His residence is usually given the courtesy title of 'Palace', though in fact it is far from being palatial—which no doubt pleases its simple occupant, even if the refugees are saddened to see 'Yishy Norbu' living at such a remove from the splendours of the Potala.

On the morning after my arrival His Holiness generously consented to receive me in audience and I found the change in him scarcely less remarkable than the change in the camp. During my first audience, sixteen months earlier, he had given me the impression of being a little unsure of himself and remaining rather on his guard against foreign observers; but now he seemed much more confident and relaxed, and this meeting felt less like an audience than a discussion between two people with an absorbing mutual interest. Our conversation centred on the problems of the refugees in Nepal, where the political difficulties of the host country create many special complications, and as we talked I realised that it would be impossible for me to enter in my diary and send through the post any detailed accounts of our work at Pokhara Camp. In this sort of situation what may appear to be minutiae can on occasions have the most disconcerting significance.

After two happy days at Dharamsala I went on to Mussoorie —a sixteen-hour journey by bus, train, bus and finally a shared taxi from Dehra Dun. On leaving the taxi at the edge of the town the first person I saw was Jigme Taring, a Tibetan–Sikkimese prince who runs the co-educational six-hundred-pupil Tibetan school and prefers to be known as a 'Mister'. During my previous visit to Mussoorie he had been away in Sikkim, but though we had never met we simultaneously recognised each other and drove together to Happy Valley, the appropriately-named centre of the local Tibetan community.

For all his illustrious ancestry Jigme Sumchan Wang-po
Namgyal Taring is a typical Tibetan—simple and gentle, with
a keen intelligence and a tremendous sense of humour. He and
Mrs Taring, who runs the Tibetan Homes Foundation, illustrate
the best side of feudalism; they feel that the thousands of peasants
in exile are partly their responsibility—a logical view, though
one that is uncommon among rich Tibetan exiles.

The Tarings' Lhasa residence was near the Potala and during
the shelling of the Palace, in March 1959, it too was partially
demolished. Their first-hand account of the Lhasa Insurrection
interested me greatly because, on reading the Gelders' book,
*The Timely Rain*, it had seemed to me that among the authors'
few plausible arguments was one supporting the Chinese claim
that the Potala had *not* been heavily shelled. Yet Mr Taring,
who was then C.-in-C. of the Tibetan Army, has a ciné-film
of the actual shelling, taken by himself before he left the capital.
As Mrs Taring quietly pointed out he had obtained this film at
the risk of his life, realising how effectively it could counteract
Chinese propaganda and foreseeing its future historical
value.

When His Holiness left the Summer Palace on 17 March
Mr Taring remained behind for two days, to help delude the
Chinese into believing that the Dalai Lama was still there. Then
he set out on foot for the Indian frontier with one companion—
the Tarings' present cook. Meanwhile Mrs Taring had fled on
horseback, also with one manservant, and months passed before
either knew that the other was safe.

It is significant that both Tarings unquestioningly followed
His Holiness into exile, making no attempt to rescue their
children and grandchildren. On first hearing their escape story,
two years ago, I was privately a little shocked by this 'desertion',
since in similar circumstances most Europeans would choose
to stand by their nearest and dearest. Yet after several hours'
conversation with the Tarings one realises that to them His
Holiness *is* their 'nearest and dearest'—not as an individual,
but as the living vessel containing the Spirit of Chenrezig.
Therefore their sacrifice of family loyalties to his needs was a
form of religious martyrdom; they each knew that in exile he
would require guidance from those few Tibetans who have

received a Western education but who still retain a religious faith as strong as that of the simplest peasant.

The most remarkable characteristic of Tibetan Buddhists is their freedom from bitterness against the Chinese. Despite the emotional scars discernible beneath the Tarings' courageous good humour neither shows the faintest flicker of hatred or anger when discussing the past; indeed they shrink from such reactions on the part of less spiritually disciplined Westerners like myself, who in this context cannot help but utter some impulsive condemnations. The manner in which most Tibetans distinguish between wrong actions and the individuals performing them—with whom they seem to sympathise as fellow-victims of Evil—made me uneasily aware of the immaturity of our susceptibility to petty propaganda.

In Mussoorie the Tarings occupy one large room, partitioned by a curtain into bedroom and living-room, which is rather less comfortable than many of the Homes run by Mrs Taring for Tiblets. The rest of this house accommodates some of the teaching staff, plus seventy-two small children. After we had gone to bed one of the children began to cry and at once Mr Taring hurried to investigate; he and Mrs Taring take it in turns to do 'night duty' in addition to working at least twelve hours a day seven days a week. My own room was a tiny cubbyhole, containing nothing but a charpoy, and it soothed me to observe such unusually austere standards being upheld by workers among the refugees.

# 1

## *The Iron Road to Rexaul*

*29 April 1965. Muzaffarpur Railway Station.*
*11.30 p.m.*

I'm now sitting in the Railway Ladies' Waiting Room being
almost asphyxiated by the stench of stale urine and surrounded
by recumbent Ladies. Some are on the floor on bedding-rolls,
others are lying on lumpy Victorian couches and two are curled
up on the table, their saris drawn over their faces. At present
I'm conscious only of being in *a* Railway Waiting Room,
enduring its unique combination of aesthetic repulsiveness,
physical discomfort and powers of suspending mental animation. Notice-boards tell me I'm in Muzaffarpur, but I could
as easily believe myself to be in Waterford or Milan.

The twenty-nine-hour journey from Dehra Dun was brief
by local standards, yet it was by far the longest train-ride of
my life and seemed decidedly penitential. The fare (one pound
eight shillings and fourpence all the way to Nepal) covered
reservation of a slatted wooden shelf, on which I slept quite
well last night, but by morning a gale-force wind was whipping
a dust-storm across the endless, arid, grey-yellow plain, and this
diabolical torture by Nature continued until dusk. Visibility
was down to about a hundred yards, the hot sky was sullen with
dust, and dust and sweat formed a mask of mud on my face.
All morning I sat in a semi-coma, reflecting that at last I was
experiencing *real* hardship; compared with such a journey
cycling to India is just too easy.

However, the worst was yet to come. At Lucknow I changed
trains and found myself sharing an eight-seater compartment
with seventeen Gurkha soldiers going home on leave. Each was
carrying a vast amount of kit and initially it seemed a sheer
physical impossibility for all of them to enter the compartment;
yet it's not for nothing that the Gurkhas have won so many

8

V.C.s and enter it they did, bravely disregarding the possibility that we would all suffocate to death long before the journey ended. At first they had appeared to be slightly nonplussed by the sight of a dishevelled Memsahib in one corner, but they rapidly decided that I was best ignored and within seconds I found myself nine-tenths buried beneath a pile of bed-rolls, haversacks, wicker baskets and tin trunks. This pyramid was then scaled by two nimble little Gurungs, who expertly inserted themselves into the crevice between the topmost trunk and the roof and immediately began to dice and smoke, dropping unquenched cigarette ends onto my head at regular intervals. I don't doubt that the Gurkhas are a wonderful people, but somehow today I never really managed to appreciate them.

Then, soon after dusk, my luck changed. When we stopped at a junction I strenuously effected an earthquake in the carriage, bringing Gurungs and trunks mildly to grief as I fought my way out through the window. No one had told me where to change trains and as it was now essential to find out I went hobbling anxiously down the platform, every muscle knotted with cramp, in search of some knowledgeable-looking individual. Having questioned three officials, who each indicated that they couldn't care less whether I ended up in Calcutta or Kathmandu, I was enormously relieved to come upon an Englishwoman strolling along the platform beside the first-class carriages. She at once assured me that I did not have to change until Muzaffarpur—and then we began to discuss our respective destinations. When the Englishwoman mentioned that she was returning to Dharan I said, 'Then you must know Brigadier Pulley?' (to whom I had a letter of introduction) and she exclaimed, 'But I'm his wife!' A moment later the Brigadier himself appeared and, when everyone had made the appropriate remarks about the dimensions of the earth, the Pulleys very kindly invited me to continue my journey in their air-conditioned coach. By then my addiction to 'travelling rough' had been so thoroughly—if temporarily—cured that it was difficult for me to refrain from hugging my benefactors.

It is now only 1.45 a.m. and the daily train for Rexaul, on the Nepalese frontier, does not leave until 6 a.m.; but I'm afraid to sleep lest I should fail to wake in time.

*30 April. Rexaul Railway Station Retiring-room.*
*9 p.m.*

This pedantically-named apartment—no doubt a verbal relic
of the era when trains were introduced into India—is equipped
with two charpoys, a lukewarm shower and a defunct electric
fan; but despite this wealth of refinements I now feel irremedi-
ably allergic to everything even remotely associated with railways.

Today's hundred-mile journey on a narrow-gauge track took
eight blistering hours. The elderly engine was falling asunder
and at each village it stopped, lengthily, to pull itself together
before moving at walking speed to the next village. Also it
killed a young man; but no one took much notice of this grim
sight and we were only delayed ten or fifteen minutes longer
than usual. The police did not appear (perhaps there are none
in these remote villages) and one gathered that the event was
unimportant. My Nepalese neighbour told me that it was probably a case of suicide, as people with family or financial
troubles frequently throw themselves under trains; and this
seemed a likely explanation, since our snail-paced engine could
hardly take anyone unawares.

This morning, on the platform at Muzaffarpur, I met an
Irish boy named Niall who was travelling to Kathmandu with
a Swiss youth named Jean and an American girl rather disconcertingly known as Loo. Loo had recently arrived in India
on a round-the-world air trip, and had been persuaded by the
boys, against her own better judgment, to sample life in the
raw by going overland to Nepal. She spent most of today
pointing out just how much better her own judgment was, and
though recriminations seemed futile at that stage one could see
her point of view.

Certainly life cannot be much rawer anywhere than it is in
these villages of Bihar. Throughout the Punjab one rarely encounters that extremity of poverty traditionally associated with
India—but here one does. And, as the hot, squalid hours passed
slowly, I began to take a more lenient view of our affluent
society. The people all around us seemed inwardly dead, mere
mechanically-moving puppets, their expressions dulled by per-

manent suffering. To look at their bodies—so malformed, starved and diseased—and to sense the stuntedness of their minds and spirits made me feel quite guilty about helping Tibetans when so many Indians are in such need. Yet one doubts if Indians ever can be helped in the sense that Tibetans can. Apart from the vastness of their current material problem the very nature of the people themselves seems stubbornly to defy most outside attempts at alleviation.

Rexaul is a smelly, straggling little border-town, overpopulated by both humans and cattle. It has an incongruous air of importance, since all the Kathmandu truck-traffic passes through its streets, yet its cosmopolitanism is limited. When I went to the Post Office—a dark wooden shack—to air-mail the first instalment of this diary to Ireland my request caused unprecedented chaos. To begin with, registration was not permissible after 4 p.m. and it was now 5.30; however, when I had flatteringly explained that I wanted to post from India rather than Nepal the senior clerk consented to make an exception to this rule. But then came the knotty problem of deciding where Ireland was—and the even knottier problem of determining the air-mail registration fee for such an outlandish destination. In the end no fewer than seven men spent twenty minutes working it all out, consulting thick, fly-blown volumes, weighing and reweighing the package on ancient scales of doubtful accuracy, checking and re-checking interminable sums on filthy scraps of paper and finally laboriously copying the address, in triplicate, on to the receipt docket—with hilarious results, since even intelligent Europeans often find my handwriting illegible. I suppose it *is* possible that the package will eventually arrive on the Aran Islands, but one can't help having horrible doubts.

*1 May. Kathmandu.*

The ninety-mile Tribhuvan Rajpath, named after King Mahendra's father, was built by Indian engineers during the 1950's. At present it is Nepal's only completed motor-road—though the Chinese are working hard on an uncomfortably symbolic continuation of it from Kathmandu to Lhasa—and it must be one of the most remarkable engineering feats in the world. Yet

the Rajpath's inexplicable narrowness (or is this defect perhaps
explicable in strategic terms?) means that trucks are often ram-
med against cliffsides by other trucks, or go skidding over precipices in successful but unrewarding attempts to avoid head-on
collisions. However, the art of truck-driving is only nine years
old in Nepal, so perhaps it is not surprising that most drivers
apparently long for a rapid reincarnation; doubtless the next
generation will have learnt that too much rakshi does not aid
the safe negotiation of six hair-pin bends per mile.

In view of the Rajpath's reputation it is understandable that
trucks are forbidden to carry foreigners. A high mortality rate
among visitors might be bad for the tourist trade, so in theory all
foreigners use the senile bus that leaves Rexaul daily at 6 a.m.
But the bus fare is Rs. 16/- while the truck fare is only Rs. 8/-,
and therefore many travellers blithely ignore the illegality of
trucks. Fortunately the border police also ignore it, or perhaps
are unaware of the law's existence—an anomaly that would be
typical of this deliciously topsy-turvy land.

This morning we left the railway station at six o'clock and
walked the two miles to the border. The next three hours were
spent wandering in and out of tumble-down customs, police and
passport offices, where courteous but clueless officials enter-
tained us to innumerable glasses of tea while trying to make up
their minds exactly *why* they wanted to interview us. One felt
that this profusion of bureaucratic formality was a game, since
none of these men seemed to comprehend the nature of his
job clearly enough to take it seriously. The whole performance
appeared to be part of Nepal's sudden attempt to get 'with it',
after centuries of deliberate isolation, and over all those glasses
of tea the stiff, alien formalities spontaneously blossomed into
flexible, indigenous informalities.

The Nepalese expertly elude the tyranny of Time simply by
refusing to allow it to affect any of their actions. We waited
endlessly for everything: for glasses of tea to be carried on trays
from the bazaar, for a policeman's bunch of keys to be fetched
from his home down the road, for an adjustable rubber stamp
which would not adjust to be dissected (and finally abandoned
in favour of a pen), for a Passport Officer to track down Ireland
(whose existence he seriously questioned) in a dog-eared atlas

from which the relevant pages had long since been torn, and for the Chief Customs Officer, who was afflicted by a virulent form of dysentry, to withdraw to a nearby field between inspecting each piece of luggage.

To me all this was enjoyably relaxing and precisely what one expects at a Nepalese border-post—though I suspect that these dilatory methods will twang on my nerves when I am encountering them daily. But unfortunately my companions reacted adversely to this subjugation of Time, and the Nepalese were bewildered to find that neither their conversation nor their tea could begin to compensate for so many 'wasted' hours. In the end I felt thoroughly ashamed of Loo's querulous impatience, Jean's contemptuous sneers and Niall's ill-tempered commands—none of which had the slightest speeding-up effect on the Nepalese. Yet no doubt I myself will behave equally badly on occasion during the next few months.

When at last we were freed we walked another mile or so to the little town of Birganj and there, after much playing-off of drivers one against another, we secured seats in the back of an almost empty truck.

By now the sun's rays were fierce and we had no protection against them as we covered the next twenty miles. This section of the Terai has been spoiled by the railhead and road, and as nothing of interest lay on either side I was all the time eagerly looking north; but the heat haze restricted visibility, and only on approaching the village of Bhainse could one see that gigantic mountain barrier which here rises so suddenly and splendidly from Northern India's eternity of flatness.

At Bhainse we stopped outside an eating-house, and without bothering to replace my boots I hopped out of the truck into the welcome shadow. Loo declined any refreshment, after one shuddering glance around the mud-floored, fly-infested interior, but the rest of us enjoyed piles of rice moistened by dahl and curds—with a very hot curry for the driver. Here the devastating poverty of Bihar was no longer apparent, though otherwise there was little to distinguish these people from their Indian neighbours; only the style of domestic architecture (already some Newari influence was evident) indicated that we had entered Nepal.

When the driver had demolished his Everest of rice he told us to wait in the eating-house, and twenty minutes later I had to walk half a mile, barefooted, to rejoin the truck beyond a toll-gate. By now the sun was directly overhead and melting tar on the road forced me to cover this distance by running about ten paces, sitting down to get my agonised feet off the tar, jumping up when my behind became equally agonised—and so on . . . and on . . . and on. The locals were vastly amused at this spectacle; but oddly enough the humour of the situation escaped me.

From Bhainse—which is almost at sea level—the road climbed steadily over the Churia and Chandragiri mountains, crossing a pass of more than 8,000 feet. On every side the slopes and crests were heavily wooded and freshly green and this abrupt ascent seemed most dramatic in contrast to the dead plains which stretch from Dehra Dun to Bhainse. At one point we could see below us the *twelve* hair-pin bends which we had rounded on our way up that particular mountain, and often the famous cable on which some goods are still brought from India to Kathmandu was visible overhead, its wires spanning the deep valleys from mountain-top to mountain-top. Until we crossed the pass no villages were visible, but at Bhainse the truck had filled up with cheerful, unkempt families who were returning home from marketing trips. These people, bred to walk everywhere, have been very quick to take advantage of the luxury of motor transport.

Even motoring up the Rajpath gives one a sense of achievement, felt on behalf of those Indian engineers and Nepalese coolies—many coolies were killed on the job—who had the brains and the guts to construct a road in direct defiance of the laws of Nature. Most Nepalese believe that the coolies' deaths were caused by enraged mountain-gods and I can sympathise with this view. The Rajpath is a triumphal example of man's ingenuity, but it is also an impertinent defacement and naturally the gods would resent having their mountains so humiliatingly brought to the heel of Progress.

We reached the pass at 3.30 and here the air was tinglingly crisp and keen. To steady our nerves we stopped for tea in a tiny hut near the forest's edge; a few moments earlier, when toiling around the last hair-pin bend, we had missed by inches a grossly overloaded jeep taking the corner at top speed.

Our descent to the Palang Valley was more gradual than the upward climb—though hardly less dangerous, for the truck's brakes were not of the best. The two-storey farmhouses scattered around the valley floor looked curiously European, with their curly red tiles and brown brick walls, and they were far more skilfully built than the average dwelling of rural India; I noticed that instead of chimneys square apertures were visible in the gable walls. The people were small, sturdy and gay, and groups of children shouted, waved and laughed as we passed; evidently many of the Nepalese are temperamentally closer to the Tibetans than to the Indians. On all sides this valley was guarded by mountains and, despite the encroachment of 'The Road', it retained an atmosphere of tranquil 'lostness'. Looking at the sunny expanse of cleverly terraced young wheat, and at the high-spirited children and bounding flocks of goats, I was very conscious of being in a new and pleasant country.

When the road began to climb again the nearby mountains became bare walls of reddish clay that reflected the slanting evening light like giant uncut jewels. I felt myself getting more and more excited as we passed the new, neat milestones saying 'Kathmandu 15 miles . . . 14 miles . . . 13 miles'—but then suddenly it was dark, and still we were slowly rounding bend after bend, though we had just passed a notice forbidding vehicles to use the Rajpath by night.

At 8.30 p.m. we stopped near the hamlet of Thankot, six miles from Kathmandu, where a tree-trunk on trestles blocks the road outside a Police-Passport-Customs check-post. Now the spice of melodrama filled the air. Our driver—using what can only be described as a hoarse whisper—instructed us to leave the truck quietly, go through the necessary hoops with officialdom, walk on a quarter of a mile and wait for him to retrieve us. We need take only our passports; everything else could safely be left where it was.

At this point my drab European rationality prompted me to wonder what the police would make of four Westerners, equipped only with a passport and two legs apiece, appearing out of pitch darkness on the rim of the Kathmandu Valley and producing visas which declared that they had entered the country a mere ten hours earlier. But at once I reproved my rationality for intruding on this first gay day in Nepal.

The check-point was enchanting—a tiny bamboo lean-to, containing an affable character arrayed in pyjamas and armed with a revolver. This officer peered briefly at our visas, by the light of a wick floating in a bowl of grease, and then politely made the required assumption that we had come from Rexaul by magic carpet. However, Loo's native honesty did cause a moment's tension. On being asked if she had cameras, transistors, tape-recorders or binoculars she admitted to one of each and Pyjamas, looking faintly irritated by such candour at so late an hour, dutifully asked her to produce them—whereupon she saw her indiscretion and stared through the low doorway in wild surmise, while the boys and I giggled cruelly. Our driver was in the adjacent tea-house, having something stronger than tea and stolidly feigning not to be acquainted with us, so any attempt to contact him would have been monumentally tactless. But Pyjamas obviously had a quick understanding and a kind heart for now he gestured grandly, saying "These things are not important"—and immediately we were released, our passports enriched by one more set of convulsed squiggles and solemn seals.

From Thankot the downhill road to Kathmandu was lined with flowering bottle-brush trees, and by the light of the head-lamps their long scarlet blossoms formed glowing curtains of colour on either side. I was a little puzzled not to see, somewhere on the valley floor, that shimmer of light which is to be expected after dark from even the least advanced capital city; but I later discovered that this was one of the not infrequent occasions upon which the urban electricity supply had quietly faded away.

It takes only a few moments to drive through the 'suburbs' of Kathmandu and by half-past nine I was standing in the city centre, beside 'Bhim's Folly'—a cigarette-like white tower erected for no apparent reason by Bhim Sen Thapa, that murderously scheming nineteenth-century ruler of Nepal who instigated the Prime Ministerial reign. The area around the Folly is the General Truck Terminal, and therefore the scene of much haggling, arguing and general commotion at all hours of the day or night; in fact it seems to provide the only sign of life in the city after dark. Already Loo and Niall had been led away by Jean, who is familiar with Kathmandu, and I now discovered that —as pronounced by me—the address to which I was going conveyed nothing whatever to any of the surrounding Nepalese. But eventually I observed two young men, clad in semi-Western fashion, who spoke some English and soon fixed me up with a cycle-rickshaw.

Half an hour later I was installed in this dingy but—by Asian standards—wildly expensive hotel. The charge is £1 per night for a large, filthy room, containing only a plank-bed and a roll of bug-infested bedding—and no breakfast will be provided. In itself the dirt leaves me unmoved, since I have survived even greater extremes of filth elsewhere, but the excessive charge moves me deeply. I only hope that it is not a reliable guide to the general cost of living in Nepal.

# 2

# *Kathmandu*

Yesterday began well when I heard after breakfast that
Sigrid Arnd—a Swiss friend first met when we were both working in India—is now living here; and last night she most generously invited me to stay in her Jawalkhel home, near Patan,
until I leave for Pokhara on 12 May.

Sigrid prefers to live reasonably close to the local level, and
she has proved that in this country one can create a very
attractive home through an imaginative adaptation of native
materials and customs. She rents a two-roomed wing of this
three-storey brick house, and the simple living-room—where
I'm now sitting—has a low, black, raftered ceiling, white-
washed walls and pale gold matting. Everything in the room
is both beautiful and Nepalese, and Sigrid's four-months-old
black and silver mongrel puppy is also both beautiful and
Nepalese. His name is Puchare ('Tail' in Nepali) and he has an
adorable personality, in addition to being a good deal more
ornamental than many an effete thoroughbred I've known. The
household is completed by Donbahadur, a Newari daily servant who shops intelligently in the bazaar and cooks like an
angel. (Many Westerners in Kathmandu won't even walk
through the bazaar, much less eat food that has been bought
there.) Donbahadur has a bubbling sense of fun, an almost
visible integrity and an awe-inspiring but quite effective
method of communicating through the medium of Swiss Ger-
man-cum-English. One senses that he approves Sigrid's appreciation of things Nepalese, which interests me; in India a
Memsahib would almost certainly lose face with the servants if
she did not maintain entirely European standards.

A small bathroom (with a cold shower but without a bath)
and an even smaller kitchen lead off this living-room, while at

the back a narrow wooden staircase, to Sigrid's bedroom, is concealed by a cupboard-like device. Outside, in the large, haphazard garden, twin giant poplars stand handsomely in one corner, and at the moment I can see Donbahadur in another corner, baking delicious bread in that mud-stove which is his contribution to the establishment's excellent system of improvisation. Beyond the ten-foot wall enclosing the garden runs a very wavy, very pot-holed and very dusty track, which unfortunately happens to be one of the valley's main roads, linking Kathmandu, Jawalkhel and Patan. At this season the frequent passage of buses envelops the garden in a veil of yellow, suffocating dust; only the tops of these vehicles are visible as they lurch slowly by, so one has the curious illusion of watching ships on a stormy sea.

Tonight, with Sigrid's blessing, Puchare and I will curl up together on a Tibetan carpet; I don't often encounter the perfect hostess who refrains from registering horror at the prospect of a guest sleeping on the floor.


*5 May.*

What a lovable little city this is! Each day I enjoy it more, though before coming here I had thought of the place as no more than a stepping-stone to Pokhara. But my vision of the Kathmandu Valley as being only slightly less dire than India was quite false. Of course there are the obvious resemblances —dust, stench, flies, ubiquitous sacred cows and mangy dogs in gutters. Also many of the women now wear either the sari or the *shalwar* and chemise, though the majority of men have retained their distinctive dress of jodhpur-type loose-seated trousers, high-necked tunics flaring out above the knees and jaunty little caps—a reversal of the common pattern in the East, where men are usually the first to abandon the national costume. However, the obvious differences between the two countries are far more important. The ordinary Nepalese seem to be without a trace of the Indians' servility, or their touchiness, or that excruciating national inferiority complex which masquerades so pathetically as a superiority complex. In the past the Nepalese suffered more injustice and cruelty under their

own corrupt and unscrupulous rulers than the Indians ever did
under the British; but at least they were spared that lethal blow
to a country's pride which can be given only by foreign con-
querors. All the other Westerners to whom I have spoken during the past few days agree with me that on most levels the
Nepalese are far easier to get along with than the Indians—
which alone would make the atmosphere of Kathmandu much
pleasanter than that of New Delhi.

Another of my misconceptions concerned the influence of
tourism on the valley. I had pictured it as having been already
spoiled by and for tourists, but despite the fact that 'everyone'
now comes here, in much the same way as 'everyone' leaves
London during the summer, it would be ridiculous, at present,
to describe Kathmandu as a Tourist Centre. However, in its
outward aspect it is already far less 'exotic and romantic' than
one has been led to believe; there are almost as many petrol-
pumps as temples, and ugly new buildings are going up everywhere. No one could call it a lovely city, yet there is an abundance of beauty to be found here, and the friendly gaiety and
inconsequential craziness of the atmosphere have completely
captivated me. This craziness is repeatedly manifested in
various Gilbertian ways. When I moved from the hotel to the
labyrinthine Youth Hostel at Jawalkhel—one of the many
tasteless ex-Rana palaces that litter the valley—I found a
multitude of h. and c. taps and some very imposing Western
flushes above Eastern latrines; but the nearest water was in the
nearest well. Also there is an intriguing urban telephone
system, installed by the Americans a few years ago in the fond
hope that local activities might thus be speeded up, and to date
this innovation has made several quite important contributions
to the national muddle. On some days it works only in some
areas and on other days it works only in other areas, so the
consequent alarms and excursions create far more tension than
would ever have to be endured if life were philosophically
geared to an absence of telephonic communication. Then there
are the foibles of the electricity system. These include switches
that have been humorously hidden in the most unlikely
corners—at floor or ceiling level, or behind window shutters—
and that function, if at all, only after prolonged and highly

dangerous manipulation. Because of the current's 'erraticism' everyone keeps a supply of candles at the ready, and this evening, at a meeting of Father Moran's Tibetan Refugee Committee in The Royal Hotel, I noted with joy that amidst so much ornate splendour our conference was being illuminated by two candles stuck on saucers.

Since Nepal was opened to foreigners in 1951 The Royal Hotel has been the centre of what passes for social life in Kathmandu. Officially it is a 'luxury hotel' and as such not at all my line of country; but one soon discovers that here even 'luxury hotels' are purged of their uniformity, and in fact The Royal is as outrageously individual as all other local phenomena. Partly this is due to a ludicrous magnificence, both in the building itself (another ex-Rana palace) and in the Grand Opera décor, which is so gorgeously 'un-with-it' that one is immediately charmed into forgiving its excesses. But mainly the uniqueness of The Royal is due to the personality of Boris, that legendary Russian whom I had already met with delight in so many books and whom I met today, with even greater delight, in person. Undoubtedly Boris belongs to that corps of larger-than-life cosmopolitan eccentrics who have been born to redeem this conforming age, yet to me the most impressive thing about him is his simple kindness. He seems essentially a benevolent rural inn-keeper, rather than the owner-manager of an international hotel, and on his account I fear the more ruthless and practical hoteliers who are now beginning to invade Kathmandu.

At The Royal I was also introduced to Peter Aufschneider and Sir Edmund Hillary. Sir Edmund looks and behaves exactly as one would expect a conqueror of Everest to look and behave, and on shaking hands with him I got a positively schoolgirlish thrill—though it is to be hoped that this was not apparent, since the unfortunate man must be bored almost to extinction by thrilled females. Peter Aufschneider (Heinrich Harrer's companion in Tibet) lives permanently in Kathmandu and now works for the Nepalese Government. He is very shy, modest and likeable—but unfortunately I'm invariably struck dumb on first meeting people who have long been admired from afar, so as a conversational unit we never really got off the ground.

Inevitably The Royal forms a hollow into which all Kathmandu gossip finally trickles and, as much of this gossip concerns the sex-life of various Nepalese royal personages, or of prominent foreign residents, the resulting pond is depressingly murky. But more interesting subjects are occasionally discussed, and here I heard that it is now very difficult to obtain a trekking permit for Northern Nepal. Apparently a certain writer recently took unfair advantage of having been granted such a permit, went to or beyond the Tibetan frontier, took a film of various odd happenings there, wrote about his exploits in European newspapers and generally so upset the Nepalese that they are now thwarting innocent travellers who wish to explore Nepal from no motive other than wanderlust. Personally I know only too well how forbidden frontiers tempt one's juvenile devilry and I have once been guilty of succumbing to their lure; yet out of common politeness to the Governments concerned and for the sake of other travellers one should surely refrain from writing up such incidents—especially in a justifiably jittery country like Nepal. No doubt these regrettable activities near the Tibetan frontier are also partly responsible for the Nepalese Government's ban on further Himalayan expeditions.

Another news item concerned the voluntary return to Tibet, within recent months, of an unspecified number of refugees who had been squatting in Eastern Nepal for the last two years. My informant on this matter was as reliable—within the limitations of the subject—as anyone could be, so I was greatly interested to hear that the uncommitted traders who still travel between Lhasa and Namche Bazaar are bringing reassuring verbal messages from those who returned to their friends in Nepal. The messages say that these ex-refugees find themselves a lot better off in present-day Tibet than they ever were in Nepal and that the Chinese, having secured a firm grip on the country, are now relaxing their first savage pressure. Possibly this news simply represents another victory for Chinese propaganda. The Communists badly need more labourers and I remember hearing, about eighteen months ago, of the Lhasa-printed leaflets then being circulated in India and Nepal, urging the refugees to return to Tibet and guaranteeing them a 'pardon' for their flight into exile. Yet it does seem psychologically probable that the Chinese régime is now evolving from its initial fiercely repressive stage, and I can't help wondering if a return home might not be the happiest solution for many of the Tibetans in Nepal. Whether they are living under the Chinese or in exile it is going to be impossible for them to preserve their ancient religious and social traditions, and in Tibet they would at least enjoy a suitable climate and altitude. I suspect that many Westerners, being unprepared to concede that the Chinese are human beings, would be enraged by this suggestion; yet it does seem a pity to let ideological biases confuse humanitarian issues.

Bicycles are among the main ingredients of Kathmandu traffic, and now I must confess that yesterday I was unfaithful to Roz. I had been advised to buy a bicycle for use in Pokhara (it would of course have to be flown there, as not even a mule-track connects the two valleys), but at first I wasn't very enthusiastic about the idea, having only seen Indian models here and knowing from previous experience how difficult it is to come to terms with these parodies. Then yesterday morning, while wandering through the bazaar, I spotted a likely-looking second-hand Russian cycle, tried it, found it congenial and bought it for £10. 16s. 8d. (Leo, a brother for Roz). Leo is sky-blue and at least twice as heavy as Roz, but he is beautifully balanced and very comfortable on rough tracks, with his huge, well-sprung saddle and broad tyres. He has a bewildering multi-plicity of accessories. None of my previous cycles sported a mirror, foot-brake, milometer, tool-case, carrier, front-wheel dynamo, automatic stand and built-in lock with two keys—in addition to the statutory bell and pump. At present the foot-brake is a menace as I am in the habit of casually back-pedal-ling when going down-hill—but I'll soon get adjusted; and this is only one of the many hazards of cycling in Kathmandu.

The traffic here is predictably unpredictable; trucks suddenly begin to back on top of you without warning, buses simply pre-tend you aren't there, taxis shave your elbow just for the hell of it, brakeless fellow-cyclists charge you at right angles and jog-ging porters, carrying pairs of laden baskets on yokes, enjoy abruptly changing course to send their loads swinging into your front wheel. All things considered it seems reasonable to deduce that the Nepalese are a people not yet 'switched on' to wheeled traffic; when I ring my bell before overtaking pedestrians, as likely as not they respond to the warning by joyously bounding across the road without looking left or right. Yet another hazard is the umbrella, which at this season is used as a sunshade. Your Nepalese pedestrian, strolling along with a friend, tends to gesture extravagantly with his umbrella just as one is pedalling past and so far these antics have twice unseated me—indeed, were I not wearing sunglasses I'd probably have lost an eye by now.

Today I realised that for cycling very slowly through crowded bazaars a heavy cycle is undoubtedly best. Roz was not built to move at the pace of meandering cattle, and on her slim tyres one has to dismount repeatedly or fall off; but one can sit on Leo when he's almost stationary, while waiting for the sacred cow and her sacred calf to deign to move out of the way—it's the difference between taking a cart-horse and a thoroughbred through city streets. Naturally I wouldn't exchange Roz for half-a-dozen Leos, but in his way he's sound enough and will keep me happy in Pokhara.

This evening I have a lump like a football on the top of my head; the height of the average Nepalese is five foot three, and local doorways are made accordingly.

### 7 May.

There are many things one 'should see' in this valley, but I secretly resent being bossed by guide-books and am therefore a slip-shod tourist. To me the little statue that one unexpectedly discovers down an alley-way, and impulsively responds to, means much more than the temple one had been instructed to admire for erudite and probably incomprehensible reasons; so I just go wandering vaguely around on Leo, finding enough incidental entertainment in the three ancient capitals of Kathmandu, Patan and Bhatgaon.

These 'cities' (by our standards market-towns) were for many centuries the seats of the rival Newari dynasties who ruled and fought over this valley before it was conquered by the Gurkhas in 1769. As a race the Newari had an exceptionally developed aesthetic sense and the ordinary people of the valley seem to have attained an almost freakishly high level of craftmanship, most notably displayed in the bronze or stone temple sculptures and in those intricate weather-worn wood-carvings which adorn so many of the older buildings. If any European city had produced in the past such a concentration of artistic achievement it would long since have been demolished, bombed or self-consciously preserved—and whatever its fate the spirit of its craftsmen would have been well and truly exorcised. But here all this beauty is taken for granted, and its survival has been entirely a matter of chance. Some corners of the cities, where nothing has visibly intruded from another age or civilisation, seem quite powerfully haunted by the force and fervour of those nameless men whose work still lives on every side; and in such corners Time can occasionally slip into reverse, so that one is no longer deliberately reaching back into the past with one's imagination but actually *experiencing* it for a few brief, bewildering moments.

By now these Newari arts and crafts have all declined and the majority of the valley's original inhabitants are petty traders or minor clerks. Some people argue that this is a consequence of Gurkha domination, yet it seems probable that Newari inspiration was already flagging by the eighteenth century and that apathy must in any case have succeeded those rich centuries of enthusiasm.

In many parts of the valley elegance and crudity clash violently—especially where the graceful Newari houses emphasise the ostentatiousness of the Rana palaces. These ugly edifices proliferated during the last century, when the avaricious ruling family were breeding like rabbits and building like beavers, and against any other background they would remain for ever intolerable; yet so strangely does Kathmandu affect one that a certain bizarre charm can be found even in such monstrous mistakes.

Another aspect of Kathmandu's crudity is referred to in *A Winter in Nepal*, where John Morris quotes Dr David Wright, who spent some years here as surgeon to the British Residency and wrote, in 1877, 'From a sanitary point of view Kathmandu

may be said to be built on a dunghill in the middle of latrines.'
Mr Morris himself found this description still accurate in 1960,
and I feel that he was being charitable when he stated that
'this is *one* of the filthiest cities in the world'. (My italics.) In
some quarters reeking water lies stagnant in square stone public
baths, and I doubted the evidence of my eyes when I first saw
people drinking this brew. After the scum has been pushed
aside and the liquid—one can hardly describe it as water—has
been collected in earthenware or brass pitchers it looks like
strong tea; what immunity (or what dysentery) these people
must have! Yet despite all this squalor most of the children
seem reasonably healthy, though many of their elders have
been prematurely aged by a lifetime of carrying unbelievably
heavy loads.

There are surprisingly few beggars about, and today I was
approached only once—by a small, Murillo-faced boy with
whom I became on very good terms *after* I had made it clear
that no baksheesh would be forthcoming. Indeed everywhere
I went I was greeted with laughter and gestures of friendship,
and for me the effervescent happiness of the Kathmandu Valley
more than counterbalances its filth.

Today I went to the ramshackle G.P.O. to register some
letters, since unregistered mail from Kathmandu rarely reaches
its destination. At present a new post office is being built, as
part of Indian Aid to Nepal, but I'm glad to have had the
singular experience of patronising the old one. The Nepalese
have no conception of queueing so one is at once caught up in
a loose maul of sturdy little bodies, each with an arm thrust out
towards the clerk, in whose face envelopes, money and forms are
waved vigorously while requirements are shouted as though by
the rules of the game the loudest demands must win. I felt a
bully when using my superior height to achieve the necessary
victory; but clearly there was no future here in being lady-
like.

When the clerk had scrutinised my envelopes he politely
asked if London was in Germany. I equally politely said 'No,
as a matter of fact it's in England,' and—still thirsting for
geographical information—he next enquired if Ireland were
one of the United States of America. Having sorted that one out

with some difficulty, since neither islands nor oceans meant anything in his young life, I asked him how long he had been a post office employee. (By now the scrum had subsided, as everyone was absorbed in our unintelligible conversation.) He grinned at this question, admitted to having started work only this morning and explained—superfluously—that he had not yet invented a formula for controlling his customers.

Before leaving the building I went into the courtyard to watch the mail being sorted. Here some dozen men were squatting on the ground surrounded by hillocks of envelopes, the majority to or from foreign countries. Between the hillocks the 'plain' was littered with stray envelopes, across which coolies and chickens and dogs and a buffalo-calf wandered casually; I deduced that these were the ill-fated epistles—addressed to obscure places like London—for which no suitable hillock could readily be found. And all the time I was looking wistfully for a few Irish envelopes with green and orange around the edges—but none appeared. Maybe the buffalo-calf had eaten them.

The weather here is much more pleasant than I had expected, with an average mid-day temperature of only about seventy-five degrees Fahrenheit and a cool breeze blowing almost constantly from the near though invisible snows. Every day since I arrived the sky has suddenly clouded over during the afternoon and an hour or so later we get a magnificent thunderstorm, with bigger hailstones and heavier rain than I've ever seen before: even in India during the monsoon we had nothing quite like it. This is a very satisfactory arrangement, as the rain lays the dust—if only briefly—and slightly lessens the stink by washing away some of the excrement and rotting garbage that accumulates on the streets. Half an hour ago I stopped writing to revel in a truly classic thunderstorm. The first crash made my ash-tray leap off the table and literally deafened me, so I blew out the candles and sat at the open window to enjoy the display. Overhead it was as though some mischievous god were switching on and off a brilliant blue electric light which revealed every detail of the garden and neighbouring house. Then the sheet lightning stopped and instead the sky seemed alive with writhing dragons of flame flashing from horizon to horizon, while the thunder roared continuously from mountain to mountain like a million lions—and then the rain came and gradually the storm subsided. I must be getting more and more animistic: this is the sort of thing that now awakens my religious fervour.

*8 May.*

At this season a permanent heat-haze veils the Himalayas, and for me one of the most unexpected things about the Kathmandu Valley is its lack of a 'mountain atmosphere'. Nor, I feel, is this merely a temporary effect of climatic conditions for Kathmandu has long been a place apart, isolated from, ignorant of and indifferent to both the outside world and the rest of Nepal. Now the outside world has enthusiastically invaded it, either for pleasure or profit, and it has been forced reluctantly to consider itself in relation to other countries—but it still ignores the mountains.

It is remarkable how the fact of coming to a country to work rather than to explore completely alters one's approach. The always exciting discovery of an unknown land takes on an entirely new texture when one is planning to settle, for however brief a period, and since it is essential to learn to live with local idiosyncrasies the tendency to criticise is blunted. Also, instead of eagerly pursuing knowledge and understanding from the moment of arrival, one waits for them to come, how and when they will. Yet I have to admit that something is missing too—the incomparable thrill of wandering for wandering's sake.

It has been calculated that Nepal has approximately a hundred and twenty national holidays per annum (apart from the fifty-two Saturdays, which are the weekly day of rest) and all these—including the King's birthday, as he is popularly believed to be a reincarnation of Vishnu—are religious festivals. So far I have failed to comprehend even dimly the religion of Nepal, where Hinduism and both schools of Buddhism mingle and subtly interact on each other; but I am consoled by the knowledge that even distinguished scholars go astray in this theological maze and have to end their expositions with a flurry of generalities.

However, it *is* clear that the Nepalese are devout adherents to something and their many and much-feared gods are immeasurably more important to them than their politicians—and very likely more useful too. Almost everyone believes implicitly in charms, and astrology determines each important decision, including affairs of state. I often wonder what happens when events belie the astrologers: but no doubt there are well-established formulae to cover up for the stars' mistakes. To us, all this is ignorant superstition in its most extreme form, and the payment of fees to miserly Brahmin priests does keep many families in perpetual debt; yet to the Nepalese these payments are a sensible insurance against disaster.

During the past week the important Machendranath Rath Jatra Festival has been in progress at Patan—about ten minutes' walk from Jawalkhel—and this morning Donbahadur informed us that the astrologers had pronounced six o'clock this evening to be the most auspicious time for drawing the god's two chariots through the streets of the town; so, having arranged to meet Sigrid beside the wooden floats at 5.30 p.m., I went early to Patan to get the feel of the occasion.

On the way I passed through the 'Street of the Pigs', a low-caste quarter where an inconceivable number of tiny black sows lie all over the place suckling an equally inconceivable number of piglets whose size, colour and shape makes them indistinguishable from rats. Here, also, dozens of naked children, manure-smeared buffalo-calves, congenitally mangy puppies and grubby chicks are to be seen tumbling around together in filth-blocked gutters, half-filled with inky, glutinous liquid. Most of the higher-caste Nepalese avoid this street—not through any fastidiousness, for their own home area could well be equally unsavoury, but simply because the proximity of pigs would make them ritually unclean. Yet the inhabitants do not seem to be in the least cowed by their inferior social status; they are now used to seeing me passing by, and today quite a few of them leaned from their first-floor windows and shouted greetings, which gave me a warm 'accepted' feeling.

In the small square where the god's chariots were parked a considerable crowd had already gathered—including many hill-people, some of whom had walked for more than a week to attend the festival. During my first few days at Jawalkhel I had often stopped to watch these chariots being assembled and decorated; each float is surmounted by an unwieldy fifty-foot tower of wood, bamboo and bast, festooned with greenery and long strips of coloured cloth. At the summits fly scarlet flags, and in a shrine at the base of the leading chariot's tower sits Machendranath, one of the 'Grand Magicians' of Buddhist tantrism, who normally lives in the Bungmati Temple, south of Kathmandu. On the night of the full moon preceding this festival he is washed in milk to prepare him for his slow, week-long journey through the city streets—a journey during which he is believed to bestow greater fertility on humans, animals and crops. If either of the towers collapses—as one did in 1953—this is interpreted as a prediction of bad luck for the coming year, and to lessen the chances of any such collapse all overhead cable wires are cut along the god's route—which perhaps explains why the electric current has been so very erratic during the past week. Within the shrine a Brahmin priest sits in constant attendance on Machendranath, and as the crowd drifts to and fro people pause to bow to the god, and pray for a moment with joined hands, before throwing a fistful of rice or a small coin into the shrine. Each of the floats has two unsteady-looking, giant wooden wheels, on which three big eyes have been awkwardly painted, and a twelve-foot shaft made from a curved tree-trunk. To the outward ends of these shafts, where they curve upward, are tied huge, carved, painted masks—grotesque and gaudy—that grin at the populace with ambiguous expressions in which threats and promises seem intermingled.

When I arrived beside the chariots scores of small boys were doing acrobatic tricks on the shafts, sitting astride the masks, climbing the towers and generally behaving as though this were a fun-fair rather than a solemn occasion. To the Nepalese Machendranath Rath Jatra is one of their most important religious festivals and this deity is very sacred, very powerful and very easily angered; yet here that subdued sense of reverence which we cultivate towards things sacred is quite unknown, and fear, worship and gaiety flow together as inseparable parts of daily life. Only for a brief, solemn moment, while they show homage, pray and make offerings, do people withdraw from the joyous tumult around them—and when they rejoin it they appear even happier after 'making *puja*'.

Sometimes a strolling musician would pause beside the chariots and play to Machendranath, and when two adolescents spontaneously started a dance near the chariots I hurried to join the circle that was forming around them. These were village lads from the hills, clad in homespun grey tunics, yet they gave an extraordinarily good performance of one of those stately temple-dances that long ago were imported into Nepal from South India. To an initiate every turn of the boys' wrists and flicker of their eye-lashes would have been eloquently symbolic; but even uninitiated spectators can enjoy the grace of these slow, formal movements, and I found myself being also very much moved by that strange beauty which so transformed the faces of two quite ordinary boys, as they became more and more absorbed in their chosen way of worshipping the god.

Afterwards I went to sit among a group of Newari women half-way up a flight of temple steps. Within this ancient square were only mellow brick dwellings, semi-ruined pagoda-style temples, their roofs grass-grown, time-damaged shrines of obscure significance, and ornate, sunken baths, where water came gushing from the mouths of brass serpents into the pitchers of local housewives, who then pushed home through the crowd balancing their gleaming pitchers on their hips. By now the sun was just above the curly-tiled roofs, the golden light was soft and one could sense an increasing excitement. With every moment the crowd grew denser and more colourful, and as the women thronged to Machendranath with their handfuls of rice they seemed to create a splendid tidal wave that was tinted red and black, and green and blue, and gold and white.

When at last the auspicious moment came for the chariots to be drawn forward, and their uneven wheels began to roll slowly over the bumpy ground, I was horrified to see the towers' incrustations of small boys remaining defiantly in position. Fortunately others shared my horror, and after a few moments the boys obediently detached themselves and leaped into the crowd.

It now looked as though all the men, women and children of

the valley were cramming the narrow streets, filling the over-hanging balconies and straddling the roof-tops. Yet as Sigrid and I were directly behind the chariots we could see every detail, including the creamy-coloured, bushy yaks' tails with which Machendranath's Brahmin attendant was being fanned by his acolytes. The extraordinary technique of moving these colossal contraptions through narrow laneways is to attach to each shaft two steel ropes about one hundred feet long, at which scores of men pull and pull, as in a tug-of-war—though facing away from the god—while a drum and cymbal band plays en-couragingly beside them, accompanying that curious chant which the men shout in unison before each straining heave on the rope. When at last the chariot has been induced to progress some twenty or thirty yards (it never gets further without a pause) the whole crowd cheers wildly, and Sigrid and I had by now become so involved that we too yelled triumphantly as the cumbersome float groaningly moved forward. Then, as the floats proceeded on their crazy but curiously dignified way, some hundred yards apart, we noticed with alarm that the front 'tower' was becoming more and more unsteady, until it seemed quite likely to go toppling homicidally forward into the crowd. But apparently this threat was familiar, as four men now climbed half-way up the swaying superstructure, from where they released two more ropes, throwing them out behind the float. Another army of men at once manned these and, by hanging on desperately, managed to keep the tower on a com-paratively even keel, though the braking effect of this pre-caution made progress even more difficult.

Now we looked back towards the other chariot and saw that it too was in trouble, of a different sort. One of the gigantic wheels had stuck in a pond of that gluey black mud which is among Kathmandu's specialities and all the efforts of its team of draught-humans were being of no avail. We began to force our way back to see how this problem would be dealt with, but then our attention was violently recalled to the first chariot, and now we really were alarmed. Here the ground sloped slightly downwards for some fifty yards, and the chariot, sud-denly becoming unnaturally frisky, was pulling the men on the brake-ropes so strongly that they had to run, while the men in front had panicked a little and were plunging into the crowd on either side. A few people fell and were trampled on slightly, but happily the slope levelled out—or Machendranath relented —before this panic spread. I hate to think what a real panic would have meant; as it was we were being pushed around fairly roughly—not out of any discourtesy, but through sheer necessity—and I felt truly *in* Nepal as I was carried along by that compact mass of sweaty little bodies, all shouting and laughing and pushing and shoving and praying and enjoying.

The god's tour, begun in warm, golden sunlight, ended by the cloud-filtered light of a half-moon. Now tiny lamps were being hung outside each unglazed window to honour the passing god, and we could see into first-floor living-rooms where lanterns, hanging from low rafters, illuminated the little shrine-niches set into the walls. Each finely carved balcony was crammed with exuberant family groups, looking down in comfort on the seething gaiety and fervour in the street and throwing their offerings of rice towards the chariot as it drew level.

When Machendranath had reached his resting place for the night—another temple-filled square—the crowd thinned out, and Sigrid and I returned to investigate the second chariot's situation. We saw at once that it was hopeless: no amount of heaving was going to dislodge the float from its mud-trap, and Donbahadur told us that the astrologers were being severely criticised for having miscalculated the most auspicious moment to begin the procession. He added that perhaps tomorrow a lorry would come to tow the chariot to its companion—a possibility which saddened me, as it seemed to foreshadow the day when the gods would succumb to motor transport.

*9 May.*

This morning I paid my third visit to the Swiss-run Tibetan camp here at Jawalkhel, where about four hundred refugees live in one-roomed mud huts roofed with straw. Most of the adults are employed in the Self-Help Handicraft Centre where they make—mainly for export to the West—carpets, coats, sweaters and boots in modified versions of the traditional Tibetan style. Both adults and children appear to be in reasonably good health, despite this relatively low altitude of 4,500 feet, and it does one good to see the families still united, instead of being split up as so often happens in India.

Yet it is becoming obvious to me that all is not well in this Nepalese province of Tibland. Since my arrival I have repeatedly noticed how uneasy is the relationship between helpers and helped—and indeed I had some forewarning of this last month in Dharamsala, where I met hundreds of Tibetans who had recently, and illegally, crossed the frontier from Nepal because of extreme dissatisfaction with conditions here. It seems clear enough that some of their grievances are genuine and that the various relief agencies operating in Nepal have not always avoided those pitfalls which everywhere await workers among the Tibetans. But unfortunately it is equally clear that a 'taking-help-for-granted' attitude is now being developed by many Tibetan leaders, in direct opposition to His Holiness's strongly-expressed wish that the refugees should strive increasingly for independence. One finds among these leaders a spoiled-child petulance if they don't always get what they want—though often their demands are quite unreasonable—and this development is something I foresaw and dreaded more than a year ago. Such an attitude was no part of the Tibland scene as I knew it in India, yet it did seem likely to evolve as a result of the pampering policies adopted by so many relief agencies, and of the deep affection and admiration which the ordinary refugee inspires in his Western helpers—including myself. It was inevitable that the totally unsophisticated Tibetans would eventually be to some extent demoralised by our well-meant but ill-judged mixture of lavishness and adulation; so now we are finding it necessary to use clumsily harsh methods in an attempt to remedy our own mistakes, much as a badly brought-up child might be sent by despairing parents to an extra-strict school. And—understandably—the Tibetans don't quite know what this is all about.

At the Handicraft Centre I met an English-speaking Tibetan youth whom I'd known in India, and after lunch he borrowed a bicycle to accompany me to Bodhanath as my interpreter on an official visit to the Tibetan monastery there. Bodhanath is four miles east of Kathmandu and we stopped for a few moments *en route*, on finding ourselves outside the Pashupatinath Temple— a site which rivals Benares as a place of Hindu pilgrimage. My copy of *Nepal in a Nutshell* had informed me that 'only Hindus are allowed to go inside the courtyard of the Temple', so we stood and stared from the arched entrance at the giant statue of the Golden Bull, who naturally has his back turned on non-Hindus, giving them a splendid view of his world-famous behind —which displays such disproportionately massive testicles that one is tempted irreverently to diagnose mumps. Just to test Pasang's reaction I innocently asked if Christians were allowed to enter Buddhist temples, and looking deeply shocked he said, 'Of course! *Anyone* can enter our temples!' He then asked the man who sat outside the gate, in charge of worshippers' shoes, if Buddhists could enter this Temple: and in defiance of my little guide-book, but in harmony with the liberal traditions of Nepal, the reply was, 'Yes, but only Tibetan Buddhists. Not Chinese'—which seemed to me a very revealing confusion of politics with theology. I rather like the idea that we Westerners so often condescending, should occasionally be slapped down by Hindu prejudices; yet there seems to be a flat contradiction between the Hindu philosophers' teaching on the Oneness of the Universe and this priestly ban on non-Hindus entering certain temples.

The Bodhanath stupa—on which are painted four pairs of enormous eyes, gazing gravely in the four cardinal directions— is one of the highest Buddhist stupas in the world; one sees it first from afar, across the flat fields, and unlike most religious buildings here it is freshly painted and in good repair. Pasang told me that it is more than 2,000 years old; but one keeps an open mind on the dates, measurements and general statistics quoted by either Tibetans or Nepalese—though this date may well be accurate enough, since Professor Tucci thinks it possible that Nepal formed part of Asoka's empire in the third century B.C.

Bodhanath is now chiefly associated in foreign minds with the rich and influential Chine Lama, a prominent character who is sometimes erroneously described as the Dalai Lama's representative in Nepal—a position that in fact is held at present by a Khampa layman named Sergay. I can think of no two men who are less alike than the Dalai and Chine Lamas; yet foreigners accept him as a bona fide example of a Tibetan lama—which error might be funny were it not so unfair to many thousands of genuine lamas. As Pasang and I cycled towards the monastery around the base of the stupa, past scores of giant copper prayer-wheels set in the circular wall, we saw a Tourist Office mini-bus decanting some dozen wide-eyed visitors outside the Chine Lama's house. Pasang then asked me if I too would like to meet him; but I declined with thanks.

The Bodhanath Tibetan monastery was built about thirty years ago and now houses some forty monks and lamas, ranging in age from a charming sixty-five-year-old Rimpoche to several Incarnate Lamas of eight or nine, who when we arrived were happily scampering around the courtyard in their long, ragged maroon robes. I visited the temple first, with some excitement, being conscious that it was the nearest I'm ever likely to get to a genuine Tibetan temple of the traditional style. And indeed it was as genuinely Tibetan as could be—filthy and magnificent and untidy and awe-inspiring, with gross, ferocious effigies of gods and goddesses lurking in the gloom, swathed in ceremonial white scarves and presiding over the hundreds of *tormas* and wispily luminous butter-lamps that had been laid before them. The monks' praying-seats lined the aisle in front of the 'High Altar', facing each other. Some had incongruous tins labelled Farex Baby Food or Andrews' Liver Salts beside them, containing roasted flour for making that *tsampa* on which the monks somehow survive during their long chantings from the scriptures—and when there are a hundred and eight thick tomes to be chanted aloud quite a lot of flour must be required.

Each member of this community has his own cell, and from the temple Pasang and I were conducted to the Rimpoche's quarters—a tiny cupboard of a room, some ten feet by four, with a plank bed, one thin blanket and a miniature shrine where eleven butter-lamps burned before a picture of the Lord Buddha. Here we each consumed five cups of heavily buttered tea—a smiling young lama stood beside us throughout with poised kettle—and reluctantly ate the damp but very expensive

Indian biscuits which, despite this monastery's evident poverty, were produced from a tin trunk under the bed.

Here one soon sensed a concentration of all that is best in Tibetan Buddhism—simple, ardent piety, cheerful courage, gentleness, instinctive courtesy and a quick sense of fun. Then, as we talked with the Rimpoche and the four other lamas who had squeezed into his cell, I became painfully aware that now I was glimpsing part of the last act in the drama of a civilisation's history. By the time the young Incarnate Lamas of this community have grown to manhood only a shell will be left of that unique tradition which bred them.

*11 May.*

Among the friends I've made here during the past ten days is a nine-year-old schoolboy with one of those beautiful young faces that misleadingly denote an extreme degree of virtue. He is a pupil at St Xavier's College, the big boys' school run by American Jesuits for Nepalese students, and he speaks quite fluent English—as do an astonishing number of middle-class youths in the valley. I first met Rambahadur outside the G.P.O., where he loiters daily to contact his clients—those foreigners who wish to change money or travellers' cheques on the Black Market. He came sauntering up to me and said—naturally out of the corner of his mouth—'Want to change?' and when I replied 'Yes, but not today', he took my hand in his, showing a touching childishness rather at variance with his spare-time profession, and off we went to have a cup of tea together and make mutually convenient arrangements. At his age the ability to conduct shrewd financial transactions has a certain charm, and the necessity to do so a certain poignancy; we quickly became friends when I noticed that he was not a scrounger, but simply worked to earn honest, if illegal, commission, and I arranged to meet him this morning to cash a £50 cheque. However, when I arrived at our New Road rendezvous I found not only Rambahadur but *four* others—two men and two youths—all waiting to capture my custom. Rambahadur looked small, forlorn and scared; but he was evidently going to stand his ground like a good little Gurkha and secretly I had no intention of

deserting him. Yet this was my chance to hold an auction and
secure a better rate, so I played the five off against each other
until, in desperation, Rambahadur promised me Rs. 32/-N.C. to
the pound. One of the men (a nasty-looking character) said
that he too could get me Rs. 32/- and when I shook my head
and held out my hand to Rambahadur the boy was at once
knocked into the gutter by a savage blow from his rival. At this
I lost my temper and gave the bully a box on the ear, whereupon all four vanished, leaving me to retrieve a sobbing Rambahadur from the gutter. And before my business could be
transacted the negotiator had to be consoled and cuddled and
mopped up. This incident struck me as typically Eastern: at one
moment Rambahadur was a tough man-of-the-underworld, all
set to do nefarious deeds down a back-alley, and the next moment
he was sobbing in my arms, a big baby with a painful shoulder.

We then turned off New Road, with its would-be Western-
style shops, and immediately were amidst that dank maze of
narrow laneways which still forms the main part of Nepal's
capital. When we came to a small square Rambahadur glanced
furtively around, though no one was in sight, before darting
through a very low doorway and beckoning me to follow him.
The domestic courtyard we now crossed was scattered with
stone gods and phallic symbols, but I had no time to study these
before being quickly hustled into a pitch-dark interior and led
up a steep shaky wooden stair to a squalid 'bed-sitter', where
Rambahadur instructed me to await developments. He then
disappeared, locking me in the little room—presumably as a
precaution against inquisitive neighbours.

For the next twenty minutes there were no developments.
The small window overlooked the courtyard, where a wrinkled,
much-bejewelled woman was now scouring brass pots and platters with handfuls of black mud, afterwards rinsing them in
sour-looking water. A dejected pi-dog, which had accompanied
her, was nosing unhappily at a heap of refuse, and then a tiny
naked boy toddled out to make his contribution to the excrement already in evidence—being afterwards called by granny
to have his bottom cleaned, also with black mud and water. In
general this scene was not uplifting and I soon turned away to
observe the interior of the room.

In one corner stood a large, padlocked tin trunk, which I rightly assumed to be the 'safe', and on top of it were piled a number of poorly-printed paperbacks in Nepali, indicating that the money-changer—who of course would also be a trader —had had some education. Several garish Hindu oleographs were pinned to the walls between a large photograph of King Mahendra with Queen Elizabeth II and a T.W.A. picture calendar for 1952. And, presumably as a demonstration of strict neutrality, small photographs of Nehru, Gandhi, Chou-en-lai, President Kennedy and Khruschev were huddled companionably in a corner by the door.

I had become thoroughly bored by these gentlemen when at last Rambahadur returned with our fellow-conspirator—a lean little Chetri who looked sharp-eyed but honest. Having scrutinised my cheque, passport and various signatures very closely he requested me to write both my local and home addresses in his 'register'—a scruffy exercise book. Then he took the key of the trunk from round his neck, walked to the corner almost ceremoniously and finally, after much muttered counting and recounting, handed me the cash in brand new notes. I couldn't help wondering what practical purpose my credentials could serve in these circumstances; if my cheque were a dud there was no method of legal redress open to him and equally, if his notes were duds, I was debarred from protesting officially. In fact this was the most pleasing part of the transaction: it demanded a high degree of mutual trust—and so far his notes have not been questioned. I also wonder, being conspicuously ignorant about financial matters, how and where such cheques are eventually cashed. It is said that in many countries with an unstable currency they are never cashed, but are passed from hand to hand as legal tender; yet this seems unlikely, for the simple reason that they would disintegrate comparatively quickly. Even now in parts of Nepal the country's own paper currency is unacceptable for the same reason.

This afternoon I spent four and a half hours buying medical supplies for the refugees in Pokhara—a fascinating experience, unlikely ever to be repeated elsewhere. To begin with most of the stocks—imported from India—have passed or are rapidly approaching expiry date and the anxious salesmen look at you pathetically when you point out that this terramycin or that sulphaguanidine has been useless since last March. They then explain hopefully that local doctors unquestioningly use these drugs every day (which doesn't surprise you in the least) and having declined to follow the doctors' example you resignedly move on to the next chemist. Naturally everything takes ten times as long as it would at home—finding the articles, searching for the semi-illegible invoices, painfully and not always accurately pin-pointing the relevant articles on the invoices, typing the account with one finger on a machine that looks like the first of its kind, checking, packing, *un*packing because that box was too small, repacking, finding straw because the other box was too large. . . . If one were new to the Asian business scene (of which Nepal is admittedly an extreme example) one would go mad within an hour; even though reasonably adjusted I very nearly did go mad after four and a half hours. But mercifully the petty dishonesty so common in India seems to be much less evident here; every night I leave Leo in Sigrid's garden—an act of faith which no one but a lunatic would make in India.

It will sadden me to leave this warm-hearted little household, which has recently been augmented by two domineering hens, bought by Donbahadur to provide Sigrid with *really* fresh eggs. At dusk they come strutting into the living-room, watched by a disapproving but discreetly unprotesting Puchare, and demand to be put to bed in the kitchen under the standard Nepalese wicker coop. Now Donbahadur is murmuring ambitiously about the advantages of owning a buffalo heifer—to provide Sigrid with *really* fresh milk. But I suspect that his stock-piling enthusiasm will be checked at this point, to avert the occupation of the bathroom by cattle.

# 3

## *Descent on Pokhara*

*12 May. Pokhara.*

This morning, when delayed by a series of typical Kathmandu
hitches, I foolishly allowed myself to fizz slightly; all passengers
for Pokhara were due at the Royal Nepalese Airways Corpora-
tion Terminal at twelve noon, but it was 11.58 a.m. before I
had got myself, my knapsack and assorted boxes of medical
supplies, dried milk and old clothes assembled at the appointed
spot. (Leo cannot travel until a day when the plane is less loaded
with freight for Pokhara.) Yet I needn't have fizzed; minutes
passed, and more minutes, and half an hour, and three-quarters
of an hour—and then an impatient-voiced young man told us
to hurry out to the bus, his tone implying that the delay was all
our fault. We next had to walk some three hundred yards up a
side-street and with so many bits and pieces in my charge I
was the last to reach the smart, blue airport bus (donated by
the U.S.A.). Disconcertingly, it was quite empty, but an exceedingly decrepit Afghan-type bus stood a little further on, packed
to the roof (part of which was missing), and now someone
beckoned to me and shouted 'Pokhara? *This* Pokhara bus.' So I
squeezed in, having paused to pick up from the ground under
the bus a British Embassy mail-bag, gravely but not very effectively labelled 'On Her Majesty's Service'. My luggage was
then insecurely attached to what remained of the roof and I
engaged a small boy to ride with it and scream loudly if anything fell off. Now all we needed was a bus-driver; and one did
appear after about ten minutes. He took a pair of sandals from
beneath the driving-seat, slipped them on to mark the resumption of his official duties, climbed leisurely into the cab, lit a
foul-smelling cigarette and started the engine. Giving a roar
like a wounded tiger the bus at once leapt convulsively across
the rough street and I trembled for my small boy on the roof:

41

but curiously enough both he and my luggage were still there when we arrived at Gaucher Airport forty minutes later.

There are eight landing-strips in Nepal, all but two—Pokhara and Gorkha—being in the Terai, and R.N.A.C. runs daily flights (weather permitting) to each of these favoured points. This means that as fares are relatively low (about £3 for a hundred-mile flight) many Nepalese villagers have graduated within a decade from the earliest-known method of transport to the most modern. At first I was astonished to see so many poverty-stricken peasants queueing for planes, but I soon realised that if one can arrive in thirty-five minutes instead of walking for ten days, spending money on food and lodging *en route*, it is undoubtedly more economical to fly.

At Gaucher Airport a wind-sock is not necessary during this season when the wind rhythmically blows columns of yellow dust across the field—a sight both horrible and fascinating. Even more fascinating is the airport's indescribable turmoil; it is entirely beyond my understanding how anyone ever gets to their prearranged destination—or ever finds their luggage on the same plane as themselves.

The Pokhara flight was scheduled to depart at 2.30 p.m., and at 2.15 I went into the small airport restaurant for a cup of tea. At 2.25 the loudspeaker made a rapid crackling noise, so indistinct that it could have meant anything in any language, and I optimistically deduced that the Pokhara flight was being called. But looking out of the window I saw our huge handcart of luggage still standing near the verandah where it had been loaded; so I relaxed again, aware that this was no reliable indication of the flight's postponement, but determined to stand by those hard-won medical supplies.

After another cup of tea I moved out to the verandah, where an ocean of humanity and luggage was ebbing and flowing amidst a despairing babel of sound as everyone pleaded with everyone else to tell them when *their* flight was departing and which plane was going where. At this stage four Dakotas (two of them venerable machines bought long ago from Aer Lingus) were enigmatically lined up on the airfield and one simply had to watch to see which plane one's luggage was put into—and go on from there. The luggage itself was a classic Asian array—

tin trunks, bed-rolls, padlocked wooden boxes, bundles tied up in filthy clothes, bulging sacks, plastic baths filled with miscellaneous objects, cardboard cartons uncertainly roped together, canvas satchels, cloth bags, biscuit tins, and wicker *dokars* (porters' baskets) shaped like overgrown weaver-birds' nests. When at last our cart was pushed and pulled to a plane by four coolies I somewhat cynically followed to supervise the loading, for here the public are allowed to wander at will among arriving and departing aircraft.

Half an hour later the loudspeaker made another of its rude noises, people began to move towards our plane—and now it seemed we really were on the way to Pokhara. Then suddenly everyone stopped moving and started to gesticulate and protest, and a young Nepalese teacher beside me announced in English that our flight had been postponed until seven o'clock tomorrow morning. To me this seemed so true to form that I wasn't even slightly surprised—nor was I half as annoyed as my Nepalese fellow-passengers. Strolling back to the verandah I sat awaiting the unloading of the plane and a reunion with my medical supplies, for which I was by now developing an almost maternal affection, having guided them through so many dangers. The young teacher came to sit beside me, his pale-skinned, fine-featured face puckered with frustration. When I asked him if he knew why the flight had been cancelled he sighed and said, 'The crew never came—this often happens after a party that is late to end. And in Kathmandu we have many parties.' He added, 'For you our country is full of difficulties—I'm sorry.' To which I sincerely replied that for me his country was a joy, and not half as full of difficulties as the West; but I'm afraid my sincerity failed to convince him.

By now our handcart had arrived back at the verandah and was being rapidly unloaded; my companion explained that the next flight, to Simra, had just been postponed as this cart was needed to load the relevant plane. Then, when half our luggage had been flung to the ground, a rumour started that our flight *might* be going after all—and instantly the confusion became unbearable, as the Simra coolies had been impatiently loading the cart with *their* luggage before *our* luggage was all unloaded and now the piles on ground and cart were inextricably muddled.

As no definite statement had been made regarding the Pokhara
flight it had become a matter of opinion whether our luggage
or the Simra luggage should be unloaded or reloaded and on
this point the coolies were disagreeing violently—so after some
moments I decided to rescue the medical supplies before they
were whisked off to the Terai.

Time passed and the coolies squabbled and bits of luggage
went flying around like shuttlecocks. But then there came a
new flurry and fuss, followed by joyous exclamations from my
fellow would-be passengers, and it was confirmed that we had
indeed been reprieved—because, as I later discovered, the
American Ambassador and his wife were booked to Pokhara on
our flight, which circumstance had inspired someone to filch
the crew from another unfortunate plane.

When we finally took off at 2.45 p.m. I was not as nervous as
I might have been, because R.N.A.C.'s multi-racial team of
pilots and engineers has established during the past eight years
a safety record that many more experienced and disciplined
airlines might envy—and this in a country where high peaks,
treacherous valleys, swiftly changing weather and scanty tech-
nical equipment increase the normal hazards of flying.

At this season cloud hides the Himalayas, and our thirty-five-
minute flight to Pokhara was quite tame. As I gazed down at
the 4,000- to 8,000-foot hills below us I longed to trek through
them instead of merely having a quick, teasing glimpse. Yet this
would be a gruelling trek in May, for now the broad, stony
river-beds are mere thirsty trickles and the terraced hillsides a
series of dry, brownish undulations, only relieved by the thick
green forests that cover the higher ridges. Few villages were
visible, for their mud-walled houses blend perfectly with the
surrounding earth: but on the highest hills we could see straggling little hamlets set amidst strips of maize, and it was possible
to follow for miles the thin connecting thread of porters' paths,
endlessly winding around the mountains.

We made a perfect landing in this broad valley and stepped
down from the plane into a chaos of Nepalese, through which
could be glimpsed five conspicuously tall Peace Corps volun-
teers, struggling through the mob towards their Ambassador
and his wife. In every direction swarmed dirty, inquisitive,

laughing children, and vigorously-elbowing, bare-footed passengers eager to embark for the onward flight to Bhairawa before our cargo had even begun to be unloaded. We were at once surrounded by predatory, dictatorial porters—mainly women, wearing tattered, vivid clothes and heavy, noisy jewels —and by a vast number of interested locals, few of whom have ever flown anywhere or will ever fly anywhere and most of whom have nothing whatever to do with passengers or cargoes. Having disentangled myself from this throng I was at once pursued by a young policeman in creased khaki, armed with a cumbersome ledger in which all arriving foreigners are requested to write down 'particulars'. For political reasons the country north of Pokhara has recently been made a Restricted Area and one gets the impression that the Government, which only opened its frontiers to foreigners in 1951, would be quite pleased to have an excuse to re-impose restrictions on all tourist travel outside the Kathmandu and Pokhara valleys.

While I was doing my duty by the ledger a tall, thin Tibetan in European dress came towards us, welcomed me warmly and introduced himself in a mixture of Tibetan and English as Amdo Kessang, the proprietor of The Annapurna Hotel—a new, one-storey, Tibetan-style building which overlooks the airfield from a rise of ground about one hundred yards away. Prayer-flags flutter happily beside the arched gateway and though this establishment is hardly a hotel in our sense of the word, its easy Tibetan friendliness more than compensates for the disadvantages that may strike the passing visitor.

Kessang next introduced his cousin Chimba, a Lhasa-born trader who has spent some years in India and speaks fluent Chinese, Hindi and Nepali—and adequate English. Chimba is now the Pokhara Refugee Camp interpreter and general dogsbody and it was a relief to have someone to take responsibility for the medical supplies while I went to drink tea with Kessang.

Twenty minutes later Chimba reappeared and offered to introduce me to Mrs Kay Webb, the infinitely resilient and resourceful English grandmother who has been in sole charge of this camp's health since last December. For three years Kay worked as doctor-cum-nurse among the thousands of Tibetans in the Mysore settlement and, though she has never had any medical training, apart from a Red Cross course, in certain respects she is the more effective for being untrained; too much conventional knowledge would inhibit one from practising those unorthodox improvisations which are often the only way to achieve results in places like Pokhara.

It was no more than a ten-minute walk over level common-grazing land to the village of Pardi—a strung-out collection of wood, brick and mud houses situated at the western end of the airstrip. Here Kay lives, on the outskirts of the village, in a two-roomed house with a rickety wooden 'staircase', a rat-infested thatched roof and uneven mud floors. She uses the downstairs room as the camp dispensary and upstairs is her bed-sitting-room, where she cooks what little food is available on a tiny oil-stove.

Kay and I had been talking for less than fifteen minutes when Chimba came rushing back to inform us that the American Ambassador and his wife would like to tour the camp—so we all hurried off down the rough village 'street' to that other stretch of level common land where some 500 Tibetans of all ages have been camping since their trek last winter from the northernmost part of the Dholpo region of Nepal. Most of these Tibetans belong to the independent nomad tribes who tend flocks of sheep and yak in the Nepalese-Tibetan frontier areas, and they have never been accustomed to discipline or control from any quarter; they do acknowledge some tenuous link with His Holiness as their religious leader, yet they were never within the political sphere of influence of the Lhasa Government or the spiritual sphere of influence of the Potala. In Kathmandu one hears many different versions of the same stories about the intractability of Tibetans in Nepal—depending on the teller's racial, religious, political, social or personal biases—and it is almost impossible to sift out the truth. But I suspect it *is* fair to say that in general the Tibetan refugee in Nepal differs considerably from his compatriot in India and is much more difficult to cope with.

At present these Tibetans are being issued with a weekly ration of U.S. Surplus Food—Bulgar wheat, cotton-seed oil and dried skimmed milk—and they are living in 120 ragged cotton tents; but we hope to provide better shelter for them before the monsoon breaks in mid-June.

During our tour of the camp I made an impulsive purchase. As we walked between the tents my attention was distracted from what His Excellency had to say by an object lying on the palm of a Tibetan's hand. The object in question was very small, very black and very vocal; its piercing squeaks fatally attracted me to Ngawang Pema's side and a moment later I had done a deal and one twelve-day-old Tibetan mongrel bitch was promised to me for all of ten-and-sixpence. I wonder what the astrologists would make of the fact that this pup and I entered Nepal on the same date—the first of May.

Penjung, the camp leader, had just invited us all to drink tea in his tent when a rainstorm broke and the Ambassador's Peace Corps escort decided that he and Mrs Stebbins had better be transported at once to the comparatively luxurious Peace Corps house some four miles away in Pokhara Bazaar. So Penjung hurriedly produced a pair of white scarves and draped them around the Stebbins' necks before the rattling Tourist Department jeep arrived to rescue the visitors.

Kay and I then had tea with Penjung and his wife and four daughters. The rain was cascading down both outside and inside their flimsy tent, where we sat cross-legged on filthy bamboo matting while chickens pecked around us, and Penjung's wife coughed incessantly, and a baby with dysentery whimpered in one corner; yet Tibetans are never as gloomy as their conditions might warrant and my happiness at being back among these people was undiminished by the surrounding squalor.

When the downpour temporarily ceased we slopped our way back to the village through slippery, ankle-deep mud—and there we found a broken-down jeep, with which two mortified Peace Corps boys were frantically fiddling while the Stebbins sat on wooden benches in a bazaar-stall, looking blissfully happy. (At the time this happiness seemed to be a brilliant exercise in diplomacy, but later I discovered that both are quite capable of enjoying such misadventures.) Kay immediately invited them to her room, where we talked—above the roar of the wind, the crash of thunder and the rattle of hail—until seven o'clock, by which time it had become evident that the jeep was very severely incapacitated. However, the Stebbins are unusually adaptable Americans who genuinely love Nepal, having now been here seven years, and they adjusted without difficulty to the prospect of dining and sleeping in The Annapurna. When we had been joined there by four sheepishly apologetic P.C. boys, Kessang produced a quite elaborate Tibetan banquet—which astonished everyone, for food is scarce at this season and most things have to be imported from India. In the end we had quite a party, enlivened by ambassadorial gin, Nepalese *rakshi*, Tibetan *chang* and Irish whiskey—a combination which may reasonably be expected to produce some rather interesting variations on the hang-over theme.

Apart from these P.C. boys the only other Westerners in the valley are the three medical missionaries in the Leper Colony beyond the airfield, the eight medical missionaries in the Shining Hospital north of the main bazaar and the MacWilliamses, a young New Zealand couple (he is a sheep-breeding expert with F.A.O.) who live on the outskirts of Pokhara Bazaar.

Before retiring I went out to the field and from there saw a vision of such supreme beauty that momentarily I wondered if it could be real. To the north, under a clear sky and a high-sailing moon, the whole Annapurna range stretched in one massive white tumult and, dominating the range—seemingly dominating the world—was the sharp-peaked, austere and infinitely lovely Machhapuchhare, home of Pokhara's tutelary deity. One should not try to trap such splendour in mere words, but beneath the moon, in the utter stillness of the valley, all those silver snows burned coldly with an overwhelming, undeniable life and spirit of their own. This silent, vital grandeur almost compelled me to kneel down and worship; and perhaps if no inbred self-consciousness intervened and it were possible to do so I would be all the better for it.

### 13 May.

I awoke at 5.30 to hear the familiar, soothing hum of Tibetans saying their morning prayers, and when I went to wash at the tap in the field the eastern sky was orange and the sun's first rays were firing the tip of Machhapuchhare. Then the new light spread rapidly over the entire range, tingeing the snows with nameless colours—to gaze on these mountains almost lifts one off the ground with joy.

This valley, which lies only 2,500 feet above sea-level, is considerably hotter than Kathmandu. Its population is estimated to be between 12,000 and 15,000, and apart from Kathmandu it is the only level stretch of land north of the Terai. Being at the converging point of most routes from central and west Nepal to India it has a certain importance as a trading centre, yet it does not seem nearly as prosperous as the more fertile Kathmandu Valley.

From Pardi the valley opens out to the south-east and low foothills are visible in the distance; to the south-west the hills are near and covered with dense green forests, and at their base —a few moments' walk from Pardi—lies the long, emerald-green lake which gives this valley its name. (*Pokhara* is the Nepali for lake.) The beauty of the place is incomparable, with sub-tropical vegetation flourishing on every side directly beneath the cold white lines of the snow-peaks, and it is not surprising that the Nepalese hope eventually to develop it into another Kashmir.

However, on a more practical plane Pokhara does have its disadvantages at present. The prices of obtainable essential commodities are astronomical, and as most supposedly essential commodities are unobtainable at any price one soon learns to regard them as inessential, which is very good for one's pampered Western soul. Sugar is half-a-crown per pound, tiny eggs are sixpence each (it takes three of them to make what looks like one scrambled Irish egg), small potatoes and onions are fourpence each and no other vegetables or fruit are to be had at this season. Fresh milk, butter, cheese, meat, bread and flour are all unobtainable, so rice, dahl, dried beans and eggs must therefore be our staple diet—and for luxuries we can import from Kathmandu Indian instant coffee of a peculiarly vile variety and stale Indian Cadbury's chocolate at one-and-six-pence per very small bar. Just now excellent Russian sweetened condensed milk is available in the local bazaar at four shillings per pound tin, and recently good quality Chinese tinned jam was also available; but the supply of these 'propaganda-type'

goods is very uncertain. Occasionally Kay treats herself to
Indian cream-crackers at seven-and-sixpence per pound—a
good example of 'give them cake . . .'. One feels that the Nepal
Tourist Bureau could use this situation as a new advertising
gimmick aimed at over-weight Westerners—'Enjoy the Breathtaking Beauty of Pokhara Valley and Regain Your Figure!'.

Today Chimba told me that I could soon move into a room
at the lower end of Pardi Bazaar—for a rent of fifteen shillings
per month—so this afternoon I went marketing in the main
Pokhara Bazaar. From Pardi the rough track climbs all the
way, past neat two- or three-storey Brahmin, Chetri and Gurung
homesteads, their ochre walls warm against a freshly-washed
background of maize-fields, bamboo-clumps, banana-trees,
orange-groves and many other trees and shrubs unknown to me.
Everywhere smug black cattle roam free, blatantly conscious of
their sacred status and looking a lot healthier than their Indian
cousins. It seems lunatic that we have to buy tinned milk from
Russia in a valley overrun by herds of healthy cows; but I can
see that these cattle are not bred as milkers: their udders are
completely undeveloped, so the little fresh milk that is used by
the locals must come from buffaloes.

An hour's unhurried walking took me to the centre of Pokhara Bazaar, and at once I fell hopelessly in love with the place.
Its attraction is not easy to define: one cannot claim that it is
especially beautiful, or colourful, or gay, or exotic—but as yet
it is utterly *itself*, a small Nepalese town (or Nepal's second city,
if you wish) where one feels immediately and intimately in
touch with an ancient, strong tradition that still determines
every action, thought and emotion of the local people. One
may be aware that in the course of many centuries much of this
tradition has become distorted, and therefore socially damaging;
yet the basic stability and tranquillity inherent in such communities—despite the perennial anxieties of debt, disease and
political unrest—appeal most powerfully and significantly to
our tradition-bereft Western hearts.

On either side of Pokhara's 'Main Street' stand dignified,
three- or four-storey tiled houses, their ground floors open-
fronted shops, and from any given point on any of the town's
streets or alleyways at least one dilapidated but much-frequented

Hindu shrine is visible. At various corners squat ragged haw-
kers, with their pathetic stock-in-trade of gaudy Indian glass
bracelets, small religious oleographs, bunches of safety-pins,
flimsy combs, heavy bead necklaces and sundry other trinkets
spread on the dust at their feet; it is to be hoped that they are
not dependent on their sales for a living. Then, half-way up
the Main Street, one is startled to see the carcass of a large
motor-truck. There are now six or seven small Willys jeeps in
the valley, but as all vehicles have to be flown in I was fascinated by this remnant of someone's over-optimism; considering the nature of local tracks and the absence of local mechan-
ics it is not surprising that the truck died young.

Even by Nepalese standards the surface of the Main Street
is incredibly rough: it looks as though it had been torn up by
some enraged god who was determined that no-one should ever
again be able to walk in comfort through the bazaar. And sure
enough I was told this evening that it had indeed been deliberately torn up a few years ago, when the local authorities were
afflicted by delusions of grandeur and yearned for a 'with-it'
paved road. However, by the time the previously tolerable track
had been turned into this present inferno of boulders and
chasms the authorities had recovered from their delusions and
lost all interest in paved roads—so the inferno remains.

At first sight Pokhara Bazaar appears to be quite an impressive shopping centre: but a brief scrutiny reveals that its stock
is virtually limited to cloth, cigarettes, matches, pens, electric
torches, lanterns, saddlery, kerosene oil, rice, dahl, dried beans,
dust-tea, rock-salt, sugar, biscuits and Bournvita at fifteen shillings per quarter pound. I tried to buy a small oil-stove for
cooking but none was available so I returned with only two
enamel mugs, three little aluminium bowls in lieu of plates, a
tiny kettle, a slightly larger saucepan and three teaspoons—all
of the most inferior material though they cost me thirty-five
shillings.

Almost everything in the bazaar has come from India
(though the rock-salt still comes from Tibet), which perhaps
explains why I paid for my purchases by *weight*. The system
by which they were weighed was most intriguing—even foreigners who have lived for years in Nepal can't begin to

comprehend it, though the Nepalese themselves take these pro-
ceedings quite seriously. To begin with little shapeless lumps of
metal are thrown onto the scales by the handful—and then, if
these prove unequal to the occasion, the merchant casually
leans forward, without bothering even to uncross his legs, and
picking a few stones off the ground throws them, too, on to the
scales. But I feel that somewhere there is method in this mad-
ness and I have no suspicion of being diddled. Indeed, I was
very gratified today when on two occasions merchants handed
me back excess rupee notes which I had given them in error
because of my ignorance of Nepali. Such gestures do a lot to
make one feel at ease in a new environment.

This evening, at sunset, I went for a swim-cum-wash in the
lake, which was too hot to be refreshing, though with the aid of
carbolic soap it served to remove sweat and dust. Even by
strictly controlling one's imagination it is impossible to believe
this lake to be clean; yet at present it is our only source of
drinking-water, so quite a lot of expensive kerosene will be
needed to boil the brew before use. It is rather annoying that
so many Nepalese favour the edge of the lake as a latrine—
obviously because they can then jump straight into the water
and combine a swim with the ritual washing enjoined upon
Hindus after defecation. But the abundant consequences of this
habit diminish even my enthusiasm for swimming. Incidentally, one good result of nomadism is that the camp here has
always been kept spotless—providing quite a contrast to the
many Tibetan camps in India, which tend soon to become
revolting manure-heaps. These Tibetans are so used to the
hygiene of camping that even the hobbling grandparents and
toddling infants go far over the fields each morning, and every
day the whole camp is cleared of litter and swept as clean as a
Mayfair street.

# 4

# Under Machhapuchhare

*21 May. Pokhara.*

It is a (long) month today since I left London and I've just
now moved into my new home, after a week of inexplicable but
not unexpected delays. (I reckon that at least half one's time in
Nepal is spent waiting for something to happen that probably
won't happen until tomorrow, or the day after—if ever.) This
unfurnished apartment is in a fairly recently-built semi-
detached house and it measures some twelve by fifteen feet—
very nice too, apart from an excess of rats. Just now a glitter
caught my eye, and looking up towards the crude wooden
beams that support the flat corrugated-iron roof I thought at
first that I was seeing fire-flies or glow-worms: but then I
realised that three monster rats were peering speculatively
down at me—no doubt wondering how securely the new tenant
would lock away her food supplies.

The mud-floored lower room, where Leo lives, is designed
as a 'shop', with a few rough shelves facing that double-door
which one bolts when coming in for the night and padlocks
when going out for the day—though this latter precaution is
ludicrous, as almost every padlock in Pokhara answers to the
same key. From the lower room an unpredictable bamboo
ladder gives access to my wood-floored bed-sitter, through a
trap-door without a door. A thin partition separates this room
from its twin over my landlord's shop and there are such wide
spaces between the planks of the partition that all my sounds
and movements are audible and visible to Thupten Tashi, the
young Tibetan teacher who is my neighbour. As I write Thupten is holding a night-class in English grammar for some of
the more studious older children and a moment ago they were
all solemnly chanting 'Where *did* you *went*? Where *did* you
*went*? Where *did* you *went*?' But one can't stand this sort of thing

53

for long so I interrupted with a cry of anguish—'Please, Thupten—Where did you *go*!' Not that I blame Thupten; the other
day I saw a Nepali-English primer full of 'quotable quotes'—
e.g., 'He is a girl,' 'This is a pictures on the walls.'

My unglazed, wooden-shuttered window is large by local
standards—four feet by three—and it looks south across level
farmland to a green curve of wooded hills. Two little niches at
eye-level in the outer wall (designed for religious emblems)
hold my kitchen utensils and toilet articles (i.e. toothbrush and
paste), and I'll sleep in a corner on a bamboo mat; at this
season bedding is unnecessary, and before the cool weather
comes I hope to have bought a flea-bag from one of the home-
ward bound mountaineering expeditions. My furniture consists of a new table and stool which were very promptly and
quite skilfully made for me by a carpenter in Pokhara. I also
have a wooden box as food-cupboard and an empty four-
gallon kerosene tin to hold my drinking-water. (These square
tins are sold at two shillings apiece in the bazaar, and because
they are easily carried on the back they have become the most
popular local water-containers.)

Tonight I feel very well-adjusted to the world around me:
the camp is almost opposite and I can now hear the Tibetans
enlivening their evening with some communal singing, while
next door Thupten's pupils are giggling wildly—obviously they
have too much horse-sense to take his English lesson very
seriously. It would be hypocritical to pretend that I could live
happily ever after in this state of Noble Savagery; yet at the
moment I am more than content to have so decisively Got
Away From It All.

*23 May.*

I find it extremely difficult to keep track of days and dates
here—not that they matter very much. Yet for official purposes
one does sometimes need to know the date and this aspect of life in
Nepal is chronically confused by the fact that the Nepalese
month begins in the middle of our month and that both calen-
dars are used indiscriminately by English-speaking Nepalese,

who rarely explain which system they happen to be using on any given occasion. This can—and does—lead to unspeakable mix-ups: yet it also provides an excellent excuse when Nepalese officials break their appointments, which they do rather more often than they keep them. Then they can say, with an air of indignant innocence, 'Oh, but *I* meant *our* twenty-third—and that isn't till next Friday week!'

Recently I have been negotiating for the employment of some of the Tibetans on the Indian Aid Hydro-Electric Project and today, on visiting the work-site, I made a wonderful discovery. This site is about 300 feet below the average level of Pokhara plain, in a very hot gorge through which a small river flows from the lake, and after my discussion with the Indian foreman I went hopefully to investigate the river. What I found far exceeded my hopes—a perfect swimming-pool, about 150 yards long, 10 yards wide and 20 feet deep. The pool is only five minutes' walk from the work-site, where my duties will often take me during the weeks ahead, yet comparative privacy is ensured by a high, grey cliff on one side and a sheer, forested mountain on the other. The water is a clear green and less warm than the lake; also one can persuade oneself that it is less filthy, because of its movement—and certainly it feels much more refreshing. I spent the lunch-hour swimming happily up and down the length of the pool, since it is now far too hot to eat anything at mid-day; but unfortunately the very steep climb up from this gorge leaves one again pouring sweat by the time one reaches level ground.

Today, near the river, I saw my first Nepalese snake. Here there is a wide stretch of rock-slabs, glittering with the distinctive local deposit of mica, and while I was walking over this my concentrated thinking on labour-relations was suddenly interrupted by a most curious noise as a snake at least six feet long swished away over the rocks from under my very toes. It travelled fast, its dry scales sounding like a distant swarm of bees, and I just had time to observe that it was olive-green, with brown markings, before it poured itself into a crevice between two boulders. When I came out of the river I looked —cautiously—into the crevice and it was still there, doubtless saying to itself that it didn't know what the world was coming

to, with all these dangerous humans clumping about, disturbing an innocent reptile's sun-bathe.

This afternoon I cycled up to Pokhara Bazaar to attempt to
sort out three different accounts at the local bank. The building
is guarded by two heavily-armed, sloppily-uniformed and chain-
smoking soldiers of the Nepalese Army, and one penetrates to
the office by crossing a dim, derelict ground-floor shop premises
and climbing a dark, trembling staircase. Some ten individuals
staff the low-ceilinged, dingy cavern which one assumes to be
the office—but only one of them, so far as I could judge, is
literate in any language. If it is accurate to say that banking is
in its infancy in Nepal, then this establishment is very decidedly
a cradle. Yet as a person inside a glass-house I shouldn't throw
stones: my own ignorance of the financial world is total, which
made the afternoon's transactions very trying indeed. I had
to fill in countless forms to send to Dublin and London, but
as they were all printed in Nepali it is difficult to imagine them
achieving the desired effect at the other end, and I have a
nasty suspicion that since neither I nor the young manager
really knew what we were trying to do they were probably the
wrong forms to begin with.

This evening Kay lent me her table-thermometer to enable
me to see the worst, and now, at 9.30 p.m., my room temperature is eighty-eight degrees Fahrenheit and all the time I am
mopping sweat off my face, neck and arms. Yet one shouldn't
complain—this is moderation compared with current tempera-
tures down on the Indian plains.

*28 May.*

Like most Asian peoples the Nepalese are very curious about
any foreigner's way of life and their respect for privacy is
nil. During this past week they have been coming in droves to
inspect my room and their dismay at what they see vaults all
language barriers. After one quick look they intimate that it is
altogether wrong for me to sleep on the floor, to do my own
cooking on a tiny temperamental stove and to wash myself and
my clothes in the river. They point out severely that I should

have at least one servant and a bigger room with a more tract-
able stair, a mud floor and a cool grass thatch. So far my Nepali
vocabulary consists of one word, meaning 'good', and gesturing
widely I repeat this adjective—at first cheerfully, then firmly
and at last, as their indignation grows, almost aggressively, in
self-defence. But my enthusiasm fails to quell their disgust, and
when they finally withdraw I can hear their condemnations
being repeated to passers-by in the street below.

European adaptability might be expected to promote har-
monious race-relations, but I can see that in this country it does
nothing of the sort. Instead the Nepalese suspect the integrity
—or perhaps the sanity—of a European who fails to maintain
European standards, either through preference for the simple
life or through lack of cash. They cannot conceive of any European *choosing* to live on their level—or below it, as all but the very
poorest Nepalese families have servants of a sort about the
house—and obviously they are embarrassed by a memsahib
'going native'. So now I am realising sadly that in such a class-
conscious and conservative society 'going native' is the longest
way round to integration.

Our local mail system is thrilling. A Nepalese postal service
does exist in theory, but as no-one cares to test it in practice the
British Embassy very nobly sends a mail bag by plane on
Fridays, for the benefit of the missionaries, Kay and myself.
Both hospitals are some distance from the airfield, so Kay and I
have permission to break the seal when the bag arrives and sort
out our own mail before Joseph, the wiry little Magar servant,
trots away with the sack over his shoulder. Undoubtedly this
ritual is the highlight of our week; it is most exciting to squat
on the dusty airfield, beside a large pile of envelopes and pack-
ages, and eventually to discover the few familiar and precious
envelopes addressed to oneself—a much more gratifying system
than the dull process of having letters pushed through one's
letter-box. But naturally there is no certainty about which
flight The Bag will come on, and at 10.30 a.m. today, when I
saw a speck in the eastern sky, I went hurtling off to the airfield
on Leo only to find that The Bag had not been put aboard this
plane. Nor did it come on the next flight, which landed at 1.40
—but two hours later we saw with joyous relief our beloved

canvas sack being tossed into Joseph's arms, from the last plane
of the day.

For a variety of reasons I find myself having to spend a prodigious number of hours each week simply awaiting the arrival
of planes. Luckily one cannot tire of a place where horsemen
on richly caparisoned steeds may frequently be seen galloping
across the airfield—briefly framed by the wing of a Dakota—
with bells ringing a wild harmony and hoofs pounding an exul-
tant reply; or where, under blue skies, a dozen women in swirling
crimson skirts gracefully pace the length of the field, half-hidden
by their baskets of sweet green grass and their enormous golden
wickerwork sunshades.

Another diversion is provided by the Gurkha soldiers. Sometimes one sees scared, barefooted youths from remote hill
villages coming to the airfield, carrying battered little tin boxes
of meagre possessions, on their way to join those elder brothers,
cousins and uncles who are 'doing well' with the British Army
in Hong Kong, Borneo or Malaya. Then one often sees Gurkhas
returning on six months' leave, after three years' service, and
invariably they look sensationally spruce among their welcom-
ing family. The grimy stay-at-homes wear unwashed, fraying
garments, while the well-scrubbed soldiers are attired in
starched, neatly-creased khaki shorts, flowered bush-shirts and
broad-brimmed straw hats. And instead of the modest little tin
box with which they departed from home they now possess at
least four huge padlocked trunks. These, of course, are left for
their wives, mothers or sisters to carry—one on each bent back,
supported by a broad canvas band across the forehead—while
the Returned Hero strides importantly ahead, an expensive
camera slung over his shoulder and a raucous transistor screaming in his hand as he chats with those male relatives who trot
respectfully beside him, carrying light pieces of hand-luggage.
Usually at this stage the hero's pocket is full of newly-acquired
rupees, for he will have paused long enough on the airfield to
sell a selection of excellent Swiss watches and Japanese pocket-
transistors at incredibly low prices.

At first one is appalled by the apparently lethal degree of
chaos which prevails on every side at the airfield. The least
timid Westerner recoils with incredulous horror from a landing-

ground on which, ten minutes before a plane is due, children are flying kites, babies and dogs are romping together, cattle are grazing placidly, mule-trains are plodding stolidly and trans-country porters are carrying loads as big as themselves.

When the plane has landed one frequently sees members of the general public standing in the welcome shade of its wings, nonchalantly smoking. Then, when it eventually taxies away, creating a gale-force wind in which the children dance joyously, no-one bothers to move and from the booking-office doorway newcomers are subjected to the harrowing optical illusion that at least twenty people are about to be decapitated by a wing. Incidentally, for the village mongrels this is the climax to their day's fun. Yelping hysterically they pursue each departing plane with a verve undiminished by the proven futility of the exercise—and just occasionally one of them is rewarded by *almost* getting his teeth into the rear wheel. Yet appearances are in this case deceptive, and though the situation seems to be so irrevocably out of control none of the accidents which should happen do happen. When a speck appears in the sky at the end of the long valley a man blows a quavering blast on what sounds like a referee's worn-out whistle and immediately frenzied herdsmen leap onto the field, hurling stones and imprecations at their cattle who, disgruntled but resigned, file off through a gap in the sagging barbed-wire fence. Meanwhile the dogs have also temporarily dispersed, the children have pounced on the babies and removed them, the mule-trains have broken into a canter and the porters into a trot and, as the plane roars low over the camp at the end of the runway, nothing or no-one remains to be killed—which by my reckoning constitutes a daily miracle.

Recently I have been chiefly occupied in supervising the building of bamboo huts, into which we hope to move most of the Tibetans before the monsoon breaks. However, at this season it is not easy to obtain the necessary matting and poles, and today we suffered yet another setback when a local farmer, who had agreed to sell us forty bamboos, announced that his astrologer had advised against the sale as it would be most inauspicious to cut bamboos on his land before the rains came. A practical streak was perceptible in this edict, since May is the least suitable month for felling bamboos; but obviously it simplifies life if one can refuse to honour one's promise on the advice of an omniscient astrologer. Everybody knows that this sort of argument is incontrovertible in Nepal, where the hour at which King Mahendra begins an air-journey is still determined by astrology as well as meteorology.

It was 5 p.m. when Chimba informed me of this development and at once we set off on our bicycles to hunt for a more amenable farmer, cycling through one of the many beautiful corners of the valley that I haven't yet had time to explore. By now the level land south of Pardi is grey, arid and harsh to the eyes—but half-a-mile north of the village one is in a new, cool green world where the narrow laneways are shaded by towering, leafy trees and where clumps of powerfully curving bamboos, more than one hundred feet tall, bend their feathered tops over fields of shoulder-high maize. At about 6.30 a strangely muted light began to come from the west and soon this suppressed sunshine, slanting through torn copper clouds, was casting a red-gold glow over the whole landscape until the circular, ochre farmsteads seemed like giant lanterns against their dark green background.

For over an hour we toiled from farm to farm along stony tracks ankle-deep in fawn, powdery dust and often blocked by droves of obtuse buffaloes who panicked at the unfamiliar sight of bicycles. At the first farm we negotiated with a timid boy of eight or nine and his great-grandad—an ancient whose skin was so wrinkled that his legs looked as though he were wearing brown nylon stockings several sizes too large. Not surprisingly these negotiations came to an unsatisfactory conclusion; and at the next two farms the owners, having discovered that we were not going to pay a fancy price, brusquely claimed to need all their bamboo for themselves. I was very aware that these Brahmins were hostile to us non-Hindus—less, I should think, because of our ritual uncleanness than because they see the infiltration of foreign ideas into the valley as a threat to their present profitable influence over the villagers. However, we were eventually promised twenty-two bamboos, of varying sizes and qualities; but tomorrow being Saturday (when it is inauspicious to fell bamboos) we can't send the Tibetans to collect until Sunday morning—by which time there may have been further astrological intervention.

We cycled home along the lakeside, past the hideous new pseudo-European Royal Palace, and the very sacred Hindu temple that rises out of the water some two hundred yards off-shore. When we were out of sight of the Palace I dismounted and asked Chimba to go ahead; then I sat for a little time by the lake. Rarely have I seen anything more lovely than that still, vast expanse of emerald water, beneath a tremendous arch of bronzed cloud, through which a few near-by peaks and crags were just discernible.


*29 May.*

At five-thirty this morning a jubilant Chimba came scrambling up my ladder (fortunately Tibetans are not at all embarrassed when confronted with semi-nude females) to tell me that the German Annapurna Expedition want forty-two porters for twelve days at Rs. 12/- per day—and are willing to employ our Tibetans. When you remember that Rs. 3/- is the average daily coolie wage Chimba's elation is understandable, and together we rushed off to the camp to choose twenty-one men and twenty-one women—a list of whose names and registration numbers would have to be presented to the Anchiladis when we applied to him for permission for the refugees temporarily to leave his district.

By nine o'clock we had made our selection of those most suitable and I had written out the list for Kay to type; but then we received a message that, for a very odd reason, only men would be acceptable. Apparently one of the Hindu hamlets *en route* to the base camp is fanatically orthodox, and recently the inhabitants have been experiencing great difficulties with their local god because some passing travellers killed a chicken in the village. Therefore it would be extremely dangerous further to provoke this god by admitting into his territory outcaste women who might happen to be menstruating at the time without heeding any of the very strict Hindu taboos that apply to the occasion. As we returned to the camp to revise our list

I noticed that even Chimba, who has his full share of Buddhist tolerance, was finding this hitch hard to stomach—perhaps because it had followed so soon on yesterday's astrological débacle!

Lately I've observed that among Nepali diseases there is an affliction, peculiar to resident Americans, known as 'Cultural Shock'. In older English this means not liking local smells and being disturbed by the national habit of flinging garbage into the streets; nor does any consolation derive from the fact that in villages all such garbage is instantly disposed of by battalions of cattle, pigs, dogs, horses, goats, hens and ducks. Fortunately Europeans are immune to this disease and, though Kay and I were both quite nicely brought up, we have long since adjusted to flinging through our windows egg-shells, potato-peelings, onion-skins and basins of filthy water, with never a thought for the passers-by—who anyway are usually protected by umbrellas at this season, which I am not when I cycle past *their* windows at dumping-time. We must take great care to break this habit before returning to countries where it might culturally shock the natives.

At noon today there was a marathon row in the street below my window. It began when one young woman accused another of having an affair with her husband—accompanying the accusation with a blow across the face. Then, within moments, an excited crowd of about a hundred and fifty mysteriously assembled, and I was looking down on a sea of bobbing black umbrellas, beneath which men and women were furiously arguing and gesticulating, each trying to shout or scream more harshly than the rest. Personally I should have thought this an exclusively family matter—but possibly these hundred and fifty protagonists did all belong to the three families involved. The argument continued for some forty minutes, and then the husband vigorously whacked both women on the back with his rolled umbrella and told them (if one may judge by his tone and expression) to go to the Hindu equivalent of Hell—or, perhaps, to become worms in their next incarnation. In Nepal a man is not expected to pretend to be faithful to his wife (though she is required to be very discreet about her own infidelities), so this should have concluded the argument. But instead of accepting their chastisement with womanly humility these two shrews promptly declared a truce and united to attack the husband with their hastily rolled umbrellas—at which point they were seized by several men, on whom they lavished kicks and scratches before being partially subdued and frog-marched away out of sight. Now I noticed that the original dispute had sparked off a variety of subsidiary quarrels among the crowd, all of whom were enjoying themselves enormously. Clearly this sort of ding-dong battle is the Nepalese peasant's favourite recreation, and one can't help wondering if the apparent lack of civilisation revealed by such scenes is not in some respects healthier than our repressive over-civilisation, in which sedatives and tranquillisers are necessary to so many.

After watching one of these not uncommon mass-arguments, or even after spending a few hours dawdling around the bazaar, waiting for someone or something, a return to the camp provides the most extraordinary contrast. Tibetans rarely raise their voices, however heatedly they may be disputing, and instead of the Nepalis' cheerfully shouted '*Namuste*' one is welcomed by a silent bow or a tongue stuck out respectfully to its full length. It is curiously moving to find the distinctive Tibetan gentleness showing through so often among these uncouth and at times unruly nomads; and in their case one cannot reasonably associate this gentleness with the practice of Buddhism, since it is obvious that they have been chiefly influenced by the cruder and more ancient Bön-po religion.

The weather is really grim now; there has been no rain for eight days and the temperature of my room, under this low tin roof, reaches 102° or 103° Fahrenheit by 2 p.m. At bedtime it's down to about 88° and I lie naked on my bamboo mat, tormented by a heat-rash, while the rats provide background music by upsetting dishes and spoons and squealing angrily at each other. At first I found it rather disquieting to lie on the floor with these brutes scampering around me—there seemed no guarantee that they wouldn't nibble at the edges of recumbent bodies—but now I've become adjusted, though I'm still afraid to chase them as they are reputed to turn savage if treated rudely; recently Kay was bitten on the finger when she tried to push one off her pillow in the small hours. But in a way

the millions of tiny, red-brown ants are even more troublesome
than the rats: they get into all the food and swarm over one at
night in tickling (but not biting) hordes. Initially I tried to pick
them out of the rice, dahl, sugar and tinned milk, but I soon
gave up—life's too short—so now I suppose cooked ant is my
chief source of protein. All things considered I don't especially
look forward to night-time at the moment. Yet on the whole
I'm very happy and one can't have perfection.

*3 June.*

Today I distinguished myself by getting hopelessly lost for
eight hours. Kay had asked me to go up to the Shining Hospital
for some medical reports and then to collect an X-ray result
from the Indian Military Hospital on the other side of the Seti
Gorge; but at the Shining Hospital one of the missionaries very
kindly, though rather vaguely, directed me to a short cut and
by 2 p.m. I realised that I was probably half-way to India.
However, as there has been no opportunity to take a day off
since my arrival I decided to make the most of this involuntary
expedition, without feeling too conscience-stricken.

On the whole my sense of direction is quite reliable, yet soon
it was clear that I was becoming 'loster and loster'—and my
compass was in my knapsack at Pardi. The sort of reasoning
which can usually be applied to such situations seems to count
for nothing in Nepal, and I'm seriously tempted to believe that
here even the sun flouts the natural laws. One complication is
that those low, wooded hills which rise at intervals from the
valley floor look identical to the newcomer, so one is wildly
misled and lured over the plain for two or three miles in the
conviction that Pardi lies just *there*—only to find oneself on the
verge of a magnificent 1,000-foot river-gorge one has never seen
before and which is certainly not negotiable; and so it goes on
. . . and on . . . and on.

Though Pardi and Pokhara have now been put on the tourist
map by the airfield one only has to travel a few miles beyond
them to reach, within the valley itself, villages so untouched by
outside influence that a white woman on a bicycle creates a
veritable sensation; and this unblemished picturesqueness has its

snags, for whenever I asked for directions the villagers were too astonished, too scared or too amused even to attempt any helpful response or gesture. Once a man did point down a track that appeared to be leading direct to the middle of nowhere, and optimistically I followed it to its terminus on the brink of yet another gorge—or perhaps at a different point along the same gorge.

All day the heat had been intense and by 3 p.m. I was feeling quite dehydrated, having covered over forty miles according to Leo's milometer. Partly for this reason, and partly because I despaired of ever disentangling the inconsequential tracks of the plain, I now attempted to descend to river-level and follow the course of the Seti—an idiotic move which involved Leo and me in a series of gymnastic feats and stamina-tests such as even Roz and I have never had to endure. And Leo is twice the weight of Roz . . . Eventually I discovered that one could descend to within about one hundred feet of the water, but no further—something which would have been obvious from the start to any moderately intelligent person. So I sat down in the shade of a tree by the cliff-edge to smoke a cigarette while reflecting on the sad fact that soon we would have to ascend somehow to plain-level and resume our war of nerves with those tracks.

However, it was impossible to remain glum for long in such surroundings. Below me the Seti (its name means 'white') was a swift, seething torrent, narrow at this season but still violently strong amidst a desert of pale, rounded stones. From the opposite cliff rose smooth-browed, forested hills enclosing the gorge in a wide, gentle curve, while behind, rising in layers to the plain, lay the rough, silent, sun-beaten countryside that we had just traversed. I hadn't expected to find such solitude within this valley; yet for hours past people had appeared only in the vicinity of the few hamlets and from here not a trace of humanity was visible. But then, when my almost pathological aversion to 'turning back' drove me on up the gorge—I was able to cycle for about a mile over the short, burnt grass and pungent herbage—a lone farmhouse appeared on the very edge of the cliff. This building, clumsily constructed of timber and stone, was a mere loft over an open-sided shelter for cattle, crops and firewood—yet in it lived an old grandmother, her

son and daughter-in-law and their five children, of whom the
younger three were stark naked and pot-bellied. Around this
pathetic dwelling (the most impoverished I've seen outside of
Gilgit) stood a few acres of poorly maize and three feeble
banana trees, beneath which a starved-looking buffalo lay
chewing the cud. (Though what that cud consisted of I can't
imagine.) The usual Nepali 'ladder'—a notched tree-trunk—
led up to the entirely unfurnished living-room, where the
family were sitting idly, sharing a local version of the hookah.
When they saw Leo and me at the foot of the ladder their
astonishment was considerable, but they responded to my urgent
plea for '*pani*' by beckoning me 'upstairs' and handing me a
brass pint-measure of river-water which tasted faintly of human
excrement (or was I imagining things?) yet which at that
moment seemed an ineffably delicious drink. With wild disregard for the probable consequences I emptied three of these
measures, while the family tried to question me and registered
incredulity at my ignorance of Nepali. They were a remarkably
cheerful group, though not one of them looked healthy, and
after their first shock of surprise they treated me as though
we were old friends.

I longed to be able to find out how they came to be living in
such isolation; it seems likely that they belong to the Siva
Bhakti tribe, which was formed of ex-slaves after the abolition
of slavery in Nepal on 28 November 1924, and which now constitutes an almost untouchable caste of people who are allowed
to marry only among themselves. It is estimated that about
50,000 slaves were freed at that time, their 16,000 owners
receiving a cash compensation from the state. The majority of
those freed became apprenticed to their previous owners for a
seven-year period, eventually settling down as labourers, and
this 'improvement' in their status often left them worse off than
before, since employers were no longer bound to provide food,
clothing and shelter. An enterprising minority, however, set
up as independent coolies and in time had saved enough money
to settle on just such scraps of wasteland as my friends of this
afternoon are farming.

Before saying goodbye I made a determined effort to obtain
some idea of where Pardi might be and at last the eldest child,

a boy of about fourteen, volunteered to show me the track for a fee of one rupee. I had already paid these unfortunates for their water (as requested) and I certainly didn't grudge the boy a rupee: yet I couldn't help contrasting this profiteering attitude towards a stranger in difficulties with the boundless generosity of those equally poor Muslims and Tibetans whom I've met elsewhere on my travels.

Leaving the shack we walked away from the river for some half a mile, through dense, knee-high, prickly bushes which tore deep scratches in my legs, to the base of a 500-foot cliff. There the boy pointed towards the sky, said 'Pardi', smiled a farewell and briskly trotted off.

Surveying the cliff it seemed to me that I had had a very poor rupee's worth of guidance; this precipice was completely overgrown with tangled shrubs and looked like a monkey's playground rather than a route to anywhere. But then, hidden beneath the bushes, I saw what might possibly be described as a track, though it more closely resembled a dried-up water-course. This ascent would have been strenuous without a bicycle and only by a savage combination of obstinacy and brute force did I finally get Leo over the top and on to the plain. By then every muscle in my body was throbbing from the fearsome contortions involved in heaving both of us over five-foot-high boulders, across four-foot-wide crevices and through thick patches of scrub, so I sat down to recover while studying our new horizons—which unfortunately did not look very new. I saw the same identical hills, rising on three sides, and the same gorge—from a different angle—and the same brand of little-used track that tends to expire at a moment's notice. In fact the only change was overhead, where the sky had suddenly become black with welcome storm-clouds. But as progress in some direction seemed advisable I mounted Leo and bumped off hopefully towards the north-west, which seemed just as good a bet as the south-east.

Twenty minutes later I rounded a hill and saw a village ahead and another river-gorge on my left; and providentially the storm broke only as we reached the outskirts of this village. Normally being exposed to a storm delights me, but now I raced for the nearest shelter—a small Gurung farmhouse—with head bent to protect my face from being lacerated by the hail which a 110 m.p.h. gale was driving horizontally across the valley. (Later this evening a stranded air-pilot gave me details of the wind's force and told me that during such storms cattle are occasionally beaten to death by the hail.) Of course this is not what we think of as hail; I measured many of the jagged pieces of ice that came shooting like bullets through the open doorway and several of them were three inches by two and at least an inch thick—extremely effective ammunition for the use of angry mountain-gods!

Certainly some god was very angry today; never have I witnessed anything approaching the ferocity of this storm, either during my previous monsoon among the Himalayas or during my winter months on a North Atlantic island. As I crouched just inside the doorway among an assortment of frightened villagers, for whom this house had been the nearest shelter, I could see my host's little field of six-foot maize being plastered to the ground within moments—then his one stack of hay was swept off its high platform and went sailing out of sight, twenty feet above the ground, creating a curiously Mary Poppins-like effect. I could sense that my companions' fear was not merely for the safety of their families, dwellings or crops: they were responding also to the spiritual malevolence which was being conveyed to them through the devastating fury of the elements. My normal reaction to any demonstration of Nature's power is a simple awe, yet I found it easy today to sympathise with these peasants' taut perception of some sinister force behind this onslaught.

Within moments of the storm breaking the temperature had dropped so abruptly that soon everyone was shivering. Forty minutes passed before the gale suddenly died and allowed us all to proceed, through almost solid sheets of rain, to our respective destinations. For the duration of the gale rain had been as continuous as hail and now all tracks were rivers, flowing between piles of greyish, unmelted ice-bullets. Then, cycling against the current through a foot of water, I realised that we had passed this village quite early in the day, which meant that though I still had no idea how to find Pardi I could at least try to retrace our original route from Pokhara Bazaar.

The whole valley—this morning parched and quivering silently in the heat—was now an ocean of noisy brown water, rapidly moving on every side as the fields are so designed that the rains pour from one to another before finally reaching river-level. Very soon cycling became impossible; I simply walked through a sort of submarine world in which the cold rain falling around me seemed no less in volume than the knee-deep, earth-warmed torrent through which Leo was being dragged. At one point we had to re-cross a river—for all I know the ubiquitous Seti again—that earlier had been ankle-deep but was now breast-high and positively dangerous. Then, incredibly, from a slight hill I saw through the curtain of falling water an aeroplane parked under a tree; and that vision could only mean that I had—as might have been predicted—lost the Pokhara track and inadvertently found Pardi. But between us and the airfield lay wide, flooded paddy-fields of such soft mud that I sank in to my knees at every step and could not possibly get Leo through. I was determined to make for that aeroplane in a straight line, lest we might find ourselves behind one more low, green hill, so I painfully carried Leo along half a mile of the narrow, slippery ditches that intersect paddy-fields, frequently falling into three feet of muddy water and feeling rather like a drunken tight-rope walker. Then, as we crossed the airfield at 6.15 p.m., the rain stopped and a startling gleam of sunshine lightened the valley.

I went direct to the camp, dreading what I might find. Inevitably it is in a shambles: most of the tents have been torn to shreds and four have been blown away, including the chief lama's. From the airfield sheets of water raced across the whole site, and to enter the camp one had to wade across a twenty-foot wide, four-foot deep torrent in which one of the children had nearly been drowned a few minutes before my arrival. All clothing, bedding and firewood are saturated and the little cooking-holes in the ground will be unusable for the next twelve hours; so these unfortunates cannot even console themselves with a hot drink, much less change into dry clothes as I have now done. When I arrived some of the torn tents were already being moved to less flooded spots, and piles of drenched possessions were stacked on the high firewood heaps all over the camp.

Many families had begun frantically to dig drains, using spoons, knives, hands and feet in an attempt to get the water away more quickly. The sodden remains of those prized cardboard U.S. milk cartons, which are used as domestic altars, were floating off rapidly in every direction and most families' weekly grain ration was soaked through. Tiny children stood shivering beside their collapsed tents, and stiff-jointed grandparents searched in vain for a dry spot on which to sit.

The whole heart-rending picture would have made a real tear-jerker had it been filmed, but for one detail which ruined it all—the unconquerable good humour of the Tibetans. Wherever I looked I saw people roaring with laughter as they waded around through the flood, and it was plain that the majority regarded this whole performance as the funniest thing to have happened in years. So I gave up feeling guilty about my own good fortune in having a roof over my head and came back here to enjoy it.

I had often wondered why all the local lanes and streets look like dried-up river-beds and now I know—they *are* dried-up river-beds. On the way to my house a knee-deep torrent was swirling furiously between the buildings—which, as in Kathmandu, are almost all raised some three or four feet above the ground—and three dead hens and a dead puppy were swept past me as I waded home.

As usual I had left my window open and the room had been thoroughly blitzed: on the floor lay rice and onions and smashed eggs, sodden papers and books, and a broken lantern and spilled kerosene. I swept up the rice, which is in any case filthy when one buys it, and lifted a neighbour's dog up the ladder to dispose of the eggs, and now I'm writing by torchlight, pending the replacement of the lantern. Luckily my 'cellar' escaped so I'm not deprived of spiritual consolation. At the moment this consolation consists of a brew distilled in Kathmandu, sold at seven shillings per pint bottle and imaginatively described on the label as 'Pineapple Wine'. Somehow such a description conjures up pictures of elderly ladies (retired missionary type) daringly sipping a beverage made from great-grand-mamma's recipe and containing ·001% alcohol: yet here this coy name disguises a spirit that would make hair grow on an egg. (A recent visitor of mine went so far as to claim that the stuff could propel a steam-roller up Mount Everest, but I feel this may be a slight exaggeration.) Most certainly 'Pineapple Wine' is *not* wine and I doubt if pineapples play any part in its production—at a guess I'd say that it's pure poteen, coloured green. For even the best heads two tablespoonfuls produce the desired effect, and it is probable that three tablespoonfuls would result in macabre hallucinations, quickly followed by death. What it does to one's inside, when taken regularly, I hate to think—but time will tell.

*4 June.*

As from today I'm living with a lama—the untented one, who presented himself on my doorstep this morning and said, 'Please may I come and live with you?' or words to that effect. At first I had some misgivings, not for the conventional reasons that might operate in Europe, but because it is against the rules for any refugee living outside the camp to draw rations. However, a lama is a lama, so after a moment's hesitation I said, 'Very well, come right in—but you must give me your ration-card and every Friday morning I'll bring you your supplies.' A big grin then spread over his face, and after many expressions of gratitude he hurried off to collect his possessions.

Half an hour later I beheld a brigade of twenty-two small boys marching towards my door, each child carrying five enor-mous cloth-bound volumes—except the last, who was carrying only three. I then did some simple mental arithmetic and realised that this was the full Buddhist Canon—all one hundred and eight volumes of it—arriving as item number one of the lama's luggage. Mercifully the other items were less impressive—an incense burner, a prayer-wheel, a prayer-drum, a *dorje*, a prayer-bell, a small photograph of His Holiness, eleven tiny silver butter-lamps to burn before it and (as non-religious goods) a dented kettle, a wooden, silver-rimmed bowl to drink from and an uncured, stinking yak-skin to sleep on. The little room down-stairs (or down-ladder) has now been transformed into a mini-ature temple, from which the exquisite scent of incense comes wafting up, and my life is further brightened by ecclesiastical music; I find the sweet melody of drum and bell so absolutely enchanting that when it starts I simply drop everything and listen.

This afternoon we had another violent storm—not as devastating as yesterday's cyclone, but a passable imitation of it. These storms are not to be confused with the monsoon, which isn't due for another week or ten days, but I'm told that they herald it annually in this region. Tonight the room temperature is down to a blissful seventy-five degrees Fahrenheit and, as my body is now free of heat-rash for the first time in weeks, I'm looking forward to a good night's sleep.

## 5 June.

Famous Last Words! I've discovered that living with a lama has its limitations, the chief of which is His Reverence's predilection for praying—with full instrumental support—from 3 a.m. onwards. Unhappily this is an hour at which the very sweetest of melodies leaves me quite unmoved so perhaps I'd be justified in asking him to postpone his Matins until 5.30 a.m. But somehow this seems slightly disrespectful, though as he doesn't conclude his devotions until 11 p.m. it might be good for his health to force him to sleep a little longer. The unfortunate thing is that these advanced lamas seem to have long since transcended our frail needs for regular meals and eight hours' sleep, and His Reverence is capable of praying non-stop for six hours without moving a muscle.

## 6 June.

This evening I learned quite a lot about my exalted guest, when he invited Thupten Tashi and me to supper. Armed with our own dishes, spoons and salt, we joined him downstairs at seven o'clock—by which time I am always ravenously hungry, having eaten very little since breakfast-time—but the meal did not start until half-past nine. However, it was preceded by much interesting conversation and nine or ten cups of buttered tea (about five cups too many for the average Western stomach) so I'm not really complaining.

Thupten Tashi is by far the best Tibetan interpreter I've ever known, and with his assistance the lama briefly recounted his own life-story. Though he had always wanted to enter a Gelugpa monastery as the only son of a rich farming family he was forced into marriage with a neighbouring farmer's daughter at the age of eighteen; but bringing a horse to the water doesn't necessarily make him drink and bringing Lama Ongyal to his bride's bed did not make him consummate the marriage. Then, after two years of domestic celibacy, he renounced his inheritance and ran away to a monastery in Kham—no doubt to the considerable relief of his still virgin bride, who was now considered free to seek a more practical mate. In Kham he studied for sixteen years under a very learned Rimpoche, before spending three years as a hermit in a Himalayan cave at an altitude of 18,000 feet. Next he returned to his monastery, did his final examinations and moved on to be a tutor or *guru* at Drepung Monastery—from which he fled to Dholpo in 1959.

Encouraged by my revelation of a very rudimentary knowledge of Tibetan Buddhism he followed this potted autobiography with a lecture on the importance of accepting the impermanence of all matter and acting accordingly. But at this stage my concentration began to be seriously impaired by most inappropriate pangs of hunger and, though the spirit was willing, I can now remember few of his profound remarks. He asked me if I believed in God, nodded approvingly when I said, 'Yes', and observed that he had heard rumours to the effect that many modern Europeans were atheists, which seemed to him a pity, as they had a very good way to God in their Christianity. Whereupon I felt compelled to admit that I wasn't exactly an orthodox Christian and on hearing this the lama looked slightly worried, and said he hoped I wasn't a Buddhist, as the Western Buddhists he'd met in Kathmandu were very unhappy people and in fact only imagined themselves to be Buddhists— which is as good an analysis of the breed as I've yet heard.

Meanwhile our supper was being cooked, on a wood fire between stones, by the twelve-year-old boy who is Lama Ongyal's personal servant, and when it at last appeared I noted that our host was not eating with us. I longed to ask if he ever ate *anything*—since as far as my observation goes he exists on buttered tea only—but fearing that the question might sound impertinent I restrained myself. The meal consisted of rice, green dahl and potatoes—a true banquet by Tibetan standards, and it tasted none the worse for the fact that I knew it to have been cooked outside the back-door almost exactly where I (and not a few Nepalese) habitually answer Nature's calls.

Incidentally, I have had the undeserved good luck to escape unscathed after my reckless water-drinking of a few days ago.

*10 June.*

This morning two Dakotas took off from the airfield loaded with the remains of the German Expedition's equipment—and this was apart from the masses of food given away today because it's not worth the freight-charges back to Kathmandu. What looked like the whole Nepalese and Tibetan population of Pardi and exactly half the European population (that's me) were at The Annapurna for the share-out, and in due course I came away shamelessly bearing a tin of chocolate biscuits and two jars of meat extract—a month in Pokhara makes you put your pride in your pocket when such delicacies are going gratis. As for the Tibetans—this evening the camp is full of the most exotic things in tubes, tins, packets and plastic bags, and the people are as thrilled by these colourful luxury containers as they are by the mysterious contents. Walking around the camp at supper-time I saw pâté de foie gras being tentatively mixed with *tsampa,* salad cream being added to tea and soup cubes being chewed as toffees and then suddenly spat out. Terrifying howls of agony were coming from one tent, where some unfortunate little girl had just been given a spoonful of neat mustard by her loving mamma.

Trade is also brisk this evening; at the conclusion of an expedition the Sherpa guides receive as 'perks' sleeping-bags, anoraks, boots, transistors, boxes of electric batteries, nylon rope and many other locally rare objects, most of which they auction in the courtyard of The Annapurna before returning home. Tomorrow the 1965 Japanese Dhauligiri Expedition is due back here—in a rather depressed state, as their two senior Sherpas were killed by an avalanche. They are reported to have even more fabulous equipment than the Germans, both in quality and quantity, so we're all agog for the morning!

Tomorrow, too, is King Mahendra's birthday, a national holiday and in theory an enormously important occasion of universal rejoicing. During the past week all the local Government officials of every grade have been busy organising the celebrations to the detriment of far more urgent practical matters. It's rather obvious that in Pokhara Valley at least the general public have no great desire to demonstrate their loyalty to the King, and for this reason it is essential to *organise* these festivities, though the innumerable complicated religious festivals seem just to *happen*, powered by tremendous popular support.

Going on my own very limited knowledge of the Nepalese political scene I would say that the King is certainly doing his best to impose some sort of order on the indescribable mess bequeathed him by the Rana rulers. Also I have tremendous admiration for the moral courage he displayed in 1960, when he admitted that feigning to operate a democratic government in Nepal was a piece of pernicious nonsense. In the nine years since the overthrow of the Ranas in 1951 Nepal had had ten different governments, each more corrupt and cynical than the other, but now at least there is some degree of stability, though few of the needed improvements have yet taken place.

One of those improvements concerns land redistribution, about which there is at present a great deal of talk, but very little action. Here the King is up against problems similar to those of the Shah of Persia: the rich Brahmin landowners, with their superstition-based influence over the people, are analogous to the Persian mullahs—and apparently even more powerful— and the King's position is not secure enough for him to defy these Brahmins effectively. In the Kathmandu Valley he seems to have the affectionate support of a majority of his subjects, but to the average person in Pokhara both the King and Kathmandu are remote and unimportant. I have met many ex-Gurkha soldiers who have been to Delhi, Hong Kong, Singapore, Cairo and even to London—but who have never been to Kathmandu. And when I ask them, 'But don't you want to see your own capital?' they stare at me and say, 'For what?' In theory Kathmandu is their capital, but in practice they feel that they owe allegiance only to their tribe—and one can see the justice and logic of this attitude. For centuries no ruling power in Kathmandu knew or cared anything about the hill-people, and even now the King is an exception in his concern for the welfare of *all* his subjects; the majority of Government officials are still completely ignorant of and indifferent to what happens outside the valley and for them 'national improvements' mean the shoddy modernisation of Kathmandu and the installation of refrigerators in their own homes.

Today I have had quite the most gruesome experience of a lifetime. Dolma, a forty-two-year-old Tibetan woman, died last night of debilitation (following prolonged dysentery) at the Military Hospital, where I went this morning to enquire about three other patients from the camp. On my way, while walking by the river, I rounded an outcrop of rock and found Dolma's severed head at my feet. I must confess that to come on such a sight unexpectedly, when less than twenty-four hours earlier this woman had been sitting with her head on my shoulder, receiving cheering-up treatment, gave me rather a shock. Nearby the four camp chiefs were dismembering the trunk with blunt little wood-axes, before throwing it into the water, and I left the scene as quickly as possible.

Here the Tibetans choose this method of corpse-disposal in preference to the chopping up of bodies on a 'cemetery-rock' for birds of prey to eat—the more popular method in Tibet itself. Some Nepalese tribes, who live at high altitudes where wood is scarce, also use the rivers as graves, and I should think the bones are picked clean very soon after the dismembered body enters the water; at the moment I have a few open sores on my legs, and when I'm swimming these attract swarms of savage little fishes. In Tibet the office of undertaker—or chopper-upper—belonged to a special caste who were shunned by the average Tibetan; but the camp has no member of this caste and the task is so unpopular that the chiefs are forced to do it themselves. However, it would be wrong to imagine that these nomads are averse to such a job out of our sort of squeamishness; they decline to do it for superstitious reasons, not because the actual chopping up of a human body is repugnant to them.

*11 June.*

Our Royal Birthday Celebrations had been scheduled to begin in the camp at 12.30 p.m., when the Anchiladis and local Panchayat officials were due to assemble and make speeches and listen to the Tibetans praying for the King and expressing their non-existent gratitude for Nepal's reluctantly extended hospitality. A large piece of tarpaulin had been borrowed from the Indian Army Pension-paying Post and under this were arrayed a table (as altar), chairs and pictures of His Holiness and His Majesty (all borrowed from The Annapurna Hotel), while scarves and garlands of paper flowers were laid in readiness to be draped over the pictures. My worry was that the mailbag plane would arrive when Kay and I were shackled by courtesy to the camp—and sure enough in it came at 12.20 p.m., its wheels seeming almost to touch the tops of the tents. I then calculated that Nepalese officials due to appear at twelve-thirty would never present themselves before one o'clock at the earliest: so I leaped on Leo, dashed through the village to collect those precious envelopes, was back in camp by a quarter to one—and found that I had ample time to read ten letters before the Anchiladis' party arrived.

The heat was intense today and all the officials looked exceedingly bad-tempered and unfestive, having already attended several ceremonies in various places—and with many more to come. I gathered that they had only consented to attend the camp 'celebrations' because of pressure from certain quarters in Kathmandu, where a demonstration of 'solidarity' between the people of Pokhara and the refugees was considered very desirable. The whole thing felt extremely phony; of solidarity there is none and our celebrations here were incredibly bogus. Amdo Kessang, Penjung and Chimba had all vigorously exhorted the people to smarten up and produce appropriate symptoms of loyal rejoicing—yet when the officials arrived no one was paying the slightest attention to the Occasion. On every side Tibetans were going about their ordinary tasks or sitting in their tents digesting lunch—and I have to admit that I was glad of this. Contrived demonstrations of insincere feelings may be good diplomacy, but they are anathema to me.

The arrival of the Anchiladis' jeep presented an extraordinary spectacle; in Asia overloaded vehicles are a common sight, but this really was the ultimate in overloading. Though the jeep in question is the tiniest possible model it brought eleven men to the camp, and as the last three emerged one began to feel that one was watching a conjuring trick. The Anchiladis immediately announced—with comically un-Nepalese time-consciousness—that they could stay for only fifteen minutes; but ten minutes had passed before Penjung's wife and daughters produced the ritual tea and expensive, repulsive Indian biscuits and toffees; and a further twenty minutes passed before a sufficient number of Tibetans could be persuaded to assemble around the shelter to watch scarves and garlands being draped on the pictures and to hear the various speeches. At the conclusion of the speechifying everyone unenthusiastically chanted a prayer for the King, and finally the schoolchildren—if they can be so described—sang the Tibetan National Anthem, recently taught them by Chimba; and that was that. I particularly liked this last touch, which could easily be interpreted as showing a certain *lack* of solidarity on the King of Nepal's birthday; but the attendant press-photographer took countless shots with his archaic camera, and as facial expressions do not reproduce well on Nepalese paper the desired effect will doubtless be obtained in Kathmandu.

Then, when the jeep conjuring trick had been repeated in reverse and the vehicle had swayed away—invisible under its festoon of men—a demonstration of a different kind started spontaneously.

Suddenly the camp realised that a picture of His Holiness was hanging beneath the tarpaulin and their reaction astonished me. Normally these nomads don't seem nearly as devout as the Tibetans one meets in India but now everyone, including great tough men with shaggy hair and knives in their belts, came rushing to prostrate themselves before the simple black and white photograph, and then proceeded to pray lengthily with clasped hands and a look of near-ecstasy on their sun-plus-dirt-blackened faces. I couldn't help reflecting that if Tibet went under so comparatively easily to the Chinese, despite the unifying force of this tenacious loyalty to His Holiness, Nepal could

go under even more easily with its lack of any such leadership.

*15 June.*

This morning I awoke to what looked like heaven—a world
mistily draped in gentle clouds that completely hid the great
mountains and almost concealed the nearer hills. It's impossible
to describe the relief of seeing and feeling this grey dampness;
of course the temperature was still about seventy-five degrees
Fahrenheit—but what a joy, after the glare of the past weeks,
to experience such cool dimness and to find clouds still shielding
us as the morning progressed! Then at mid-day the sun re-
asserted itself and shone until about five o'clock when (cheers!)
the monsoon started—not with any spectacular storm but just
as a steady downpour, accompanied by incessant rumblings of
thunder and frequent glares of blue sheet-lightning. On my way
home from supper at Kay's house I fell repeatedly on the slippery,
flooded road, in the coal-black intervals between lightning
flashes that clearly and beautifully illuminated the whole width
of the valley; and now the din of heavy rain on the tin roof is
so deafening that I can hardly hear myself think.

I've refrained from giving details of the trials and tribulations
involved in erecting monsoon huts for the camp—but the number and variety of these trials and tribulations would drive Job to
drink. Between Nepalese procrastination and Tibetan laziness
the whole operation is taking ten times as long as it should and
today it was possible to move only half the camp from badly
leaking tents into less badly leaking bamboo shelters. I suspect that
in this case the Tibetans' laziness is a form of passive resistance;
these nomads obviously prefer the seclusion of their traditional
tent life, however inadequate the available tents may be, to the
sort of communal existence they will have to endure in the new
shelters—and as someone who values privacy far more than comfort I secretly sympathise with them. Having never experienced
the persistent damp of a monsoon season they don't yet realise
that their removal to less unsuitable accommodation is literally
a matter of life or death—especially as many of them are
already in a weakened condition because of the debilitating heat
of this valley and an ill-balanced diet.

*16 June.*

Rain was still step-dancing on the roof when I awoke and the room temperature was down to seventy-two degrees Fahrenheit. Today Pardi seemed strangely hushed without the intermittent roar of planes landing and taking-off—life in this remote Central Nepalese village has at least one feature in common with life in Hounslow or Southall! However, as Nepal has a very mild version of the true Indian monsoon it is unlikely that we'll ever be cut off from Kathmandu for more than a week at a stretch. This morning the rain stopped at about ten o'clock and until it started again this evening the damp heat was rather exhausting—though luckily the sky remained overcast.

For the past four days I've been enjoying two pairs of fish-hawks who have come to live on the wooded precipice overhanging my swimming-pool. They are falcon-sized, with glorious red-gold plumage, and it is wonderful to watch them swiftly swooping down to skim the surface of the green water, and then rising triumphantly against the blue sky with a silver fish in their talons. Here too I have twice seen a giant blue and silver kingfisher, looking like a tremendous sapphire as he flashes in and out of the water. The valley also has many other types of hawk and a great variety of unfamiliar sweet song-birds, as well as jays, tits, crows, finches, swallows and of course the very important, very ugly scavenging vulture, with its brilliant hooked yellow beak, ungainly walk and unpleasantly avid expression.

Last week two unusual patients were presented to me in camp—a pair of fledglings whose mother had been killed in the forest by Nepalese hunters and who were then rescued by Dawa, a firewood-gathering Tibetan. There was a certain pleasing incongruity about this great hulking fellow—looking as tough as Tibetans come—when he advanced towards me tenderly carrying these two tiny objects wrapped in a filthy rag. His trouble was that they wouldn't eat the Bulgar wheat he offered them, so what to do? When I advised insects Dawa carefully put his charges inside his *chuba*-pouch and hurried off on an entomological expedition—instead of getting on with his shelter-building work. And rather to my surprise the fledglings have survived and are now happily hopping around Dawa's tent to the delight of his three-year-old son.

Already I can see that the worst side-effect of the monsoon is going to be a nightly insect-plague. Nepalese shutters have little square ventilation holes near the top and through these fly an inconceivable number of insects, attracted by my lamp. At present the table and everything on it are literally being made to move by the creatures; I have just stopped writing to count eighteen different varieties, from enormous, exquisite moths, bright green two-inch grasshoppers and horny russet beetles, to mosquitoes and winged ants and half-a-dozen weird objects that I can't even attempt to identify. The combination of buzzes and bangs and whizzes and whines and bumps and drones adds up to quite a din. What is worse, the floor is swarming with big black ants—in addition to my permanent army of tiny red ones —and with cockroaches. I must admit that when sleeping on the floor cockroaches seem to me expendable, though I'm not neurotic about them as I am about spiders. Luckily—almost miraculously—spiders seem to be the only form of insect life *not* represented in the room at the moment.

Incidentally, my rats are becoming impossibly truculent— and obviously their mothers brought them up not to eat poison. Last night one of them knocked a zinc bucket off a tea-chest on to my head, so today I have a big lump above my ear; on moonlit nights it is positively depressing to see so many grey shapes scurrying around the room.

# 5

# *Tibetans on Trek*

*18 June. Pokhara.*

About a hundred and fifty more bamboo mats are desperately needed to complete the new shelter, but we have already bought all those available in the valley. However, I heard today that it should still be possible to buy some in Siglis, a village two days' walk from here, so I instructed Chimba to leave at dawn tomorrow morning with twenty-five Tibetans and to bring back as many mats as could be wheedled out of the villagers. I had expected him to rejoice at the prospect of even so short a trek for, like most Tibetans, he has an inborn inclination both to wander and to trade; but he showed an odd reluctance to go to Siglis and on being questioned as to the reason he declared that the track was exceptionally difficult at the best of times and would be downright dangerous now that the rivers were rising. This seemed a fair enough argument, yet it did not entirely convince me. When I enquired further he admitted that there was also a possibility of trouble with the Nepalese in Siglis, where the raiding exploits of Khamba brigands have made Tibetans so unpopular that the villagers would be more likely to attack our party than to trade with them; at which point I suddenly and delightedly saw that here was a perfect opportunity for me to combine duty and pleasure by accompanying the party as a pacifying agent, while getting my first experience of travel in the hills. Chimba at once agreed to organise the expedition if I came too, so tomorrow morning at six o'clock we will all set off together.

Today I found that the river had risen about five feet during the past twenty-four hours, transforming my placid pool into a frothing swirl of water. I got myself wet by cautiously going in at the edge of the torrent and hanging on to a rock while the water raced powerfully over me; then I pulled myself out, soaped all over and re-immersed for a rinsing-off session. All the time the river was rising fast; while rinsing and dressing I left my soap on a little ledge of rock some six inches above the water and within those few moments it was swept away and the ledge completely covered.

### 19 June. Toprung.

This seems a very appropriate name for a hamlet near the summit of a 6,000-foot hill overlooking a deep, narrow valley; but my spelling is purely phonetic and it may be that Anglo-Nepali experts have an entirely different way of writing the word.

Our early start didn't come off today, because of persistent heavy rain, and it was seven o'clock before we marched out of camp in a pleasant grey coolness. Then there was another delay, caused by several men disappearing into The Annapurna on some obscure business connected with the private trading they hope to do in Siglis, so it was almost eight o'clock by the time we crossed the airfield.

Siglis is due north of Pokhara, according to my Swiss map of Nepal, yet because of the terrain's intractability we began our journey by walking more than five miles due south along the valley floor, before turning east for two miles up a broad side-valley. Here flowed an erratic river which we had to ford often, but in spite of a very fast current this was not difficult as the water never came above thigh-level and the bed was of firm gravel. Though this valley is about half-a-mile wide it is not cultivable, being merely a dried-up river-course which later in the season will be entirely submerged, and its stony surface was not appreciated by the barefooted Tibetans. Many of them had started out proudly wearing formidable mountaineering boots, acquired from various expeditions, but soon these unbearably unfamiliar prestige symbols had been transferred from feet to shoulders. Now the sight of so many bare feet on such cruel stones caused me considerable vicarious pain, so I urged a temporary resumption of boots; but this idea was at once rejected and in consequence we made slow progress during the next ninety minutes.

On either side of the valley rose steep, heavily-forested hills and occasionally we came to hillocks of grass on which a few handsome black cattle were grazing under the care of inquisitive, skinny children. By now the sky was almost cloudless and the heat considerable, so I often lay in the river for a moment without bothering to remove my shirt and shorts—a sensible idiosyncrasy which provoked uncontrollable mirth among the Tibetans. The fact that none of us had ever been to Siglis was giving the trek a faint tinge of adventure. Chimba had spent the previous evening searching for locals who knew the track and discussing it with them—but the Nepalese are not very precise in their directions and now he wasn't even pretending to be sure of where we went next.

Near the head of this valley we forded the river for the fourth time and then began to follow one of its tributaries up a steep side-valley, which was cultivated here though later it narrowed to a ravine. At the confluence of the rivers stood three solid Gurung farmhouses and all their occupants, of every age group, were now working at full pressure in the flooded paddy-fields, ploughing them with bullocks in preparation for the replanting of rice seedlings.

To me such evidence of harmony between nature and man is wonderfully soothing. During the long hot days preceding the monsoon little work can be done and the people sit about idly enjoying themselves; then suddenly the rains come and overnight the landscape is utterly changed and the whole tempo of life altered to a most urgent activity. Here man, to survive, must co-operate fully with Nature, and it is impossible to see this severe yet dignified work-pattern as inferior to that of an industrial community in which men labour as dully in November as in May, obsessionally conscious of their individual 'rights' while remaining stuntedly unaware of themselves as part of a whole. Increasingly one senses a threat to racial sanity in this artificial sealing off of ourselves in a solitary compartment where pride in technological ingenuity replaces the old, instinctive recognition of our links with the rest of creation and our dependence on 'the gods'. Yet, even if it were possible to go back, any such denial of the good in our civilisation would be still more destructive than the present indiscriminate worship of both good and evil.

I had lingered to watch the ploughing and now, hurrying to catch up with the rest, I tried to imagine the unimaginable—life in 2065. Probably the most we can hope for is a gradual growth beyond this current adolescent idolatry of man's omnipotence towards a new, deliberate recognition of the necessity to worship *something* other than ourselves.

The paddy-fields all lay on one side of the river—by now I was too foxed up to know whether it was the north, south, east or west bank—and the only path was along the top of a narrow irrigation ditch, now sealed to retain the rain. As we advanced in single file the soft clay often crumbled, sending some unfortunate toppling into knee-deep liquid mud, and every one of the workers and animals was covered from head to foot in this thick dark liquid—which was all very well for the men, who wore only loin-cloths, but can't have been too pleasant for the women in their voluminous skirts. The men of our party are wearing ragged gift-parcel slacks or shorts—they reserve their *chubas* for festive occasions—but the women have not yet discarded the traditional Tibetan clothes. However, six out of the ten girls are dressed in the unusual Dholpo divided skirt, which neither Kay nor I had ever seen among the Tibetans in India; at first glance these garments look like ankle-length gowns, but they are in fact very loose pantaloons which allow great freedom of movement when walking or climbing.

As we ascended this valley the incline became much steeper and the river swifter and noisier among its tumble of rounded rocks. When the paddy-fields had been left behind I overtook the Tibetans, whose walking pace was apparently geared to that of laden yaks, and soon they were all behind me and I was happily alone in a fresh and lovely world of high, forested cliffs, glinting water and herb-sweet air. Occasionally fifty-foot waterfalls came leaping strongly off the cliffs, and in places the valley broadened enough for the path to wander briefly away from the river's edge across new green grass between silvery rocks. After about forty minutes I came to another fording place—and now I saw why Chimba had been apprehensive. Here the current was so powerful and the water so discoloured that it was impossible to judge depth and one had to feel with a stick before taking each step, all the time bracing oneself against the force of the water. But this river was no more than fifteen yards wide and I was soon across; the most disconcerting thing during such fordings is the shifting of stones on the river-bed beneath one's feet.

I sat on the bank to smoke a cigarette and de-leech my legs while waiting for the Tibetans. Surprisingly, most of the girls made quite a fuss about the fording and it was comical to see those tough nomad youngsters giving an excellent imitation of nervously giggling mid-Victorian ladies whose carriage has broken down on the way to a dinner party. Possibly this display was being put on mainly to attract the men's attention—though one can see that for non-swimmers such a crossing could be rather frightening. The ability to swim would almost certainly prove irrelevant if one were swept away by a mountain torrent but it does illogically give one an extra degree of confidence.

Chimba decided to call a halt here as many of the party were already 'creating' about being leech infested; this was the Tibetans' first monsoon so these pests were unfamiliar to them. Foreseeing several septic legs by the time we got home I hastened to explain that never must a leech be forcibly detached from the skin; either salt or a lighted cigarette are the only answers. As we have nothing but rock salt with us—and salt is in any case too expensive to waste on leeches—I went around from leg to leg with my cigarette, assuring the Tibetans that contrary to appearances they were not going to bleed to death within half-an-hour. Pasang, one of the more argumentative men, pointed out that he had already pulled his leech off and that his leg was *not* bleeding—nor did he appear convinced when I explained that this was exactly the point, and that bleeding was essential after the wretched creature had been removed. I didn't even attempt to explain that the bleeding was so copious only because leeches inject an anti-coagulant before beginning their meal.

Soon after this rest-halt we left the river and began the toughest part of today's walk—a climb to the crest of a 6,200-foot hill. (My natural impulse is to call this obstacle 'a mountain'; but by local standards it is of course a mere mole-hill.) For much of the way up—through dense forest—the track was not a track but a stone stairway; so if you can imagine ascending a two-mile stairway with very deep steps you will have some idea of how we felt on the crest.

By now it was apparent that these Tibetans have become seriously debilitated after six months in an unsuitable climate on an inadequate diet. Though travelling light and bred to walk far in rough country they made very slow progress at this stage, and for their sakes I'm thankful that on the way home, when they will (we hope) be carrying heavy loads, the journey will be mostly downhill. I waited for them at each porter's-rest —those stone squares, usually built around the base of a large tree, where a man can sit on one ledge and rest his load on the ledge above. The comfortable fixing of heavy and often unwieldy loads can be quite complicated so these rests are designed to take the weight off the body without the removal of the load. Many of them must be centuries old, for on the shiny stone seats one can see where the impress of countless buttocks has worn into the surface.

On the crest of the hill I again walked briskly ahead—and then suddenly came to one of the eeriest spots I have ever known. Here the path overhung a deep ravine, and where it turned right to climb the next ridge a tiny Hindu shrine, covered with stale bloodstains, had been built in the shadow of a gigantic, fantastic tree. The weird distortion of this tree gave it such an unnerving personality that spontaneously one thought of it as a demon in disguise; and to add to the unreality of the scene the monster roots were growing around a colossal black rock, about a hundred feet high and thirty feet wide, that had become detached from the mountainside and was poised un- naturally above a sheer, thousand-foot drop. These complex roots were as thick as a man's body and they clasped the rock with a nightmarish, writhing ferocity that produced an extra- ordinary effect of repellent beauty. Even on this brilliantly sunny afternoon the place was merely twilit and in the absolute silence of the forest the steady, quiet dripping of water off the rock sounded ridiculously, but definitely, sinister. I am not given to psychic reactions and perhaps, had I been forewarned, I would have had my shield of scepticism in place and felt no more than interest at observing a curious natural phenomenon. But as it was this corner of the forest frankly scared me and I'm

not surprised at the erection of a shrine to propitiate the spirits
of the tree and rock, who obviously have extremely unpleasant
dispositions. I rang their heavy iron bell three times as a pre-
cautionary salutation and its curiously amplified echoes were
still resounding as I climbed towards the crest of the next ridge.

Such encounters with the mysterious can be at once stimulat-
ing, chastening and annoying. It is always exhilarating to
glimpse regions that can't be mapped, and it is healthily humbl-
ing to be challenged by subtleties against which rationality is no
defence. Yet it is irritating, too, to be proved still vulnerable to
influences which one is supposed to have long outgrown; and in
the end one is left with just another big question mark. After
firmly deciding that rocks and trees do not have spirits the only
alternative explanation for such 'atmospherics' is that over many
centuries enough people have come to this place with enough
awe for its visible peculiarities and enough terrified belief in the
power of its spirits to leave an enduring deposit of fear and unease in the shadow of that root-gripped rock. But this leads on to
speculation as to *why* certain natural phenomena should so
overwhelm the minds and imagination of men—and if one
doesn't then think quickly about something else one is back
where one started.

Now the track was climbing through maize-fields to a little
village built on a series of narrow shelves just below the top of
the ridge. There appears to be a vast amount of marble available locally, and this has been used here to create a uniquely
beautiful village. For the final quarter of a mile the track was
very steep and as I ascended a stairway of smooth marble slabs
I had the illusion of approaching a royal palace rather than a
primitive hill settlement. This marble is of many soft colours—
pink, white, green, yellow, fawn—and discovered amidst the
glory of the surrounding heights and depths it is intoxicatingly
lovely. Then I found myself walking between the houses on
shiny marble paving-stones, instead of the usual rough paths,
and—most striking of all—I saw, on the ledge below, roofs of
multi-coloured thin marble slates, glowing with a gentle lustre
in the clear air.

I waited for the Tibetans in the centre of the village and
when they had joined me Chimba explained that the local

people were Gurungs, who would be less unhelpful than the orthodox Hindu Chetris in the next settlement; so we agreed to eat here. He and I then sat on the verge of a minor precipice and ate our hard-boiled eggs and raw onions, while the rest of the party dispersed throughout the village to beg for the use of fireplaces on which to prepare *tsampa*.

Rarely have I picnicked amidst such enchantment. In addition to the marbled splendour of their roofs these houses had smooth walls of handsome stone slabs, so cleverly cut that no mud was needed to stop up cracks, and each separate stone seemed to be tinged a different shade of brown, cream or grey. Yet it was the texture of the stones and the apparent simplicity of the well-proportioned structures—which in fact must require consider-able skill—that pleased me most. It is interesting that the availability of such unusual building materials has inspired local craftsmen to attain a much higher level of artistry than is evident in any of the neighbouring villages; and Chimba tells me that in all his Nepalese travels he has never seen anything comparable with this little settlement.

No milk was to be had here, but when we had finished our meal Chimba proudly produced tins of powdered milk and Swiss drinking chocolate (both scrounged from the German expedition of happy memory) and while we were drinking this delicacy one of the many eagles that float continuously over these valleys swooped down with talons outstretched and seized a hen which was pecking nearby at our eggshells. What fierce-looking birds these are, seen close to and in action!

When we continued after an hour's break the path first went downhill through terraced maize-fields, then crossed a river be-fore climbing steeply through more forest, and finally levelled out to swing around the shoulder of another mountain and bring us to this small village of grass-thatched ochre-washed Chetri houses.

My crossing of the above-mentioned river made the day for the Tibetans. The 'bridge' was a single, narrow, slippery tree-trunk, about thirty feet long and some fifty feet above a flooded river-bed crowded with hideous-looking boulders. A single slip could mean nothing but death and after one horrified look I said, 'No, thanks—perhaps in my reckless youth but certainly not now'. The Tibetans were tickled pink by such cowardice and several of them at once volunteered to carry me across on their backs; but I emphatically declined this terrifying though noble offer and while they all trooped over without a second thought I investigated alternatives. There were none. So I despairingly sat astride the damn thing and cautiously propelled myself across, which device had the Tibetans literally rolling on the ground with mirth. But it did get me safely, if slowly, to the other side.

It was only 5.30 p.m. when we arrived here and as two hours of daylight remained we intended walking further; but on en-quiring about shelter we learned that none existed between Toprung and Siglis, which is seven hours' walk away. So, as sleeping out without tents isn't very healthy during the mon-soon, we are now billeted on the unwelcoming though not overtly hostile villagers. We will sleep on various verandahs at the approximate cost of one penny per sleeping-space and I'm among the honoured few who are to be accommodated on the verandah of the village store, which sells nothing but cigarettes, matches and cloth, plus kerosene at certain seasons. The weary Tibetans were jubilant at this unexpectedly early halt and it suited me too. While wood was being collected to boil big saucepans of tea for our *tsampa* supper I set off on an exploratory walk to the top of this mountain, revelling in the cool evening air and in the dramatic splendour all around me.

The steep track of slippery yellow-red mud led me past several farmsteads set amidst fields of seven-feet-high maize. There were many goats about, and the usual Nepalese prolifera-tion of undersized poultry, and despite the terrain quite a few cattle—mostly working bullocks in excellent condition. Here rice and maize are the chief crops, and even at this altitude there were a few banana trees, though their fruit was small and as yet unripe.

While walking along the mountainside, away from the track, I was often looking down into farmyards on the terrace below and glimpsing vignettes of domestic life—a young father ab-sorbed in play with his two tiny sons, an elderly husband yelling abuse at his cowed wife and menacing her with an axe, or a grandad milking goats while keeping one eye on his toddling grand-daughter as she romped ecstatically with a pure white, newborn kid. Watching such scenes unobserved, one can forget the many gulfs that separate race from race and find security in our common humanity; then someone notices the foreigner and the moment of comforting union is gone. Every activity is neglected while curiosity seeks satisfaction and again the gulfs appear—wider and deeper in Nepal than in any other country I have known, because here, outside of the Kathmandu valley, it is uncommon for people to come halfway to meet the friendly stranger.

It would be futile to try to describe this region, for in exclusively mountainous countries every beauty is too extreme to be conveyed by any words that I might choose. None of the books or photographs studied before leaving home had even slightly prepared me for such majesty. Truly this is something that does have to be seen to be believed, and that once seen must be continually yearned for when left behind, becoming as incurable a fever of the spirit as malaria is of the body.

When I arrived back in Toprung village it was still quite bright at this level—but the immensity of the valley far below was already filled with a solid-seeming, dark-blue dusk and above the opposite mountains towering clouds were gathering fast. Now it is half-past nine and for the past two hours sheets of water have been streaming from a black sky.

*20 June. Siglis.*

It was a relief to get up at 4 a.m. and escape from the hordes of bed-bugs that had tormented me all night. Their invincibility made sleep impossible; I merely dozed lightly, woke to swear and scratch furiously, then dozed again, woke again, swore again, scratched again and so on through what felt like a week of nights. But on either side of me Tibetans were sleeping deeply, their total immunity affording thousands of bugs a blissfully undisturbed banquet.

For me one of the advantages of Tibetans as trekking companions is that their conception of essential equipment matches my own; within ten minutes of rising we were on the track again, walking by moonlight for the first quarter of an hour.

Then quite suddenly it was light and we could see banks of silvered cloud softly rolling up the valley below us. As the rain had just ceased the whole world was dripping and rushing with water, and for the first half of our long descent to river level the path was in fact a swift stream, calf-deep, through which we scrambled among shifting stones and rough rocks. It is difficult to decide whether these paths are streams converted into 'highways' or vice versa. This area of the mountain was a mere tangle of scrub, neither forested nor cultivated, and once we lost our way and went scrambling down a few hundred feet in the wrong direction before Chimba, using some sixth sense, realised our mistake and led us up again.

Today leeches were much more plentiful than yesterday, and the Tibetans made an absurd fuss about this minor annoyance; to hear their screams and roars one would imagine them to have been attacked by tigers. It was obvious that if I were to burn off every leech immediately its host noticed it we'd never get any where so, as the leech's sucking is completely painless, I told the party to ignore the creatures till we had arrived at Siglis, where we could hold a mass de-leeching session.

The latter half of our descent was from paddy-field to paddy-field—a relaxation after the rough track, yet tiring in its own way because for much of the time we were dragging ourselves through knee-deep sticky mud. Each terraced field was about twenty yards long, ten yards wide and three or four feet high; stepping stones were sometimes set in the dykes, and it was only by finding and correlating these that we could follow the route, since our track as such was no longer in existence.

We were still about three hundred feet above river level when we rounded a corner and saw Siglis—a tiny cluster of houses near the summit of the next precipitous mountain. I reckon that the village was then about two miles away as the crow flies—but eight miles as humans walk.

From here the central valley broadened out for some miles to the north and was noisy with the speed of a wide, frothing river—which fortunately did not flow between us and our destination. Now we could also survey the narrow side-valley separating us from the Siglis mountain, and the tributary that here went raging down to the main river looked sufficiently

daunting to set the Tibetans muttering prayers. I brightly remarked that when we got down to this torrent we would probably find quite an easy fording spot—but I was wrong. In fact
it proved to be far too swollen for any attempt at wading, and
there was a long delay while we searched for a spot where we
could cross by leaping from boulder to boulder. Eventually
Chimba found such a spot, though as the boulders in question
were all rounded—and entirely submerged—no one considered
this leaping game to be very amusing. I was then tempted to
worry in a fussy Western fashion about the state of this river by
tomorrow and the safety of the Tibetans when re-crossing it
with heavy loads; but happily my temperament is in some
respects more Eastern than Western, and as the Tibetans themselves were obviously not looking this far ahead I reminded myself that 'sufficient unto the day . . .'

The sky was now cloudless and clear early sunshine filled this
wild world of powerful mountains, racing waters, scattered
rocks and new green growth. I longed to be alone here: yet if
I had had to choose my companions I would have chosen these
Tibetans, who are so attuned to such remoteness that they never
come between it and me as even the most congenial of Western
companions inevitably would do.

About half-a-mile from the river we came upon an isolated,
impoverished Gurung farmhouse which also acts as a 'transport
café', and here we stopped (having had no breakfast) to drink
glasses of ginger tea before tackling the brutal climb to Siglis.
This was my first taste of ginger tea, which is popular among
those Nepalese who can't afford the real thing, and I found it
most refreshing.

The track, now quite distinct, continued level along the valley floor for another mile or so. Then directly below Siglis,
which was no longer visible, it turned left and went up and up
and up, and still further up, until it seemed that we were
doomed to spend the rest of our lives dragging aching bodies and
rumbling bellies up an everlasting incline. Yet there was—at
least for me—the reward that always makes such efforts worth
while; even non-mountaineers know the ineffable joy of *going
higher*. A peculiar triumph tingles in the blood when at each
stop one looks down and sees how much farther away is the

valley from which one started. Why this triumph should result from perpendicular rather than horizontal progress it is not for me to say; no doubt the psychologists have a word for it—but I don't particularly want to submit the ingredients of this special joy for clinical analysis.

Significantly, Chimba and I—the only adequately nourished members of the party—arrived here soon after eleven o'clock, an hour ahead of the rest. Siglis has a population of about 4,800 Gurungs, and during the past few years it has had a school of sorts, now closed because the teacher left since the government had forgotten to pay him any salary for fifteen months. Nor is this an exceptional case; all over Nepal recently-opened rural schools are folding up for the same reason. There is only one tiny store-cum-teashop, doing the usual trade in cloth, cigarettes, matches and, providentially, those nauseating Indian biscuits which are so inexplicably prized by the Nepalese. When we arrived I immediately devoured a whole pound of (literally) mouldy biscuits, while Chimba boiled a saucepan of rice on the storekeeper's fireplace.

I got through my biscuit marathon sitting outside the store on the edge of the terrace (inevitably every laneway here is a terrace) overlooking the valley far below. From this height the river's roar is inaudible, and I savoured with gratitude the uniquely calming stillness of high places. Away to the north, at the head of the valley, gleaming snow peaks soared above the nearer mountains and directly opposite Siglis—beyond the river—I could see another high village; it looked deceptively near, though for the duration of the monsoon no communication will be possible between these two settlements.

I had felt myself being almost weakened by the sun, which at 9,000 feet begins to have an odd sting in its heat, but as we ate our rice a procession of plump grey clouds came floating up the valley in a stately way; and soon long, coiling wisps of vapour had detached themselves from the main mass to send their cold moisture eddying through the village. Then, as we de-leeched the exhausted Tibetans—who came crawling up the laneway in twos and threes, characteristically laughing at their own fatigue—rain began to bucket down in a true monsoon deluge. Luckily, however, the efficient Chimba had already arranged for us to be accommodated in the local Panchayat headquarters, on the terrace below the store, and we hurriedly retreated from the downpour.

This new building is a very unsound erection of wood, stone and mud, with a leaking corrugated iron roof. Such roofs are tremendous prestige symbols here, each iron sheet having been carried on a man's back from India, and their impracticality is equalled only by their ugliness—which is the more distressing for being found in the midst of so much beauty. I cannot help suspecting some political significance in the extraordinarily bad workmanship of this Panchayat headquarters. The men who built it would certainly have done more skilful jobs on their own homes; but the Panchayat system is a political imposition from Kathmandu and the haphazard construction of its local head-quarters reveals indifference to the innovation—and may well be a deliberate, oblique protest against Government interference.

After my buggy night at Toprung, followed by a hard climb and a heavy meal, I was now almost asleep on my feet, so while the Tibetans prepared their well-earned *tsampa* I curled up in a corner on the lumpy mud floor and slept soundly for three hours.

On our arrival here Chimba had tried to circulate the news that we had come to buy mats, but at this season the farmers are so busy that virtually no one—man, woman or child—is to be found in any village between 5 a.m. and 7.30 p.m. (When you have to climb down two or three thousand feet to reach your fields you do *not* come home to lunch!) A small group of us set off to tour the village at 5.30, but we met only tottering, tooth-less, totally gaga great-great-grandfathers, who had long since forgotten what bamboo mats were, so we soon gave up our futile braving of the savage mastiffs who were chained to stakes in front of every homestead.

Siglis is quite unlike the ochre-washed, straw-thatched vil-lages of the lower slopes. Here the houses are built of enormous stones plastered over with brown mud and the majority are roofed securely with weighted slates. Steep, uneven steps lead up from one row of houses to the next and this evening each of these stairways was a miniature waterfall. At first I had won-dered—rather stupidly—why the original settlers, with a whole mountain at their disposal, had chosen to build at this height;

but now, studying the village, I realise that it was sited on the rockiest part of the mountain, where cultivation of any crop would have been impossible.

At dusk we borrowed a lantern from the storekeeper and set off again to attempt to trade. For the past half-hour people had been streaming back from the fields, carrying antique wooden ploughs over their shoulders and driving sleek black bullocks before them, and I was fascinated by the agility of these great animals as they climbed the narrow steps between the houses. Our camp had attracted great, though not very friendly, interest from the passers-by and we now found that though many mats were available few of the villagers were willing to sell them to Tibetans. Despite Chimba's warning I was somewhat taken aback by the degree of sullen hostility shown towards us; whether it would have been more active without the restraining presence of Authority, obscurely represented by me, it is impossible to say, but undoubtedly my activities as liaison officer were useful, if not essential, and when I had solicited the aid of the co-operative headman we began to make some progress. Eventually he assured us that all the mats we needed would be brought to us early in the morning—but it remains to be seen how effective his influence is. It's now nearly ten o'clock and the Tibetans are snoring happily around me; I only hope that the bugs in our bedding have been sufficiently atrophied by the cold for me to sleep too.

*21 June. Toprung.*

The headman's influence proved so effective that at 4 a.m. laden villagers began to queue outside the Panchayat building and by 8 a.m. we had purchased eighty mats (heavy rain meant that no one was going early to the fields). Then the supply dried up abruptly—doubtless because the weather did likewise—but we were promised forty more mats this evening. I then decided that fifteen of us, including all the girls, should return today, leaving ten to follow tomorrow. It would have been fun to wait and explore further, but Chimba had to stay as interpreter, and one of us two had to shepherd the fifteen, so I led the party off at 10.30 after a hearty 'brunch' of *tsampa*.

Each Tibetan was carrying a roll of five or six heavy mats—supported by a broad band around the forehead—which made me feel dreadfully guilty about carrying nothing: but it's no use pretending that I could carry even one mat (they measure eight feet by three) on any of these tracks. It was agony merely to watch the Tibetans struggling down that unspeakable path with those unspeakable loads; I myself found the descent difficult enough, and as one's thigh muscles are the brakes on such a gradient I know that mine will be very stiff tomorrow.

Soon after we left Siglis a cloud sat on the mountain and the chilly, driving mist made me feel quite homesick for Ireland when I saw it move across the green turf and grey rocks. By the time we got to the Gurung tea-house another real deluge was in progress, so we each had two glasses of the ginger brew while waiting for it to ease off. On the way down the sole of one of my canvas boots had come partly adrift, and now Tsiring—at sixteen the youngest of the party—noticed this unimportant detail, registered horror, demanded the boot, produced a large needle and strong thread from his pocket and expertly repaired the damage while we were drinking our tea. As good nomads these Tibetans set out on even the briefest trek equipped for all such emergencies.

They also have a commendable passion for buying hens and chickens and, as they had each acquired at least two birds in Siglis, every roll of mats now contained its quota of poultry—which complained loudly at halts, to the wonderment of the Gurung farm birds.

Next came that damnable river, which had risen so much since yesterday that our crossing via the boulders could not be repeated. After a long search we came on a place, much further upstream, where by a combination of rock climbing and jumping we could quite safely cross—without loads. Everyone then unloaded, some of us went to the other side and each roll of mats was passed from hand to hand up the rocks and over the water and down the rocks to level ground—an operation which delayed us more than an hour.

Knowing that no other danger spots lay between us and Toprung I now went ahead of the rest, grateful for an opportunity to be alone for a few hours. Already the sky was clear again and the sun dazzled on a sparkling exuberance of growth; even Ireland could not surpass the brilliance of the green that clothed these mountains. But even since yesterday the rains had wreaked havoc on the path above the paddy-fields, and somewhere amidst those minor landslides I took a wrong turning which eventually brought me to the village—after many bewildered wanderings in various directions—from below instead of above.

On those lower slopes I had loitered to watch the rice planters at work. This one week in the year is the most critical period of the Nepalese farmers' lives, when transplanting takes place after the original shoots have suddenly sprung up and the first rains have irrigated the terraces. Each tiny field has a hole in the dyke through which the water pours out until a foot's depth is left, when the hole is adroitly blocked with mud and the ploughing begins. Next the dyke is re-opened to allow the surplus water to flow away and in the residue of soft mud the young shoots are transplanted, before another closing of the dykes brings the water level back to six inches. I had never before realised what swift and skilful labour is required for this operation. When you see every individual tiny wisp of rice stalk being planted by hand you begin to understand why the entire population of a village has to slave at the task from dawn to dusk. Men and boys do the ploughing on one level while half the women and girls bend over the dry terraces, gently but speedily uprooting the tender shoots and throwing them onto the terrace above, where the rest of the womenfolk replant them, about six inches apart, at the most incredible speed; so rapidly do these workers' hands move that you can hardly see them. It's consoling to think that no machine is ever likely to be invented for a job that demands such a combination of skill, speed and gentleness.

The general standard of health in all these villages is pretty low—though not as low as in the average Indian village. This morning I spent half-an-hour talking to the compounder at the tiny, ill-stocked Siglis dispensary. (No hospitals, doctors or nurses are to be found outside the Kathmandu and Pokhara valleys; and even within these valleys most of the worthwhile medical care is provided by missionaries.) This young man, a native of Kathmandu, was the only person in Siglis who spoke any English but, unlike the majority of Kathmandu-born officials who find themselves stationed in the hills, he did not complain about his present 'primitive' surroundings. Instead he gave the impression of being genuinely interested in his work, though he admitted that with his limited knowledge and experience and his minimal medical supplies he could really do very little to alleviate local suffering. He told me that venereal diseases—either inherited or contracted—were responsible for most of the villagers' complaints. His estimate was that eighty-five per cent of the population was riddled with V.D.—hence so many blind, deaf, deformed or imbecile children. Whether or not Siglis is an exceptional village in this respect I wouldn't know; one can only hope so.

To my sleeping-bag now—but I fear *not* to sleep, remembering what our previous night at Toprung was like.

*22 June. Pokhara.*

It was another hellishly buggy night, as I had expected, and at 5.30 a.m. when the rain had just ceased, I set off alone, leaving the Tibetans to their lengthy preparation of a *tsampa* breakfast. An early meal is contrary to local trekking custom but the Tibetans, unlike the Nepalese, are used to a meal soon after waking, and because of this party's poor condition and heavy loads I thought it advisable for them to fill up before starting for home.

The next two hours provided one of those strange interludes —curiously apart from the rest of existence—which occur only when by some blessed chance a heightened receptivity coincides with a rare degree of beauty in one's surroundings. I know that I shall never forget this morning's walk through the forest. There seemed to be some magic in those short hours, some wonder beyond what was apparent to the senses.

Half-a-mile beyond Toprung I was walking through a density of high greenness with which man has never tampered—an entirely solitary world where supple lengths of grey vapour, weaving between great trees, seemed to possess an eerie substance and purpose of their own. A dawn hush still lay over the mountains, and on this mantle of silence were embroidered the urgent rushings of new-born streams, and the myriad harsh or melodic bird cries that are the voice of the forest. Far below me a motionless pillow of cloud hid the depths of the valley and beyond this gulf the dark blue outlines of the opposite mountains were half revealed, then obscured, then again half-revealed as their sheaths of mist shifted—until quite suddenly the sun was dominant, and the long, smooth lines of these crests lay free against a clear blue sky. Now the whole scene was changed by this vigorous golden light that came pouring over the mountain-tops. As the warmth rapidly increased one could feel the earth's eager response and around every corner were freshly-blossoming shrubs, their white, blue and deep pink flowers unfolding as one watched, to bloom with a most sweet radiance against the dark green of the undergrowth.

Only when I reached the 'marble village', and paused to de-leech myself, did I come out of my trance. Between this village and the valley floor the track had been so transformed by floods, and the landscape so altered by new growth that I got lost twice, in a mild way, and was eventually forced—by the remains of a real landslide about half-way down the mountain—to find a new route to the river. I left signposts of specially arranged sticks for the Tibetans, to save them from repeating my optim-istic mistakes in search of short-cuts, and this evening I was gratified to learn that these markers had served their purpose.

This detour involved a descent through literally pathless forest, a long scramble down terraces of muddy paddy-fields, the fording of a waist-deep, violent river and then the ascent and descent of a new hill (which by this stage felt extraordinarily like a mountain). And all these manœuvres were simply in order to reach another point along the river where it was possible to cross back to the main Pokhara track from which the landslide had deflected us.

It was 4.30 p.m. when I at last got home, painfully hungry and with both boots blood-filled from leech bites. 'Going for a walk' in Nepal really is quite something!

# 6

## *Animal Spirits*

*25 June. Pokhara*

Yesterday my pup Tashi briefly joined this multiplying household. Though a happy and healthy infant her growth has been almost imperceptible during these past weeks, and when Ngawang Pema insisted on handing over possession I very much doubted her readiness to leave home. Tibetans suckle their own offspring until the mother's breast has been repeatedly lacerated by sharp teeth so I thought it unlikely that the minute Tashi had already been prepared for life without Mum—and the next twenty-four hours proved me right. She was cowed, miserable and resolutely on hunger strike; her piteous whimpering would have taken a tear from a stone, so this morning, after a sleepless night for all concerned, I returned her to Mum with my compliments.

One hopes that soon she will grow just a little. At present she is so furry-toy-like that on several occasions last night, when she moved suddenly, I imagined myself to be at last in the D.T.s. An appreciation of religious music would also help; as yet she is positively allergic to it and the lama's sacred melodies had an extremely deleterious effect on her. Every time he started a new bell-and-drum duet she compulsively accompanied him, producing noises that sounded incredibly like the cacklings of a hen which has just laid. Yet Tashi makes music too, with every movement, because like all Tibetan pups she had seven tiny tinkling bells tied around her neck on the day her eyes opened. These serve a dual purpose—the keeping of evil spirits at bay and the prevention of straying during nomad treks.

It's now 1 a.m. because this evening we attended an uncanny ceremony at the camp—the exorcising of evil spirits by Dawa, a monk magician.

When the ceremony began it was already dark outside, but the shelter was brightly lit by the flames of a huge log-fire and by the 108 butter lamps that flickered at the monk's right-hand side as he sat cross-legged on a little mound of yak skins, facing west, with about twenty relatives and friends of the 'possessed' around him.

Dawa spent the first fifteen minutes chanting more and more rapidly and wielding his drum and bell more and more quickly as he invoked the gods to enter into him and speak through him. Next he began to tremble all over—at first slightly, then in shuddering paroxysms as he turned north towards Tibet. At this point Thupten Tashi clutched my arm and whispered, 'The god is coming!' transmitting to me as he spoke a morsel of his own fearful belief. Now the acolyte, Dawa's young servant, stepped forward and placed on his master's head a bizarre cockade-cum-mask of bedraggled peacock feathers and streamers of dirty, coloured ribbon. This signified that the god had taken possession of his oracle, and at once the monk ceased to be a familiar neighbour and the Tibetans prostrated themselves before him as before a picture of His Holiness.

During the few moments preceding the donning of the head-dress Dawa had been unmistakably going into a self-induced hypnotic trance and now, suddenly, he leaped to his feet, tossed the mask of ribbons off his face, and with staring eyes began to speak very angrily, loudly and clearly. At this stage my blood began to curdle slightly, for instead of using his native Dholpo dialect Dawa was now speaking Lhasa Tibetan, which is even further from our camp speech than BBC English is from the broadest Scots. I asked Thupten where this uneducated monk could possibly have learned such polished Tibetan and the answer was that he never had learned it, but that all mediums use it when possessed.

Soon my blood curdled still more, as Dawa became thoroughly infuriated and went rampaging around the hut shouting hoarsely and waving his arms wildly until everyone had fled except Thupten and the blasé acolyte, whose function it was to placate the god by respectfully prostrating himself, and throwing little bowls of water or handfuls of flour into the air.

Dawa's frenzied perambulations eventually brought him to our corner, where he stood over us shaking his drum and bell cacophonously while he roared maledictions; now I could see the foam around his lips, the sweat trickling down his face and the truly terrifying gleam in his eye. Then, swerving away from us, he kicked violently at the altar of cardboard boxes on which the votive lamps were burning; this seemed to me a very rash thing for a god to do in a bamboo hut, but luckily the little flames went out as their containers fell to the ground. Possibly gods can ordain safety precautions in conjunction with their tantrums.

Then abruptly Dawa subsided, trembling, onto his yak-skins, and as everyone came creeping cautiously back I asked Thupten why the god had been so angry. He replied that it was very necessary to condemn certain people in the camp for habitually having evil thoughts, which gave evil spirits a foothold in the community and caused many deaths. Other camp defects had also been censured, including disobedience of His Holiness's commands that the refugees should strive to be self-supporting, and our washing of children in the local river, which is the home of an important god who objects to this pollution of his residence. I was greatly intrigued by the undiluted animism of this last complaint—and indeed by the whole confusing con- glomeration of Bön-po rites, ancient primitive magic and prac- tical politics. I hate to think of His Holiness's reaction to any such ceremony; but at least he was being remembered, if only in his rôle as earthly leader of the refugees.

Next came the exorcism of the sufferers, and now Dawa was back to normal; although in theory he was still inhabited by a deity all the symptoms of trance had vanished. His first patient was Droma, an adolescent girl who complained of great pain in the chest and back. (She is at present being treated by Kay for acute indigestion.) This youngster sat in front of the monk for about ten minutes with her eyes closed tightly and a look of terror on her face—which did not surprise me, as she was being emotionally pulverised by a fearful description of the par- ticular demon she was harbouring. Then she lowered her *chuba* —keeping her breasts covered with unusual modesty because she is unmarried and Dawa a celibate—and the acolyte handed his master a saucer-sized copper disc which had been standing upright in a sacrificial bowl of flour. With this Dawa tapped her back vigorously, while making loud, yelping noises to frighten off the demon. (Had I been a demon they would certainly have frightened me very far off.) Next he spat all over her torso, muttering incantations between each spit—and then the exorcism was over. As Droma prostrated herself three times, before giving Rs. 5/- to the acolyte, I felt a slight sense of anti-climax; somehow one expects demons to move house less unobtrusively.

The next two patients were babies whom Kay has been treating for severe dysentery, but who are not improving because their mothers will insist on breast-feeding them.

Dawa's second trance was even more violent than the first and, though there was no verbal outburst when the god arrived, he flailed around the hut waving drum and bell wildly and once hitting me on the side of my bemused head. Yet no one fled during this display of divine wrath, though everyone cowered and covered their eyes with their hands as the medium approached them; evidently it is the god's spoken message that really frightens the people—and that most scared me, if scared is not too strong a word for the chilled unease felt in such a situation. After some ten minutes of violence Dawa abruptly sat down, and when his uncanny rigors and involuntary moanings had subsided the exorcism of the babies began.

The first one received the same treatment as Droma but the other, who is very debilitated, was subjected to a long and complicated rite. So far Dawa's face had been entirely hidden by his mask, except when the patients were being spat on, but now, as this naked baby was being presented to him by its terrified mother, he tossed back the streamers to reveal a sub-human, snarling expression, not at all modified by the flickering firelight. Then he leant forward with a jerk, giving a perfect imitation of a savage dog growling, and bit the baby between the shoulders.

The rituals that followed were exceedingly complex. With his left hand Dawa pressed to the baby's back the ends of those filthy ribbons that are always attached to prayer-drums, while in his right hand he held the drum and sucked vigorously at the ribbons where they were attached to its centre. After each suck he spat into a little brass bowl handed him by the acolyte, and then appeared to drink a mouthful of water from another brass bowl—though in fact I think he retained the water in his mouth to provide the next spit. This process was repeated eleven times, after which he did the copper-disc demon-scaring act as with Droma, before bending low over the infant and laying his head on its stomach. Then he jerked upright, tossed his mask back, spat once more into the bowl—and with the air of a grimly self-satisfied conjurer announced that the cause of the disease was now lying in the bowl for all to see. A murmur of admiration and reverence greeted this announcement and everyone crowded forward to gaze into the bowl, while the baby's mother wept and laughed with relief. Yet I myself again felt thwarted; it is disillusioning to find that an evil spirit looks like a dead water-beetle.

Finally Dawa set about freeing himself of the god. A motionless, coma-like trance was followed by incantations and music that gradually worked up to the most frenzied crescendo of the evening—then suddenly the bell and drum were dropped and Dawa fell to the ground and lay twitching convulsively and grunting and groaning like a man who is attempting some Herculean feat. Then, after one last horrible gurgle, he relaxed and lay still, his eyes wandering around the hut with the slightly dazed expression of a normally tired man.

Immediately the spell was broken and the acolyte, reverting to being a servant, began to pour tea for us all. As an excited chattering broke out among the Tibetans Dawa slowly moved back to his seat, politely acknowledging the presence of Kay and myself in the normal Tibetan fashion—though previously he had given us no sign of recognition.

I can't say that this display impressed me as a religious rite, though I consider myself fortunate to have seen it. Recently, however, our genuine lamas have been praying a great deal over sick children or adults and these ceremonies are impressive. Usually the lamas improvise a temple in one of their tents, converting an American Surplus Food box into an altar on which they lay as many butter lamps as the patient's family can afford, and little bowls of cock's blood and rice and flour, and figures of gods—here made from dough instead of the traditional butter —and the inevitable conical *tormas*. Then two or three of them sit at right angles to this altar and, fortified by buttered tea, spend all day chanting reverently from the scriptures and producing beautiful, eerie melodies with their drums, bells and human thigh-bone trumpets. These sessions are sometimes concluded by the printing of prayers on the skin of the sufferer, over the affected part, using the wooden printing-blocks with which prayer flags are made.

However, though Dawa's activities were hardly edifying they should not be regarded as sheer fraud. His trances were undoubtedly genuine, and what he said during his 'sermon' revealed a sincere, if not very sensible concern about the camp's welfare. Admittedly his medical hokey-pokey had all the hallmarks, to Western eyes, of a blatant fake designed to dominate the people by fear and earn dishonest pennies, but in these contexts it is never wise to assume that what seems self-evident to Western eyes is therefore true. In his book *Adventures of the Mind*, Dr Arturo Castiglioni observes that 'the magician's voice is in reality nothing but the echo of the voice of the hopes and desires of the crowd . . . their (the magician's) tricks are employed (tricks that are often necessary to the effect and are sometimes practised even in the most modern medical suggestion) to increase their power and success. But faith is indispensable; only the certainty of accomplishing the desired result . . . can determine great success. Men with a critical and developed spirit are never true magicians . . . only confidence in the success deriving from his own personal power, or from the supernatural factors to which he attributes his power, can exercise the spell that compels crowds.' Therefore those accusations of charlatanism so readily made by foreign observers are hardly fair. Magicians like Dawa do indeed use their special aptitudes to make money; but so do Harley Street specialists, and if the magician is not deliberately deceiving he cannot be censured for claiming a fee which, judging by tonight's performance, he has certainly earned the hard way.

*3 July.*

Yesterday I returned from a hectic four-day visit to Kathmandu; it's difficult to decide which was the more exhausting part of it—the refugee business that took me there, or the excessively alcoholic social whirl that on four consecutive nights marked my return from the wilds.

After seven weeks in Pokhara the city seemed a good deal more like a capital than when I first arrived, and now that the rains have started the whole fertile valley is lush with new beauty. The weather reminded me of showery, warm midsummer days in Ireland, when light breezes send lots of grey-white cloud moving slowly across a very blue sky. Everything everywhere looked exuberantly green, the people seemed to have an access of vitality and the air was blessedly dust-free. Yet even the rains have their disadvantages, and now the whole city reeks still more odiously of stale urine; but that is an unimportant detail compared with the golden light that comes slanting between clouds on to freshly leafy trees, tumultuously blossoming shrubs, neat, vivid paddy-fields, glowing red-brown houses and the burnished roofs of pagodas by the score.

I had booked my return seat for 1 July, but that morning the monsoon was going full blast so my forenoon was spent writing and my afternoon strolling about the valley beyond Jawalkhel. Here it struck me as paradoxical that the Newars, who created one of Asia's greatest cultures and who as farmers remain far in advance of most other Nepalese tribes, still do all their tillage with a short-handled, shovel-like iron hoe identical to that used five or six thousand years ago. Yet that oxen-drawn wooden plough used so skilfully by the hill-farmers would be perfectly suited to the broad, flat fields of the Kathmandu Valley. Hardly less extraordinary is the cultivation in the valley of virtually every kind of vegetable and fruit known in temperate and sub-tropical zones, while throughout the rest of Nepal, even in similarly favoured areas, almost none of these foods is produced.

I arrived back here early yesterday morning, and after lunch decided to re-establish communications with Tashi. Then reasoning that she merits refugee status, being the daughter of bona fide exiles from Tibet, I took the rest of the day off to help this particular refugee to adjust to her new environment. She spent most of the time on my lap while I wrote letters, and hours passed before her look of puzzled distress began to fade. Then, towards evening, the hoped-for happened and she wagged her tail. Admittedly it was a brief and doubtful wag, but a wag's a wag for all that, and this manifestation of dawning contentment enchanted me.

Another night of whimpering would have been excusable, yet when I lay on my straw mat Tashi came toddling along and climbed, with an effort, on to my stomach where she curled up matily and went fast asleep. Unmistakably I had been accepted, and it was not directly her fault that I failed to sleep equally soundly last night.

Before Tashi's advent the rats had not disturbed me more than once or twice a night, but in the small hours of this morning I came to the morbid conclusion that they would regard a plump pup as a nice change of diet and from thenon it seemed my inescapable duty to remain at least semi-alert for rescue purposes. So it seems unlikely that I will enjoy another night's sleep until Tashi has at least attained rat-size.

As yet she is much too young and insecure to be left alone in new surroundings; this morning she wailed piteously when I went out to the field for three minutes so, taking the hint, I carried her everywhere today in that cloth shoulder-bag which is habitually worn by all inhabitants of Nepal. The effect delights both camp and village—a minute black-and-tan head and a pair of very bright eyes peering out of a pouch at navel level. When I called on Kay and said, 'I feel like a kangaroo today,' she promptly replied, 'You look like one too.'

### 6 July.

Yesterday the whole camp was in a ferment of preparation for today's celebrations of His Holiness's thirtieth birthday: and ferment is very much the *mot juste* as half the work consisted of making *chang*, which normally is not available in this camp. It had been horribly humid and overcast since morning—the first such day of the season—and at four o'clock the rain came bucketing down. This was wretchedly bad luck, as already an enormous photograph of His Holiness had been brought from the Khamba headquarters in the bazaar to The Annapurna, and in the intervals of supervising *chang*-fermentation everyone dressed up and went to pray before it.

This morning the heavy rain continued until after ten o'clock. Our ceremonies had been due to start at 7 a.m. but when I went to the camp at 6.30, to see how the new huts were withstanding their first real test, the preparations—interrupted by rain yesterday—were not half completed.

Along the cart-track that bisects the camp two rows of carefully-laid white stones marked the route down which His Holiness's picture would be carried from The Annapurna, and small cairns of stones had been built to support the platters upon which incense would smoulder as the picture passed; but the two big tents, rented from the Indian Army camp to serve as temple and kitchen, were not yet erected. However, cooking had already begun in the biggest of our remaining camp tents and I passed a few giant cauldrons of boiling cottonseed oil, into which hundreds of circular Tibetan pastries were being dropped, allowed to simmer for a few minutes, and then fished out on the end of forked sticks, which various dogs licked with relish in between fishing operations.

When the heavy rain eased off the entire camp went marching up the length of Pardi Bazaar. An hour later they came marching back behind the four camp chiefs, who were carrying the palanquin—made from tea chests—that contained the gaudily coloured photograph of His Holiness under a canopy of traditional orange cloth. (It is a fortunate coincidence that the recent Japanese expedition used canvas of the exact hue prescribed by the Mahayana School for such ceremonies.) No attempt had been made to reproduce the Tibetan flag—which has an extremely involved pattern—but a tattered standard of red, blue and yellow was being borne on a bamboo pole at the head of the procession; and it was an oddly moving sight to see the camp marching along behind, all out of step, and to hear them singing their stirring National Anthem, all out of tune.

As we entered the camp clouds of incense came towards us—

the more pungent because of the muggy, windless air—and I made some remark to Kay on the pleasantness of this aroma; but she replied curtly that she hated it. And then it struck me how much easier it is for anyone who has been brought up a Catholic to 'take' Tibetan ritual, which for so many non-Catholic Christians is merely a revolting mess of incense-burning, bead-telling, genuflecting, incomprehensible chanting, and all sorts of crude superstitions like throwing blessed water around and lighting joss-sticks in front of religious pictures. Watching Buddhist ceremonies makes one realise how close Catholicism has remained to the East—which means that in this era of religious 'getting together' the Catholic Church has a shorter journey ahead of her, on one level, than some other Christian denominations. It seems odd that the majority of northern European Christians have felt compelled to turn Christianity into a bleak, sterilised affair, with a high resistance to the germs of mystery and of awe. And often people who have been brought up in this tradition of 'common-sense Christianity' become uneasy at ceremonies that allow for those unknown and 'un-guess-atable' elements which lie at the heart of every religion. Yet their brisk scorn of 'all this nonsense' seems to betray an unadmitted fear that the whole thing may be more complex than they would like to think.

The six camp lamas—between them representing the Nying-mapas, Gelugpas and Sakyapas—received the palanquin into the temple tent with music and chanting. Then the photograph was placed on its altar and Kessang offered it a volume of scripture, a bowl of rice, a massive *torma* and a bell surmounted by a statue of Dorje. Next Kay and I were given little handfuls of raw rice to throw at the picture, and then the lamas, the other guests and finally every man, woman and child came to lay a white scarf before it, each bowing low after their presentation. Obviously none of our nomads had ever before taken part in such formal ceremonies and, though there was no lack of devotion, their etiquette simply wasn't equal to the occasion. I pitied Kessang who, as Master of Ceremonies, was responsible for maintaining some semblance of order and reverent behaviour. Most of the men attempted their obeisances while wearing bear-skin or wide cowboy-type hats—a *faux pas* in itself, and one which was made almost intolerable for Kessang by the gales of laughter that greeted the frequent falling off of hats at the crucial moment. Then, when the women's turn came, many of them attempted to obtain special blessings for their infants by placing them on the pile of scarves that now lay in front of the photograph, from where they could touch the image of His Holiness. But Kessang was more lenient about this breach of etiquette and merely made disapproving noises, without taking action. Then came the best sight of all—scores of tiny Tiblets marching up with their scarves and, having presented them, folding their hands and bowing solemnly before turning away.

During this long drawn-out rite the six lamas and four monks (including our magician Dawa) were continuously chanting prayers while beating drums, blowing conches and ringing bells. Occasionally one of them would stop to swallow some tea or eat a mouthful of the boiled, sweetened rice that was among today's rather alarming delicacies; but only when the scarf presentations had been completed did they down instruments and really get to work on the banquet—of which even my ascetic lodger partook, though with more restraint than the rest. And all this time Tashi lay silent in her bag, so it seems reasonable to deduce that her appreciation of music is maturing faster than her body.

After lunch wooden jars of *chang* appeared, their brass ornamentation highly polished for the occasion, and this development prompted Kay to make her excuses and retire with dignity. A couple of hours later I also retired, without dignity, but feeling very happy indeed after four or five pints of what James Morris has so aptly called 'that species of alcoholic porridge'.

During the afternoon the drizzle turned to another downpour that has not yet eased off; but when I went on my evening tour of the camp I found everyone happily dicing for Tibetan currency, so they are enjoying themselves after all.


*12 July.*

Kay's medical statistics are certainly proving the unsuitability of this climate for Tibetans; between 1 January and

27 May there were only three deaths, but since then there have been eighteen, the majority from dysentery.

Today one baby died while its parents were bringing it to the Shining Hospital. They at once returned here with the tiny corpse and stood weeping in the middle of the road beneath my window; when I went to them the mother was still holding the infant to her bare breast in the frantic hope that after all it wasn't really dead. I had to emphasise that it was and gently force her to cover the little face from the swarming flies— whereupon the father threw himself full length on the muddy road and began to sob his heart out. I then took them up to my room and gave them neat whiskey, which merely made them choke and seemed to do no good; yet perhaps it did help them over the shock. This baby was the youngest of a family of five, but they couldn't have been more grieved if it were their only one. However, it's likely that their grief will soon fade; most of these primitive Tibetans feel such things intensely for a brief period and then recover overnight.

The general decline in camp health during these past weeks has been most depressing. Even the toughest are now afflicted with rheumatism, dysentery, boils, abscesses, scurvy (vitamin C deficiency), swollen legs (vitamin B deficiency) and a variety of worms. Nor am I immune; what I had imagined to be two septic bed-bug bites on my right leg are in fact scurvy sores and I have an impressive cluster of five boils on my behind—all small, but not conducive to comfort.

This morning when I cycled—painfully—to the Military Hospital, I saw the most harrowing sight of a lifetime—a two-year-old Gurung girl at such an advanced stage of malnutrition that she simply didn't look human. Her mother has had mastitis for the past five months, and apparently no attempt was made to wean the child. The family lives four days' walk away, and this morning mother and daughter arrived at the hospital in a large *dokar*, having been carried down to the valley on father's back. The woman's breasts were in an appalling condition; it's impossible to understand why she didn't come for treatment months ago. And the little creature's skin was like that of a nonagenarian—yellow, dry, creased and just hanging on the sharp bones, while enormous glazed eyes stared without seeing from the tiny skull. One had the nightmare feeling that the child had already been dead a long time, though it was still capable of small, feeble movements. The idea of euthanasia repels me, yet today I found myself involuntarily longing to suffocate this little girl.

One notices quite a number of drunks around here, many lying senseless by the wayside, almost visibly enveloped in *rakshi* fumes. Often too they are to be seen swaying and stumbling along the streets, provoking angry frowns from the orthodox Brahmins and good-humoured jeers from the more tolerant masses.

At the hospital today the doctor told me that stomach ulcers caused by over-indulgence in *rakshi* are among the commonest local complaints. Personally I would have thought mere *indulgence* sufficient to ulcerate any stomach, since this Nepalese potion is even fouler than my 'refined' Pineapple Wine, against which the doctor also warned me, saying that it tends to produce sudden, total blindness.

Tonight the monsoon is being positively hysterical; coming home from supper at Kay's I was wading knee-deep through rushing water, in pitch darkness. On such nights umbrellas are just a nuisance and in any case mine, being an Indian model, leaks fluently, while my storm-lantern (also an Indian model) goes out within seconds of encountering a storm. I only hope my roof doesn't spring too many new leaks. At present rain is coming through in just three or four places, which constitutes a manageable situation.

*16 July.*

Tashi is proving to be a true Tiblet. On the third day of our joint life I decided to test her powers of self-propulsion and she followed to heel perfectly, proceeding in a series of absurd rubbery bounces.

A week ago she had her first swim, in the lake. I hadn't meant her to join me but when the poor little mite saw me swimming away from the shore she gave a scream of horror and, after a moment's terrified dithering on the bank, plunged gallantly into this new element. Her silly up-curling tail remained high and dry, and began to wag ridiculously above the water as I turned back to express appropriate appreciation of her loyalty.

By now the writing is on the wall. I can no longer delude myself that when leaving Pokhara it will be simple to find a kind home for Tashi and say a fond farewell. Obviously my future career, for the life-span of one dog, is going to be hideously complicated by Quarantine Regulations, International Canine Vaccination Certificates, Bye-laws governing the Import and Export of Livestock and Rules affecting the Transport of Domestic Pets by Land, Sea and Air. In a word, I've bought it —and all for ten-and-sixpence!

Even now there are complications, for Tashi has strong views about squatting only on grass, and she consistently spurns the statutory box of clay. Therefore, small pups being very lavish of urine in tiny instalments, much of my time now goes climbing down and up the ladder answering her calls of Nature. Even at night, when she awakens me by nipping my nose, she insists on bouncing across to the grass on the opposite side of the road instead of squatting sensibly in the shelter of the verandah—a fetish which means that at this season I spend half the night towelling her.

Her capacity for destruction is tremendous and, as my room affords nothing which is both destructible and within reach, she much enjoys visiting Kay's room. There she wreaks havoc on precious Kleenex sent from London, on beloved pots of cacti which have been driven all the way from Mysore, on vitally important documents and on priceless plastic bags irreplaceable within a radius of a thousand miles. Kay's forebearance is endless and she merely remarks that 'pups will be pups', but as I take the old-fashioned view that a certain amount of repression benefits the young of all species Tashi is regularly beaten on these occasions. However, she imagines that my hidings are a sort of pre-bedtime game, and one's austere disciplinary mood receives a severe shaking when she rolls over on her back, ogles expertly, and holds her right forepaw in her mouth—this being a trick calculated to disarm the most unfeeling of dog-trainers.

Yet on the whole Tashi is obedient, and today was the first time she disgraced me in public, forcing me to pretend cravenly that we were total strangers. One of her obsessions concerns shoe-laces, which she believes to have been tied in every case so that she may enjoy the satisfaction of untying them. But outlets for such a mania are few in this region of bare feet and therefore she rejoiced at today's appearance on the airstrip of a very correctly attired Chinese Communist Delegation. (What they were delegated to or from I never discovered.) When the plane landed and the twelve comrades emerged many of Pokhara's V.I.P.s were there to greet them, most of Pokhara's armed police were there to protect them (from Tibetans?), and immediately several Kathmandu and Peking press-photographers came scuttling around to arrange groups to prove how dearly the Chinese and Nepalese love one another.

During these preliminaries Tashi had been calling on friends nearby—one of whom habitually wears shoes—but now she came bouncing along to make sure I wasn't going too far astray. The photographers had just attained perfection—Chinese arms around Nepalese shoulders, solidarity smiles on all faces—when Tashi suddenly realised that she had a whole row of stationary shoes at her disposal. Ecstatically she raced up and down the line before deciding to be formal and begin on the leader of the Delegation—so that as camera shutters clicked an irritated frown replaced a solidarity smile on the most important Chinese face.

A very curious feature of this Chinese 'courtesy call' was its length. After precisely seventeen minutes the Delegates re-entered their plane—never having left the airstrip—and headed back to Kathmandu. Perhaps the Nepalese authorities felt that it could be dangerous to allow them through the bazaar, where armed Khamba guerilla-fighters, on leave from the frontier area, are always to be found. And undoubtedly these Tibetan soldiers would enjoy nothing more than a busman's holiday.

As I was writing this last paragraph a head appeared through my trap-door and I recognised a pleasant young man who lives nearby and whose dysentery I treated successfully last week. A moment later he was in the room, followed by his mother, who complained of a violent pain in the right breast. Even by lamplight it was obvious at a glance that she had a very neglected abscess: but in case I didn't get the message she shot a stream of pus from the nipple right into my face—a proof of infection I could have well done without. Dispensing three aspirins, I strongly advised her to go to the Shining Hospital tomorrow and explained that I could do nothing to help. Unfortunately most Nepalese and Tibetans believe that just because you have a white skin (or had before you came to Pokhara) you can perform medical miracles.

This morning Krishna, my landlord, told me that soon I must move to the room next door, which has now been vacated by Thupten Tashi. These two rooms are to be let to Krishna's newly-married brother-in-law, who will set up his own minute shop downstairs—doubtless stocking cigarettes, matches, rice, soap and biscuits, like all the other minute Pardi shops.

*24 July.*

Last night in the small hours I was awakened by the most blood-curdling wails, sobs and shouts. They seemed to be coming from the lean-to at one side of the house—a shack which shelters a tailor's family of five, though it consists only of a grass roof, two bamboo-matting walls and an earth floor. Evidently someone was either being murdered or going mad—both common fates around here—but as in neither event could my intervention help I promptly went asleep again. A couple of hours later the eerie sounds recurred, while I was breakfasting, and by then a group of expressionless villagers was standing on the street staring into the shack. Joining it, I saw that the tailor's old mother had indeed gone mad and was being held down with difficulty by her son and daughter-in-law, while their baby lay screaming unheeded on a pile of filthy rags in a corner. Then suddenly the seizure was over, the old woman lay panting but still and the neighbours drifted silently away.

Many events which would be regarded as crises at home are witnessed with indifference here. A few days ago I saw a man attacking his wife outside their house; as his rage increased he tried to pick up a heavy stone for quicker results, but his son, aged about twelve, struggled desperately to restrain him, and eventually mother and son were victorious. That afternoon I again went up the street and saw husband and wife sitting in their doorway amicably stripping corn-cobs together. Yet in our countries a likely result of this fracas would have been the husband's arrest, the wife's removal to hospital for shock treatment and the son's removal from his unsuitable home to an institution.

Initially I had been ashamed of my own placid lack of reaction to such scenes: it seemed my duty at least to feel alarmed or upset. But it appears that we unconsciously and very quickly take our cues from our environment, and in Asia there is felt neither the need to evade life's grimmer aspects nor the obligation to become involved in the misfortunes of others.

Last week I had my own little experience of how close physical violence lies to the surface of Nepalese life. I had gone to the bazaar, taking with me as porter a gentle fourteen-year-old boy named Pema, and as I was haggling about the price of dahl for the Tiblets' Lifeline-subsidised midday meal I heard jeering shouts and looked out to see Pema being attacked by about twenty small Nepalese boys. At first I paid no attention, thinking 'boys will be boys', but when Pema was thrown on his back in the gutter and the gang began to stone him I realised that this was in fact a minor race riot. (Tibetans are understandably very unpopular in the valley.) Leaping down from the shop I went round an intervening house to surprise the gang from the rear, grabbed their leader and was about to thrash him when a screaming fury of a woman frantically attacked me. With one hand she tried to loosen my grip on her terrified son while with the other she beat me over the head, using her empty *dokar* as a weapon. At once a dense crowd gathered round us— amused, curious and, as far as one could judge, quite neutral; the main thing seemed to be that a free entertainment was being staged. I soon wrested the *dokar* away and hurled it into the crowd but Mamma, though unarmed, was not deterred (more power to her) and she continued to shriek abuse at me and to pull and scrape at my arm, which now has a deep four-inch scratch as souvenir. Yet despite her 'tigress-in-defence' efforts I managed to give the little bully four hard ones with my cycle pump before releasing him.

Unfortunately there was no interpreter to explain that had twenty Tiblets attacked one Nepalese boy I would have been

equally angry with the Tibetans; so the incident was bad for
Irish-Nepalese relations. It was also bad for the reputation of
the local missionaries. Bazaar gossip is such that before leaving
Pokhara, an hour later, I was told that one of the Shining Hospital nurses had just beaten up (almost unto death!) a helpless
little boy who annoyed her by begging for money. Somehow I
wouldn't have thought that even a Nepalese crowd could possibly mistake me for a missionary.

Yesterday I moved house, which took me all of fifteen minutes.
The move should have happened four days ago, but this being
the rice-planting season Krishna hasn't once opened his shop
during the past week, and he only appeared yesterday morning
for long enough to hand me my new key.

The three differences in this room are: (1) a red mud floor
(freshly plastered by Krishna's mother since Thupten left), (2) a
tiny back window that does open, and (3) eight leaks in the tin
roof instead of four. But (1) and (2) more than compensate for
(3). Two open windows lower the temperature and smooth
mud provides a much more comfortable bed than unsym-
metrical boards—though it also raises the floor level by about
a foot, so that my head almost touches the roof. Today I plugged
the leaks with candle-grease and so far this device is working
quite well.

Inevitably Tashi fancies that the mud floor was laid specially
for her to dig up, which she did with great gusto when briefly
left alone yesterday. This would be bearable if I were a Nepalese
housewife—the local women lay a new floor weekly—but in my
case excavations have to be severely discouraged or we'd soon be
living amidst a heap of rubble.

Clothing is the one essential obtainable here at a reasonable
price. Recently I bought seven yards of brown cotton for
nine and fourpence and now my tailor neighbour has made me
a pair of shorts and two shirts for five shillings, so I've acquired
three new garments at a total cost of fourteen and fourpence.
Kay says that wearing shorts and shirt of the same drab material
makes me look like a convict—but who cares?

*31 July.*

Yesterday I developed acute dysentery and retired to bed early; but as my new neighbours had just moved in this didn't do me much good. I haven't yet got round to taking a census, but going on aural evidence the family includes an aged bronchitic grandparent of uncertain sex, a discontented infant with a rasping, penetrating wail and several adults who disagree peevishly about most subjects that come up for discussion. To add to it all Tashi insisted on yapping shrilly at regular intervals. I tried to explain that we were no longer paying rent for the next-door room, but she didn't even begin to get the point and her hackles never subsided the whole night through. However, the rain was so heavy and continuous today that no work could be done and I slept for most of the time; at this relentless phase of the monsoon ordinary life here comes to a standstill.

# 7

# Conflicting Views

*21 August. Pokhara.*

The past three weeks have been dominated by illness and wetness. I had planned to go to Kathmandu on the 7th of August but for ten days, from the 6th, Pokhara reverted to its pre-aeroplane isolation—perhaps fortunately, since I was then being victimised by a particularly debilitating belly-bug.

Had one *known* that no plane could come for ten days this isolation would have been quite pleasant; but when one is due to leave on the first available plane and has to keep a constant watch on the sky, lest an unexpected flight should arrive, the prolonged uncertainty becomes decidedly wearing. Yet I was in a favoured position—living beside the airstrip—compared with those would-be passengers who were enduring a damp, aimless existence at The Annapurna, where the seasonal shortage of supplies was defeating even Kessang's ingenuity.

By the 8th of August no less than nine foreigners were awaiting the Kathmandu plane. Alan MacWilliam sat there champing to get to Delhi for urgent consultations; Peter Johnson lounged disconsolately in a corner ticking off the wasted days of his fortnight's leave which, after eighteen months' Peace Corps work in a remote hill village, was to have been spent under Calcutta's bright lights; a diabetic Indian engineer lay on his charpoy predicting—correctly—that his insulin supply would never hold out; a visiting American female missionary paced up and down the verandah insisting that the deficient diet was sapping all her energy—though her perpetual motion contradicted this—and, to refine the tension, a German couple who had been doing soil research near by were accompanied by three bored and petulant children—and were themselves unsoothing beause they persistently ascribed the absence of planes to Nepalese inefficiency. By the end of these ten days The Annapurna's atmosphere had become so charged with frustrated animosity that it was dangerous even to look at any of the would-be passengers, much less address them, and only a Tibetan proprietor could have retained his poise as did Kessang.

During this period the whole valley lay inert beneath water, providing an extraordinary contrast to the usual noisy 'to-ing and fro-ing' that starts daily at dawn. For most of the time our Pardi 'street' was knee-deep in brown floods and soon grass began to grow freely on the mud floor of my little hallway—luckily for Tashi, who was thus spared frequent swims to her customary squatting site.

My first action on arriving in Kathmandu on the sixteenth of August was to book a return seat for the twentieth; but no R.N.A.C. flights took off either yesterday or today and it was only through Swiss kindness that I got home this afternoon in a microscopic Pilatus Porter.

When the three Swiss and I reached Gaucher Airport at 9 a.m. we were told that the forecast seemed doubtful and we spent the next four hours waiting in the so-called restaurant, from whence the pilot made periodic excursions to survey the sky. At 1.30 p.m. a favourable radio report came through from Pokhara but, since Kathmandu remained completely cloud-obscured, my private opinion was that tomorrow should be regarded as another day. Yet the pilot declared cheerfully that it was worth having a bash at it, meaning that we could turn back if conditions worsened.

Flying in a Pilatus Porter is rather like being in a winged motor car; there is room for a passenger on the front seat, and one literally does get a bird's eye view of people working or walking on the hills below. Yet for me this trip was a most ghastly experience. As we climbed over the city I was unable to distinguish that narrow gap in the mountains which is the only exit for Pokhara flights and I badly needed the fifteen-minute respite of clear weather that followed our escape from this inferno of vapour. Then another menacing wall of cloud loomed up directly across our route and as we went into the middle of it I thought of my dear ones while the pilot yelled to Kathmandu, 'We may be turning back, stop. Just seeing how far it goes, stop. Hold on for two minutes, stop. Am warning

Pokhara, stop.' All of which sounded to me remarkably like
Famous Last Words—stop! Yet oddly enough, after those two
(very long) minutes the vapour did begin to thin, and Kathmandu was told that everything looked lovely in the garden.
Next Pokhara was advised that now they could safely send a
plane back—which meant that when we plunged into another
cloud ten minutes later I suffered the extra terror of imagining
a collision with the returning Dakota. But mercifully the Pokhara valley itself was unclouded and we landed here at 2.30 in
bright sunshine.

I received an astonishingly warm welcome from my Pardi
neighbours. Obviously they have at last accepted me, on much
the same basis as they accept the serenely smiling blind beggar-
boy who wanders alone round the valley, or the ragged Indian
lunatic who speaks Oxford English and sits in tea-houses for
hours on end, holding heated discussions with himself about the
relative merits of Hinduism and Christianity.


*31 August.*

Last month I discovered that Bhupi Sherchan—a young
Pokhara friend of mine who is Nepal's best-known poet—pos-
sesses a copy of Ekai Kawakuchi's *Three Years in Tibet.* This is
the rarest of all books on Tibet and I have long been scouring
the bookshops of Britain and India for a copy of the English
translation, published by the Theosophical Society of Madras
in 1906. At first it seemed as inexplicable as it was thrilling that
the valley's meagre stock of English volumes should happen to
include a Kawakuchi; but then Bhupi told me that this copy
was presented to his grandfather by the author who, on his way
to Tibet, had received much kind assistance from the powerful
Sherchan clan—one of the richest merchant families in Nepal.

During the earlier part of this month, while animation was
suspended, I spent much of my time reading Kawakuchi and
came really to love this brave, eccentric and very devout
Japanese Buddhist monk, who combined profound learning
with the most engagingly childish foibles. In 1900, having
mastered the Tibetan language, he disguised himself as a lama
and risked his life by illicitly entering Tibet to study the country's

religion. Then, having serenely survived many arduous and varied adventures he went home to write this unsurpassed account of life in Tibet at the turn of the century. And his book so enchants me that I must quote a few relevant extracts before reluctantly returning it to Bhupi.

In March 1899 Kawakuchi passed through this valley and wrote: 'Pokhara looked like a town of villas at home, the site being chosen because of the beauty of its natural scenery. Bamboo-covered ravines, flower-roofed heights, rich in green foliage, picturesque because of a rushing and winding stream, itself set in the midst of high mountains—such were the characteristic features of Pokhara. The stream's waters are milky white, probably on account of their carrying in them particles of mountain clay. In all my travels in the Himalayas I saw no scenery as enchanting as that which enraptured me at Pokhara. Another thing notable about that place was that it was the cheapest spot in Nepal for all kinds of commodities.'

With all of which, apart from the last sentence, I heartily agree. And as the rise in prices and addition of an airstrip have been the only major changes in Pokhara since 1899 one is comfortably aware that were Kawakuchi to return here in his present incarnation he would at once recognise his 'enrapturing' valley.

Further on in the same chapter he reaches Tsarang, the home of many of our camp Tibetans, and then he writes:

'In point of uncleanliness, Tibetans stand very high among the inhabitants of the earth, but I think the inhabitants of Tsarang go still higher in this respect. In Tibet people wash themselves occasionally, but they almost never do in Tsarang. In the course of the year that I lived there, I only twice saw a person wash himself, the washing being confined even then to the face and neck. The skin all over the body has on it a peculiarly repulsive shine of polished dirt, so to say; but what can they do when it is a custom to laugh at persons who wash their faces nice and clean, and to deride them as being very dirty in their habits? Not only in their appearance, but in all they do, the natives seem to have absolutely no idea of cleanliness. To say that they think nothing of making a cup of tea for you with the same fingers with which they have just blown their noses, is to give only a very mild instance of their filthiness; and I have no courage to dwell here on their many other doings, which are altogether beyond imagination for those who have not seen them done and are too loathsome even unto sickening to recall to mind. The natives hereabouts are merely creatures of animal instincts; they think of nothing but eating, drinking and sleeping, their minds being otherwise filled with thoughts pertaining to sensual love. They occasionally spend their evening in listening to a lama preaching, but only occasionally. They change their clothing but once a year, and if any of them is brave enough to wear the same suit for two years, that person is made an object of high praise. And as they never wash their wearing apparel it is always shiny with grease and dirt. Indifferent as they are to their appearance, they are very painstaking in preparing food, as also in making their sleep comfortable. And their ruling passion is that of carnal love, and that applies to all ages from the very young to the very old. Like all uncivilised people they are intensely superstitious; to them a lama is omnipotent, for they believe he can cure diseases and divine all future events.'

With most of this, too, I agree—though one doesn't notice our Tsarangs being inordinately disposed to 'carnal love'.

Anyway our Japanese friend has a 'thing' about sex, and consequently about Tibetan Buddhism in general. Towards the end of this same chapter he writes very scathingly on Padma Sambhama and the Nyingmapas: 'His teaching is a sort of parody on Buddhism proper, and an attempt to sanctify the sexual relations of humankind, explaining and interpreting all the important passages and tenets in the Sacred text from a sensual standpoint, and in the Tibetan rhetoric in which I took lessons I found this lewd and detestable teaching largely incorporated.' At which point one begins to wonder if the Japanese monk—alias Tibetan lama—was not in fact a disguised Presbyterian clergyman!

This morning the sky was cloudless when I cycled up to the bazaar at six o'clock—and what a sight the mountains were in that clear, early sunshine! One appreciated them all the more, not having seen them for so many weeks; even Roget—if he were among those present—would be unequal to those Himaayan snowpeaks. They *are* majestic, and I can't help it if everyone else has said so already. This really is the only adjective that begins to convey the impression received as one cycles up from Pardi, going straight towards Machhapuchhare itself—a king of snow and ice soaring far above the rest, high and mighty, into the blueness.

*3 September.*

Today I had my first quarrel with local officialdom; however successful I may be in social contacts with Asians I seem doomed to repeated failures in professional contacts, where resounding ethical clashes so often occur. This is an enormous problem, to which one can rarely find a solution both honourable and practical. Common sense and tolerance dictate some degree of flexibility and on minor points I do accept the irritating necessity to jog along in a haze of compromise. But then comes some major point that compels me to act according to my own principles, and it must be bewildering for the Nepalese when I suddenly revolt and begin rigidly to oppose them. Perhaps it is a mistake ever to compromise, even on minor points; yet one's work here would come to a standstill if one didn't. I can't claim that any reasoned decision is taken at the moment when I stop jogging along; I merely rebel instinctively against an utterly repugnant course of action, and from that point on the certainty that one is right by one's own standards makes further compromise impossible.

This whole problem centres on the difficulty of determining the extent to which we are entitled to impose our standards on an Eastern people. My own feeling is that normally we are not entitled to do this to any extent, and I would be the first to protest if others were bullying the unfortunate Nepalese. Yet when Eastern nations misguidedly insist on importing Western institutions that are wholly unsuited to their society, and expect us to provide the essential funds and personnel, then surely we *are* entitled to demand a minimum of conformity to our standards. However, in most cases this is an unrealistic demand, and therefore many Western field-workers, with a far wider experience of the problem than mine, have by now concluded that the whole elaborate structure of Aid to the Developing Nations should be dismantled and either forgotten or reconstituted.

It was obvious this afternoon that our 'frankness' appears to the Nepalese as simply the most atrocious form of bad manners. They feel shocked, hurt and saddened when a spade is called a *spade*, and today they were clearly writing me off as an unspeakable barbarian from some cave-man civilisation—which indeed I am, in many ways, compared with them. Yet my natural aggressiveness was being rigorously curbed in their honour and I referred to that spade very gently—though I couldn't quite bring myself to call it an agricultural implement. However, this offensive frankness at least gives Asians the opportunity to understand our reasoning, whereas we are forever groping in twilight towards some faint understanding of theirs.

Only once has a Hindu sincerely tried to explain to me his thinking on honesty, and that explanation was not very illuminating. I was staying with an English couple in Uttar Pradesh when this young Brahmin came to dinner. He was a most delightful person—warm-hearted, courteous, witty and well-informed—and during the past two years he had been virtually adopted by my elderly friends. Soon we all began to discuss the hoary topic of Indian dishonesty and in an effort to enlighten us the young man said: 'Look at it this way—I'm an educated Brahmin and a very good friend of this family, yet if I came into the house when it was empty and saw Rs. 100/- on top of that bureau, I'd almost certainly steal it, but if I only knew that the Rs. 100/- was locked inside the bureau I would *never* steal it, even if I could easily break the lock and was sure of not being caught.'

Naturally enough this concrete example was received with some rather half-hearted laughter, whereupon the young man frowned impatiently and went on: 'You don't like to believe me, but this is true. The theft would have been the fault of whoever left the money lying around. I'd feel I'd done wrong but I'd think I couldn't be expected to resist such a temptation. And then the carelessness of the owner would counterbalance my own guilt and I'd be happy.'

By this stage my host and hostess were plainly feeling upset so I hastily changed the subject, much as I longed to pursue it.

The only perceptible vestige of decency in this exposition was the admission that some guilt would be felt, though it could be suppressed so expeditiously. Possibly the uneasiness revealed by so many Hindus in their relations with Europeans is partly based on envy of the values upheld by our more obstreperous consciences. Individual Hindus cannot be blamed for following their traditional code; yet when that code is so out of harmony not merely with Christian morality, but with a universally applicable natural law they are bound to suffer from the repercussions of their too easily quieted consciences.

These clashes of standards are a normal hazard in the East and what most disheartened me today was the full realisation of how ill-equipped the Nepalese are to tackle organisational problems. Only when one has had a close up view, over a considerable period, of how their minds work can one appreciate the crucial difference between a race with a tradition of logical thinking and a race with no such tradition. And this is the chief obstacle to successful co-operation on any project. Ordinarily we completely take for granted our heritage of logic, since any moderately intelligent Westerner will think coherently, if not profoundly, about a given problem; but even the best educated and most intelligent of the Nepalese seem to lack this method of approach. Their various theories may be sound, and their various practical schemes constructive, but any co-ordination of either theories or schemes is non-existent and would require a major miracle rather than a Western adviser. Instead of looking at all of a problem first, and then dealing with its component parts in relation to its entirety, the average Nepalese deals with each aspect as a separate issue and makes various decisions which, if they were acted upon, would promptly cancel each other out—so perhaps it is fortunate that in Nepal decisions are rarely or never acted upon. But coping with this sort of thing day after day is enough to depress the most ebullient and I don't wonder that so many Western workers simply give up trying.

These disillusioned experts often dismiss the Nepalese as being colossally and irredeemably stupid; yet this is a most unjust over-simplification. Here we are not up against inferior brain-power, but brain-power that operates on a different fuel, travels on a different gauge line and is going in a different direction;

and it may be that the illogical Nepalese will have the laugh on us at some not-too-distant date, when they are as happy as ever and our civilisation has tripped itself up and broken its neck in the progress race.

*5 September.*

It is interesting that many of Pokhara's leading citizens profess to be Communists; this morning one of them openly discussed with me his sympathy for China, and he is the fifth to do so. None of these men is poor and three of them are among the richest in the valley, and are continuing to do very well under the present régime, so their new allegiance cannot be attributed to discontent. But—significantly—all five have received that fatal half-education, clumsily modelled on a Western pattern, which cuts the mind adrift from its traditional moorings without beginning to equip it to steer safely through alien waters. And now their support of Chinese Communism is being rather self-consciously flaunted as proof of both an *avant-garde* outlook and of ability to withstand Western pressures. This last point seems to be of major importance, and one finds an obsessional defiance of the United States in their attitude. Invariably they argue—more or less coherently—'America hates China and we resent American efforts to dominate us, so let's show these dollar-splashers that it's not as easy as they might think to buy us.' Clearly this childish yet forgivable reaction against America is the Nepalese Communist's most powerful incentive, and it is surprising that the inevitability of such a development was not foreseen years ago. On the one hand are the Americans, full of pity and dollars and naïve enthusiasm, supplemented by a pathological hatred of the Chinese and a total incomprehension of the Nepalese; to these 'do-gooders' the spending of money on a country is the obvious way to 'rescue' it, but as yet the Nepalese seem quite unprepared to follow where the dollar leads. Then, on the other hand, one has the Chinese talking across, instead of down, to their Nepalese 'brothers', sharing with them a state of undevelopment which they can justly claim to be improving through their own efforts, preaching opposition to a capitalism of which the Nepalese know nothing except that Americans are capitalists, and smoothly gearing their propaganda to Asian thought processes and emotional reactions. It would be strange if those Nepalese who sincerely believe that their country needs reform did *not* look north-east for support.

In Kathmandu there are several Nepalese-run Chinese Communist bookshops which sell propaganda literature in Nepali, Hindi and English. Many of these publications are incongruously luxurious, yet the prices remain artificially low. Books that would cost twenty or twenty-five rupees if imported from the West are to be had for five or six rupees, and I recently bought for one rupee (eightpence) a well-produced, hard-back volume of Rewi Alley poems entitled *Who is the Enemy?* This was published last year by the New World Press, Peking, and the blurb begins—'Rewi Alley is a citizen of New Zealand and of the world. He is now coming to the end of his first four decades in China.' And immediately one wonders if the implication is that Chinese Communism bestows an exclusive longevity which will enable Rewi Alley to enjoy a second four decades in China. The final sentence of the blurb says that these poems 'are quite frankly political,' and this is so true that at no stage do they come within light-years of being poetry. Some of them are defaced by a jeering, almost obscene blasphemy that makes the Western reader wince; but the majority—especially those on the Vietnamese war—do have that beauty which sparkles from sincerity whatever its setting. Only a fanatically obtuse reader could dismiss them as mere crafty propaganda. On every page the writer conveys his absolute commitment to the peasants of Asia and his unwavering faith in the benefits that Communism can bring them; and one feels the strength and warmth of a real compassion consistently coming through these semi-hysterical phrases. Too often we think of Communism as a cold, systematic, conform-or-die ideology that inhumanly sacrifices the individual to the theory; yet the writings of Rewi Alley and of many of his 'comrades' show that it is as essentially human as any other political phenomenon in the history of mankind. Throughout this little book one hears the thumping of its indignant, puzzled, aggressive heart, and one knows that many of these people do care for the poor, however misguidedly, and whatever brutalities may result from their passion of loathing for all 'Imperialists'.

Last night we citizens of Pardi were treated to some Western-style propaganda when a British Embassy official staged an open-air film show to enlighten the locals on Life in Modern Britain. The films were so ludicrously inappropriate that one marvelled at the responsible authorities ever having fallen into such an abyss of idiocy; but at least the performance afforded me a splendid evening's entertainment, as I sat there viewing it through the eyes of a Nepalese peasant.

Life in London was represented by the Trooping of the Colour, so the audience must naturally have assumed that city to be a most civilised place, where the majority of the male population wear gorgeous uniforms and ride around on glossy horses—always in military formation for reasons best known to themselves. Next we saw rousing shots from a performance of *Macbeth* produced on Cornish cliffs in Elizabethan costume, with a bloody dagger much in evidence—which latter detail will no doubt have done a lot to strengthen the links of friendship between the Gurkhas and the Great British Public. This was followed by the Quatro-centenary birthday celebrations at Stratford-on-Avon, showing scores of robed Lord Mayors from all over Britain, and next came the Eisteddfod, showing dancers from many countries in their national costumes, with bevies (or should it be covies?) of druidically-garbed druids in the foreground. Then, as a Grand Finale, we were given the Highland Games, with kilts flying while bagpipes squealed. Such is the image of Britain Today as the Pokhara Valley is seeing it this week. Doubtless my neighbours now think that the clothes worn here by Westerners are designed for tropical use only, and they must certainly imagine that Britain has at least as many national holidays as Nepal.

*8 September.*

This evening it was my turn to prepare supper and when Kay arrived at half-past seven, carrying her rarely-used transistor radio, she was breathless with excitement. For an instant after her announcement that a war had started I experienced a sick 'This-is-it' feeling, but as she went on I realised that the war is just more bickering than usual between India and Pakistan.

Undoubtedly it will cause many sadly unnecessary deaths on the battlefield and some inconvenience here, but it is hardly a war in contemporary terminology.

Already the bazaar price of kerosene has gone up to two pounds per gallon and there is a possibility that all internal R.N.A.C. flights may be stopped because Nepal is dependent on India for her petrol supplies. We have just spent two hours listening with great difficulty to snatches of English Language news giving very dissimilar interpretations of the situation from Pakistani, Indian, Nepalese, Chinese, American and British viewpoints. Peking is being even more lurid than usual and describing America as 'a vicious wolf' and 'the most rabid oppressor mankind has ever known', America is being no less puerile on a slightly more sophisticated level and everyone else is also reacting according to form. The whole thing leaves one sunk in depression. I myself believe in Pakistan's moral right to Kashmir and, as one of the 'Fighting Irish', I would say 'Good luck to them' if I thought the Pakistani Army had so much as an even chance of securing that right by force. But this futile skirmishing can only bring further misery to two already destitute countries.

Yet the country I pity most at the moment is poor little Nepal, who is now shaking in her shoes (or would be if she wore them!) between China plus Pakistan and India plus America. The English Language news from Kathmandu was struggling desperately to be neutral but betraying an unmistakable pro-Chinese bias—perhaps partly because there is a Nepalese Mission in Peking just now and the delegates' families want to see them again. However, we are in no danger here. Even if a full-scale conflict were to develop between China and India it is most unlikely that Nepal would be directly involved in any fighting.

Tonight Kay is understandably worried. She had been planning to drive her jeep down to South India at the end of the month, but by then no petrol may be available for civilian use; so she will probably leave within the next few days.

*15 September.*

Kay took off on the eleventh and must now be on her way down the Rajpath. Jill Buxton is the only other grandmother of my acquaintance who would blithely drive a twenty-one-year-old jeep singlehanded from Kathmandu to Mysore, through a country at war. Whatever else may be said about Britain's export trade there's nothing wrong with its line in grandmothers.

Today the war is a week old but Peking's jamming is so efficient nowadays that no news trickles through from the Big Wide World. This seems healthy; presumably anything too drastic would have made some slight impression, even on the Nepalese.

The bazaar Black Market is now thriving; obviously Nepalese merchants are born profiteers—once they get a whiff of war beyond the horizon everything becomes a racket overnight. In theory the Government has imposed price control, but in practice Kathmandu's laws never do impinge on Pokhara's daily life.

This morning I myself was out to corner Russian tinned milk for the eighteen Tiblets who are suffering from malnutrition and who, since Kay's departure, have been coming to my room early every morning for their egg-flips. I did manage to get forty one-pound tins; but these won't last very long so I also got thirty tins of the Indian product, though this is far inferior to the Russian and costs even more.

At the moment I am a bit shaken, having just seen the killing of a rabid dog on the village street. When leaving the camp after my evening tour I heard the most frightful shrieking sounds ahead—and then a herd of buffalo came galloping wildly towards me across the common-land. People were fleeing in all directions and a moment later I saw a very nice dog, belonging to a local trader, racing round and round in circles making this hideous noise. At once I looked frantically for Tashi, who was well behind, frolicking with other Tibetan dogs, and having rushed back to pick her up I stood near the tents wondering what would happen next. There wasn't long to wait: three young men climbed on to the roof of a house, with armfuls of sharp-edged bricks, and the grim execution was soon over. But the fact that this poor little creature was one of Tashi's best friends is creating a certain amount of suspense.

By now Tashi has become quite an elegant young lady, her earlier furry cuddlesomeness having been replaced by a silky strokability. Her general architecture is reminiscent of a Dachshund whose parents' genes have been a little wide of the mark; she has a ridiculous brown feathery tail which curls up and over her back and her regular white and tan markings are very handsome indeed.

On the delicate question of Tashi's breed there are several schools of thought. When she was two months old a local 'expert' pronounced her to be a smooth-haired Tibetan terrier; but I have always questioned this diagnosis. Then, a few weeks later, a visiting Indian, who obviously knew something of Eastern breeds, defined her as a Miniature Himalayan Sheepdog— which theory is reinforced by her breeder's occupation of shepherd. Privately, however, I am of the opinion that she is a perfectly good Tibetan mongrel. Yet if one is besotted enough to go to the immense inconvenience and expense of transporting a dog from Nepal to Ireland one has to pretend, as a face-saving device, that the dog in question belongs to some exclusive Central Asian breed of enormous snob-value. So, on the form which I have filled in this evening to begin the tortuous process of obtaining Irish citizenship for Tashi, her breed is boldly given as Miniature Himalayan Sheepdog.

A week ago the more tiresome aspects of being possessed by a Nepal-born dog began to obtrude on the idyll. I am due home in December and a letter of enquiry to the Irish Embassy in Delhi brought a fearsome array of lengthy documents by return of post. These made it plain that our Department of Agriculture is allergic to alien quadrupeds, and the pages of grim regulations are clearly intended to eradicate all the imprudent affections indulged in by Irish citizens abroad. But an Irish Government Department should know better than to attempt to thwart the desires of an Irish citizen. My determination to 'import a domestic pet of the canine species [dog to you] into the State from a place abroad' hardened rapidly as I read these formidable strictures; even had I actively disliked Tashi they would have inspired me to import her 'separately confined in a suitable hamper, crate, box or other receptacle which must be nose and paw proof and must not contain any hay, straw or peat-moss litter'. It was in an aggressive mood that I completed the preliminary form and wrote the preliminary letters to 'the approved quarantine premises' and the 'approved carrying agents', while Tashi lay peacefully asleep by my feet, unaware that during the next few months a lot of people were going to make a very big fuss about a very little dog.

# 8

## *A Thief and a Goddess*

*23 September. Kathmandu.*

Two days ago I came to a Kathmandu where, outside the
Embassy compounds and The Royal Hotel, no-one would suspect our southern neighbours of being at war. The Royal has
been completely deserted by the seasonal swarm of rich tourists
who briefly visit Nepal on their Round-the-World-Air-Trips,
and poor Boris is looking very dejected. Because of his own
legendary soft-heartedness it costs a great deal just to keep that
vast hotel ticking over; all other hoteliers have dismissed most
of their staff, but Boris argues—'It's not the servants' fault that
there's a war on. They work hard and loyally when I need them
so how can I turn them out now?' No wonder they are loyal to him!

I spent three hours at the airport this morning excavating a
consignment of Multi-Purpose Food from among the mountains
of supplies that are now accumulating there. Ironically the
present crisis has speeded up the arrival of goods from Calcutta;
most passenger-flights have been cancelled so R.N.A.C. has
taken to transporting the freight back-log instead of losing
money on idle planes, and now the airport is crammed with
bales, crates, chests and cartons of every description. The 150
tins of Multi-Purpose Food had been awaiting transportation
at Calcutta Airport for the past seven weeks and might have
been there for the next seven months had the more profitable
passenger traffic not been stopped.

*24 September.*

Today I spent over nine hours at the airport waiting for 'a
departure' that never departed. Weather conditions were suitable for the Pokhara flight so there was a possibility, from
8 a.m. onwards, that we might take off at any moment—if this,

that or t'other did not intervene. But they did intervene—apparently all three of them—and at 5.20 p.m. the Pokhara flight was cancelled.

Then came the struggle back to Jawalkhel with my usual elaborate refugee-luggage. The present consignment is made up of three boxes of dried milk weighing 60 lb. each, six tins of Multi-Purpose Food weighing 40 lb. each and two boxes of medical supplies weighing 20 lb. each—plus a *dokar* of fresh vegetables for the Shining Hospital, weighing 30 lb. and a cloth shoulder bag of personal luggage weighing 2½ lb. Amidst the chaos of Kathmandu Airport it is not easy to guard so many separate pieces for nine hours; in fact this can only be done by building a pyramid and then sitting on it, like Patience on a monument, smiling at delay. It is even less easy to get it all back to base, while horribly aware that somehow it must be dragged to the airport again at dawn; the damnable thing is that no official Left Luggage Office exists either at the airport itself or at the R.N.A.C. Terminal in New Road.

At 5.30 I tried to scrounge a friend's car, but the telephones in the relevant district were dead. Then, at 6.15, the airport bus wheezed along, my luggage was loaded up and by 7.50 I had got it all unloaded and brought into the Terminal office, where I attempted to telephone Sigrid. Having failed I called for a taxi, loaded up again and finally arrived back here at 8.15, feeling crabbed.

*25 September.*

Life is getting easier; today I only spent six hours waiting at the airport.

Being Saturday this is Sigrid's day off, yet she most nobly rose at dawn and drove me and my beastly luggage to New Road, where we were told that the departure of the airport bus had been postponed from 8 to 10 a.m. I then said another provisional goodbye to this most long-suffering of hostesses, whose stoical endurance of my comings and not-goings is beyond compare; when I arrived back at Jawalkhel yesterday evening she at once soothed me by seeming so pleased that I *hadn't* got to Pokhara!

The bus eventually decanted me and my baggage at the airport at 11.30 a.m. and, having reconstructed my pyramid, I perched hopefully on it until 5.30 p.m. when my patience was rewarded by an announcement that the Pokhara flight had again been cancelled for undisclosed reasons. I then repeated the luggage-shifting performance, which is now becoming merely another daily chore, and at the Terminal office I was advised to report there tomorrow morning at 6.30 and told that a seat was guaranteed for me—but there was no guarantee of a flight to Pokhara.

*26 September.*

Perhaps a flight did go to Pokhara today, but this passenger was not among those present. By a painful coincidence I've done it again and fractured two ribs in a bus—though mercifully they are not the two that were cracked a couple of years ago in an Afghan bus. Yet I mustn't let this become a habit . . .

The misadventure occurred yesterday on the way back from the airport but, as sometimes happens with rib injuries, the extent of the damage was not immediately apparent. This bus had distinct affinities with Afghan models, and all our luggage was piled high in the centre of the chassis, between the two narrow wooden benches. The driver was little short of a lunatic, and when a sacred bull suddenly ambled into view from behind a line of grass-carrying porters we were going far too fast to cope safely with this everyday contingency. The sudden braking threw me violently against a tin of that dratted Multi-Purpose Food but, though the pain was momentarily severe, I thought no more of the incident until I woke in agony at midnight, about an hour after going to sleep.

Sigrid was still out at a bridge-party—as usual not knowing whether her guest was here or there—but she came in soon afterwards, made calming noises, bound me tightly in sheeting and, by administering three codeine tablets and a glass of neat brandy, convinced me that this was the most minor of injuries. Then, after a slight battle about the advisability of my annexing the bed upstairs, I again lay on my Tibetan rug, beside a most sympathetic Puchare, and was asleep within moments.

This morning Dr Gyr sent me to the Nepal T.B. Centre for an X-ray to confirm his diagnosis of two fractured ribs; but on arriving there, after a torturingly joltful car journey, I found no X-rays can be taken until tomorrow as this is a National Holiday. However, I hope to be fit to fly to Pokhara on Tuesday.

*28 September.*

For about a week after The Event, simple rib-fractures have a way of feeling less simple each day; even had Dr Gyr not banned any travelling in the immediate future I would have cancelled my booking for today's hypothetical Pokhara flight.

Yesterday morning I dutifully kept my appointment for 9.30 at the T.B. Centre, only to be told that the generator had just developed a weakness and couldn't reasonably be expected to function before 1 p.m. Eventually, at 2.45, I was dealt with by a very pleasant but fascinatingly witless young radiologist who, when the picture had been developed, spent five minutes intently studying it—though even I could see at a glance that it didn't happen to include the particular ribs specified by Dr Gyr.

Last night the pain was acute but by now it has diminished considerably, after a day spent reading and sun-bathing in the garden.

During Sigrid's office-hours her house becomes a sort of club where Donbahadur and his friends meet to sing and play on the long Nepalese drum, to teach each other curious versions of the English and German languages, to flirt blissfully with other peoples' wives, to drink tea and gossip affectionately about their respective employers—or to spend hours in the garden preparing kites for competitions, as they were doing today.

The kite-flying season opens after the monsoon and now, all over the valley, one sees 'defeated' kites hanging sadly from tree-tops or electric cables. Yesterday I watched three duels being fought simultaneously in the blue sky far, far above. Usually the strings are invisible and it's utterly absorbing to follow the extremely skilful manœuvrings of these soaring, swooping, fluttering protagonists—whose owners are never seen, so that one imagines each kite to have an alert little built-in brain.

Donbahadur is a local champion and today he was preparing his kite for an important contest due to take place tomorrow, if the present deliciously fresh breeze persists. His string is over one hundred yards long and every inch of it, above the first five or six yards, has now been coated with the powdered glass which will perhaps cut his opponents' string tomorrow. This seemed to me a most tedious process, but clearly Donbahadur was loving every moment of it. His friend Tulbahadur, the milkman, helped him to extend the string to its full length, winding it tautly around trees and bushes, and then Donbahadur fetched from the kitchen Sigrid's best saucepan, in which he had boiled a mixture of flour, water and not too finely ground glass. This paste was most meticulously applied to the string and, when the sun had quickly dried it, every inch was expertly tested to ensure that the caked flour was holding each tiny splinter in place. Then, while the precious string was being gingerly wound back onto its reel, I unobtrusively took the saucepan to the bathroom to remove all traces of its lethal contents.

*30 September.*

This date will be remembered as my most horrible day in Nepal.

I had just sat down to breakfast when an odd exclamation came from upstairs and then a dead-pale Sigrid appeared through the little mock-cupboard door. 'I've been robbed,' she said. 'Everything has gone—jewellery, cameras, films—everything.' Immediately I felt a cold sickness at the centre of me, caused not only by natural distress on her behalf but by the immediate, devastating realisation that the burglar's success was entirely *my* fault.

Yesterday evening I was writing at the living-room table when a not very helpful section of my brain registered footsteps directly overhead. I thought vaguely, 'Sigrid must have come home while I was in the loo'—and went on writing. Moments later I heard bangings against the outside wall of the house directly behind my chair; but I was registering these sounds only superficially, and was automatically rejecting them, as one does all disturbances to concentration. My animal sense of hearing had assured me that they were either directly overhead or directly behind me; yet when Sigrid came in my malfunctioning human reason contradicted the evidence of my senses simply because it did not seem possible that anyone could have been upstairs. There is no valid excuse for this moronic behaviour but Sigrid, being Sigrid, now says 'not to worry', and claims that it is her own fault for always leaving cupboards unlocked and windows wide open. I might feel better this evening had she shown less magnanimity and given me my deserts.

When Donbahadur heard the news he was almost as upset as we were. Tulbahadur was in the kitchen (he seems to breakfast here more often than not) and immediately we all went to Patan in Sigrid's car.

The police station is among the oldest and loveliest of Patan's Newari buildings. In a wall-niche on one side of the main entrance stands a statue of Hanuman, the Monkey God, and this ancient sculpture is regularly smeared by the devout with red and yellow powder and paint. The eaves of the building are supported and the lintels decorated by very detailed carvings of naked gods and goddesses being no better than they should be —a form of art often alleged to be obscene, though to me it seems more witty than smutty. One can understand that it might not be considered the most apt sort of embellishment for a European police station; but if the Nepalese have retained enough balance to see the humour in sex this is surely a matter for congratulation rather than criticism.

Inside the building a rickety stairway led to the top-floor office of the Chief of Police; his unstable desk occupied one corner beside the small windows, the exquisitely carved shutters of which were lifted inwards and hooked to the low rafters during the day. The officer himself was fat, elderly and badly pock-marked, with a shaven head and steel-rimmed spectacles. On our arrival he gazed silently at us, his expression conveying some deep-rooted dislike for robbed memsahibs, and after a moment told us through Donbahadur that we would have to await the appearance of the police interpreter—who might or might not report for duty before lunch-time.

The four of us then sat on a bench near the window, and

an hour later we were surprised by the arrival of Lal Rana, the young interpreter, whose relative punctuality made me suspect that the Chief's pessimism on this point had been a ruse to drive us impatient foreigners away. Lal Rana was amiable but inept; when Sigrid attempted to make her statement he—and all his colleagues—showed far less interest in the crime than they did in her and my ages, occupations, passport numbers, home addresses and next-of-kin. Then the interpreter proudly announced that the police had 'a panel of local thieves' whom they would now proceed to question—whereupon Sigrid suggested, a trifle acidly, that were they to pay just a little attention to her description of the stolen articles their investigations might prove more fruitful. At once it was generally agreed that a list of the missing goods would indeed be helpful; then Lal Rana suddenly got very excited, said that of course they could take fingerprints too and dashed off to collect the relevant apparatus. This was bought last month from the Lucknow police, who had decided to replace it by some rather more up-to-date equipment; and when I saw it I realised that the Lucknow police had not made their decision prematurely.

Four other police officers followed us back here on foot—two clad in shabby uniforms and two in vivaciously striped pyjamas. It was not clear to me which pair were the senior officers; one could interpret the wearing of pyjamas while on duty either as a privilege reserved for higher ranks or as a mark of lowliness in the force—and none of these five men seemed to have any authority over the other four. However, they all revelled in the crime and went prowling around Sigrid's bedroom with preposterously exaggerated caution, taking great care to wrap towels around their hands before touching the woollen curtains; but in the end it was Sigrid who observed the many burnt matches on the cupboard shelves and the floor, though neither she nor I—much less the police—was able to make any astute deduction from this clue.

We next went outside, to gaze on the place of entry, and innumerable photographs were laboriously taken with a gigantic camera that almost creaked. Then the police departed—'to be pursued by investigations', as the interpreter put it; but the investigations were so obviously incapable of 'being pursued' constructively that Sigrid at once telephoned an influential Nepalese friend—and we soon received a message summoning us back to the police station.

There we found that a lavishly-uniformed and very tough-looking young Senior Officer had been sent from Police Head-quarters at Singha Durbar to take charge of the case—and already his presence had transformed the atmosphere. When-ever this formidable youth moved a finger everyone gave a series of palsied jerks which were probably the local version of coming to attention, saluting and clicking heels; yet I can't say that from a practical point of view the efficiency of the establishment was noticeably higher. However, we did have our finger-prints taken, which was perhaps an advance in some direction; and then we were all questioned about our move-ments yesterday, while Lavish Uniform sat looking threaten-ingly at his subordinates and listening to us without comment.

It soon became evident that the local police, unnerved by His Nibs' presence, were intent on proving Donbahadur the culprit. Sigrid and I simmered furiously as they persistently tried to trip him up; we would as soon suspect each other as Donbahadur, who has been on the verge of tears all day because his 'Memsahib's nice things gone'. Yet our angry intervention would not really have helped, so we confined ourselves to direct-ing indignant or sympathetic looks at the officers or their victim.

It was almost five o'clock when we left the police station, having been dismissed by His Nibs as though we were a pair of rather unpromising recruits. Immediately Donbahadur sug-gested that we should consult a Hindu soothsayer who lives nearby and we agreed that this might be more—and couldn't be less—helpful than consulting the Patan police. After a com-plicated drive through narrow alleyways we stopped at the entrance to an untidy, shrine-crowded courtyard and found the Brahmin priest sitting cross-legged in a corner of his first-floor room. Before him stood a low table, covered with geometrical signs, and when Donbahadur had briefly explained our prob-lem the soothsayer picked up a handful of dry earth, scattered it over the table, consulted a dog-eared book that had been lying on the ground beside him and began to draw or write in the earth with a four-inch glass cylinder. Meanwhile an old woman who was threshing rice in another corner went on tossing her trayfuls of grain, ignoring us, and the setting sun turned the chaff to a golden cloud.

Looking at Donbahadur, standing near the soothsayer, I was reminded of a European going to the doctor with some minor ailment, describing his symptoms, and then trustfully awaiting the scribbled prescription. This was magic in action, yet the atmosphere was utterly prosaic.

The Brahmin did not spend more than four or five minutes on his calculations. Then he laid down the cylinder and announced matter-of-factly that the stolen articles would not be sold immediately, but would be kept hidden in the thief's Patan house. He added that a young man who habitually wears black Western trousers and occasionally visits Sigrid's office had been implicated in the crime; and he concluded by foretelling that this young man would openly visit Sigrid's house at midday tomorrow. Donbahadur then paid the Rs. 1/- fee and followed us downstairs, translating the Brahmin's remarks when we reached the courtyard; and even he had to admit that this consultation had not got us very far.

*2 October.*

Yesterday, at 12 p.m., a young man in black pants walked into the living-room with a message for Sigrid; and he does go to her office occasionally on business, though he has never before been to her house. His appearance in the doorway made me feel a little odd for a moment, as black Western trousers are not commonly worn here, and Donbahadur, when called from the kitchen to take the message, concealed his agitation very inadequately; but the snag is that one can't have a man arrested on this sort of 'evidence'.

There were no other robbery developments until this afternoon. Today, being Saturday, Sigrid spent her time in the bazaar, doing private detective work, and as I was reading in the garden Lal Rana came rushing excitedly towards me. When he heard that Sigrid wouldn't be back until dinner-time he hurriedly explained that there was a suspect now loitering in the road just outside the gate and that he very much wanted to know if this man had been seen around the house or garden in the recent past. I immediately stood up—too quickly for comfort—and was already half-expecting an extension of the coincidence when I came face-to-face with Black Trousers outside the gate. By now I felt too addled even to try to sort any of it out. Though the young man greeted me most effusively I fancied some awkwardness in his manner; yet I firmly told myself that this was probably imaginary and, on returning to the garden, I merely reported his innocuous visit yesterday. Whereupon the Interpreter departed, saying that he would return later to interview Sigrid again.

One result of Black Trousers' appearance at midday yesterday has been the complete restoration of Donbahadur's faith in the soothsayer; last evening he went to him twice for more high-powered consultations, and in consequence the case is now being given the full magical treatment. Yesterday an image of dough was baked and today the Brahmin is busy chanting sinister incantations over it—these being calculated to make the thief shake violently and incessantly until he has been arrested. (Donbahadur has of course warned the police to look out for a man who can't stop shaking.) Yet if Black Trousers is the culprit something must have gone wrong—either with the baking or the chanting—since he was quite unshaky this afternoon.

The other part of the campaign is being conducted here; inside Sigrid's bedroom cupboard a big bowl of incense has been smouldering aromatically all day, and over both the cupboard door and the room door strangely-inscribed pieces of paper have been nailed to the wall. No doubt this is the ultimate in childish superstition: yet it is evident that both Sigrid and I are suffering from an excessive responsiveness to atmosphere and are taking the *puja* much more seriously than either of us would admit, even to the other.

By now the whole police investigation has acquired that patina of unreality which characterises most aspects of life in Nepal; if the circumstances were different one could thoroughly enjoy this weird kaleidoscope of improbable police-stations, detectives clad either in pyjamas or much-beribboned uniforms,

uncannily accurate soothsayers, archaic equipment, boyish enthusiasm, blatant corruption and utter inability even to attempt
to find a thief.

At present Kathmandu's weather is the only pleasant feature
of life. The nights are refreshingly chilly and every morning the
valley is filled with a thick grey mist that recalls Autumn at
home. All day the light has a glorious, exhilarating clarity, and
towards evening it is especially lovely. At half-past six today,
when the valley was already dark, two billowing masses of
cloud to the east were still glowing a deep pink—and beyond
them in the far distance the world's highest snow-peaks were
also lingeringly pink against a starry, royal-blue sky.

*4 October.*

For the past eight days the whole country has been celebrating Dasain (also known as the Durga Puja) and by now we
foreigners are really feeling the draught. The G.P.O. has shut
down completely; three days ago the electricity supply expired
and we were informed that it could not be revived until
6 October; Singha Durbar has put up its shutters, leaving
various Top-Level negotiations in a state of internationally in-
convenient suspension; and almost all servants, peons and
chokidars are *chuti*, making communication extremely difficult
—only now do we realise how much we depend on peons
delivering chits when the telephones are unwell. The whole
thing is irresistibly enchanting and I am particularly taken by
the idea of a capital city where the G.P.O. closes down uncom-
promisingly for days on end to give everyone a chance to say
their prayers; one wonders if there is any other capital in the
world so immune to the practical pressures of modern life.

My rib-injuries have been stationary, at a rather painful
stage, during the past few days. At first I had attempted to cultivate a stiff-upper-lip disdain for painkillers, but I have long
since come down from that particular high horse and am now
devouring them greedily every three hours. Today I took a
double dose at 5.30 a.m. before setting off with Sigrid and Don-
habadur to watch the annual sacrifice to Durga at the Kot; yet
I soon realised that this precaution had been unnecessary, since

the ceremony to placate the Black Goddess of Destruction is a
more effective painkiller than any number of tablets.

There is a certain flavour peculiar to Nepalese functions that
I can never define in a word; it is made up of casualness, gaiety,
indiscipline and a wonderfully unsophisticated spontaneity—
which mixture might be expected to provoke among Western
spectators a patronising amusement. Yet somehow it doesn't,
because in spite of everything these functions are *adequate*. The
Nepalese are not trying to do something and failing—they are
just not trying. And the chief impression received is of an elated
unconcern and freedom—probably nothing will go according
to plan, but anyway the plan didn't matter much in the first
place, so who cares?

The setting of the Durga Sacrifice is unexpectedly drab; on
three sides the Kot—a military square—is surrounded by new
concrete army buildings, lamentably roofed with that corrugated iron which so often disfigures the Kathmandu scene. We
sat on one of these roofs, looking towards the ancient slum house
that forms the fourth side of the quadrangle; half its tiled roof
collapsed long ago, and an eager crowd was watching the scene
from the top floor. Under the long verandah on our left a
shoddy strip of striped matting had been placed beneath a sofa
and two armchairs; these were covered in a spectacularly repulsive chintz, as though they had come direct from a refined
seaside-resort guest-house, and beside them were placed three
slick 'contemporary' occasional tables, each supporting a pea-
cock-blue tin ashtray. On either side of this suite stood rows of
plain wooden chairs—completing the arrangements made for
the reception of H.M. The King and assorted members of the
Royal Family, who were expected to arrive at any moment.

An uneven line of twelve soldiers faced the Royal Enclosure,
each holding a bugle. At irregular intervals these youths bugled
what sounded vaguely like signals—but nothing specific ever
seemed to happen as a result of their odd noises. Despite the
fact that this is an exclusively military occasion everyone was in
mufti apart from these buglers, and a group of soldiers on the
flat roof to our right who formed a brass band.

By seven o'clock the scene was set on the parade-ground.
Innumerable very young bullock-calves and frisky kids had

been led or carried into the arena, and many of these sacrifices were now being stroked soothingly and fed with greenery to make their last hour a happy one. Three rows of furled flags were standing upright, some twenty yards apart, and enigmatic chalked signs had been drawn on the ground around them. There were no statues or other religious emblems in evidence, and one had the impression, when the sacrifices started, that they were being made directly to the flags. Strong wooden killing-posts stood at about a yard's distance from each row of flags and beside these were heaps of dry clay for scattering on the ground when it became too slippery with blood. There were a number of other foreigners sharing our roof-top, and already the women among them had begun to wail sentimentally about the poor little darling kids who were soon to be so cruelly slain. How unrealistic can you get! I'm perfectly certain there wasn't a single person there who had ever declined a plate of roast lamb.

On the ground, at the base of the flagstaffs, men were laying circular trays piled with fruit, vegetables, eggs, bread, grain, flowers, leaves, little mounds of red and yellow powders—and sometimes a sod of earth from which young rice was sprouting. These men were of every sort, from ragged beggars and peasants who brought tiny tin trays, meagrely laden, to prosperous merchants and senior Government officers whose enormous brass trays were almost too heavy to be carried single-handed.

Donbahadur had told us that the King himself would kill a white calf at seven o'clock, thus opening the ceremony; but at half-past seven we decided that His Majesty must have remembered another engagement. By then three young privates, clad in off-white singlets and blue denim shorts, were busily beheading calves at each post, using a larger and less curved edition of the ordinary kukri. The animals' heads were tied to the posts and held steady by one man, while another gripped the hind-quarters; personally I would have been very nervous indeed were I holding the head, and seeing that fearsome weapon flashing down so swiftly within inches of my own neck. Yet in the course of over fifty killings we didn't see even one slight miscalculation, each head being severed with a single clean stroke. As the heads fell they were thrown towards the bases of the flagstaffs, where for moments they lay with ears violently twitching and mouths opening and shutting—a sight which slightly unnerved me at first, as I am not accustomed to watch sacrifices. All the bodies were dragged around the flags in a circle, with blood spurting, and when they had been brought back to the slaying-post they were flung together beside the heap of clay. Many of these carcasses continued to move for an astonishingly long time after death—and they were not merely twitching, but kicking so vigorously that it was difficult to drag them on the ritual round. I longed to be able to experiment by leaving one on its feet after decapitation; probably it could have walked quite a few steps before collapsing. Stories about perambulating, headless bodies have never previously convinced me, but now I find them quite credible.

Shortly before the slaying started the buglers and the brass band had begun to play different tunes simultaneously; one could just discern that each was murdering a popular European march, yet the musicians themselves were obviously being reduced to paroxysms of joyful pride by their own performances.

At about 7.45, when the three privates had got well into their stride and lots of blood was flowing smoothly, a Very Important Person wearing horn-rimmed spectacles and a benign expression came wandering alone into the arena. At once the killings stopped and everyone began to salute wildly, like so many toy soldiers gone mad. Then twenty men who had been mingling with the crowd, clad in ordinary Nepalese costume, plus swords, agitatedly began to unsheath their weapons—and as these no-longer-bright swords were held aloft in a crooked row one could see that at some stage the dew had rusted them. The brass band now stopped playing and while the buglers blew a fanfare the V.I.P., looking faintly embarrassed, solemnly turned to salute the empty sofa and chairs. Then, as the fanfare blasted its uncertain way to its ragged end, the swords were lowered and the V.I.P. lit himself a cigarette and sauntered over to talk to a group of men just below us.

Now the tempo of the ceremony quickened, as more and more animals were led in for sacrifice and the kukris flashed faster and faster and gory men ran around the flags with their carcasses, instead of walking, and piled trays almost obscured the flag-staffs. Then, to augment the excitement, two members of the brass band exchanged their instruments for ancient muskets which they frequently fired deafeningly in the air— while their colleagues and the buglers continued to vie with each other by massacring Sousa.

Smells are always a prominent feature of Nepalese events, and this morning these were cumulative. When we first arrived at the Kot it was permeated merely by the everyday stench of stale urine: but then people began to burn incense on tall, bronze stands beside each row of flagstaffs, and soon we couldn't decide which was the worse—urine or urine intermingled with incense. Next came the pleasant pungency of clouds of gun-powder smoke and, as the ceremony proceeded, steaming rivulets of fresh blood thoroughly confused the issue. Yet— oddly enough—by that time the total effect was quite appetis-ing.

An old Rana army officer was sitting beside me, looking gloomy, and when I made some enthusiastic remarks about the general scene he said curtly that this ceremony is not what it was. During the Rana régime it had been compulsory for every citizen of Kathmandu to sacrifice *something*—if only a pigeon or sparrow—in honour of the Goddess Durga, but now tire-some democratic ideas have infected the atmosphere and the King has announced that only those who really wish to placate the goddess need do so. Possibly she is feeling a little peeved as a result, because it is estimated that the number of sacrifices has dropped to about 25 per cent of the pre-1951 figures; yet she may realise that this is a consequence of prices rising, rather than of devout fear diminishing. In 1950 a chicken cost half a rupee, but now an egg cost three-quarters of a rupee and a chicken twelve or fifteen rupees.

When we left the Kot at nine o'clock the slaughtering was still in progress—the original three privates having been re-placed by three others—and Donbahadur said that it would continue for many hours; but the air of festive excitement had already faded and one felt that the rest of the ceremony would be a mere routine killing of animals such as might occur in a butcher's yard.

Donbahadur now announced that he was going to buy a

chicken to do *puja* for Memsahib's car. He explained that all
the valley's motor-vehicles are included in todays' ceremonies,
to ensure that Durga will not use them during the coming year
as instruments in her destruction campaign; and considering
how recently motor vehicles were introduced to Kathmandu this
reveals surprising adaptability on the part of Nepalese Hinduism. The chicken was duly bought on our way back to Jawalkhel and Donbahadur spent the next hour threading a long
garland of yellow flowers to lay on the car bonnet, mixing the
inevitable coloured powders with water from the sacred Bag-
mati River and sharpening the carving-knife. Then the three
of us processed out to Sigrid's little beige Volkswagen—closely
followed by Puchare, who is always interested in chicken killings
from irreligious motives.

Donbahadur opened the ceremony by sprinkling coloured
holy water all over the car and laying flowers and fruit along
the front bumper. Next he laid the garland on the bonnet,
before drawing with his fingers weird hieroglyphics on the
dusty doors and wheels, while praying *sotto voce*. Then came the
big moment, when he took the chicken from Sigrid and cut its
neck over the flowers and fruit. Finally he again went slowly
around the car, letting the blood trickle onto the roof, sides and
wheels—obviously where Durga is concerned it's always a case
of 'the bloodier the better'.

Our part in the ceremony brought it to a companionable
conclusion. A little pile of rice lay on the sacrificial brass tray
and when this had been mixed with blood Sigrid knelt before
Donbahadur, who stuck a lump of the concoction on the middle
of her forehead and put a red flower in her hair. My turn came
next, before Donbahadur applied the same treatment to himself. The blood congeals very quickly and even now (10.30 p.m.)
my piece is still in place—which indicates that Durga will not
destroy me during the year ahead. Unfortunately, however,
Sigrid's mark fell off quite soon, so now poor Donbahadur is
slightly apprehensive about the fate of his beloved Memsahib.

To complete our celebrations we had the chicken for lunch;
it was very tastily curried, but conspicuously anaemic.

*5 October.*

Quite suddenly my ribs have begun to mend; today I needed no pain-killers and my seat to Pokhara has been booked for the day after tomorrow.

This afternoon I took a test-walk to Patan, and on the way, while passing along a narrow street of three-storey, mud-brick farmhouses, I saw a madwoman dancing and singing—with distinctly lewd overtones—in front of one of these houses. She was surrounded by a little group of smiling, but not leering, onlookers, and many other interested spectators were leaning far out over their carved balconies up and down the street. Almost everyone was dressed in festival style—complete with vivid *tika* marks in the centre of the forehead, garlands of fresh flowers around the neck and bright blossoms in the hair—and one immediately sensed that the madwoman's display was being accepted—not cruelly, but casually—as a sort of bonus minor entertainment quite suitable to a day of relaxation and rejoicing. Lunatics are a common enough sight in a country where there are no mental homes, and many of them reveal their insanity by these frenzied and often slightly *risqué* outbursts of song and dance. In Europe the sight of a madwoman roaming the streets would now arouse the most extreme pity, embarrassment and horror, so it does seem a little strange at first to observe onlookers enjoying this pathetic exhibition. Yet though they laugh, and sometimes engage in what appears to be deliberately provocative repartee, one is aware of no derision or real unkindness; indeed the onlookers are obviously sharing in the lunatics' crazy pleasure in singing and dancing— and one wonders if some of these mad men and women are not better off than our hidden lunatics, who must live for ever in discreet isolation from their fellows.

At Patan the Durbar Square was thronged with holiday crowds, full of the joys of life, and on walking up a statue-lined side-street I met an extraordinary little procession slowly making its way towards the main temple in the Square. It consisted of fourteen men dressed up as women, each wearing a huge, painted mask from which hung fantastic cloaks of waist-length horse hair, dyed red, green, pink, yellow and brown. These goddesses were preceded by two men, one of whom held aloft an enormous blazing torch, from which flames were leaping dangerously over the heads of the crowd, while the other carried in his arms a sheaf of bay-leaves surrounding what was evidently a very ancient, precious and sacred bronze plaque depicting Durga in various contortions of rage. The goddesses were walking in single file, with curious rhythmic jerky movements, and each one was accompanied by a normally dressed man who held 'her' right hand with his own left hand, while a large sword was carried jointly by the couple. The procession was followed by a man playing on a drum decorated with two pairs of mountain-sheep horns and at frequent intervals, when cymbals joined the drum, the goddesses stood still and their escorts moved away a few paces. Then, waving their swords, the goddesses danced briefly with slow, solemn motions of the arms and legs. At the conclusion of each dance devout people came forward from among the crowd and ritually fed the performers by pushing tiny wafers of wheaten bread under the masks into their mouths, and presenting them with water in what looked like earthenware coffee-cup saucers, which the goddesses smashed on the ground after drinking.

Even without these halts progress would have been slow, as the narrow street was packed with excited, reverent, laughing spectators who were continually pressing forward to touch the goddesses—and who were especially anxious to bring their babies and small children into contact with these divinities. I followed the procession for almost an hour, being accepted by the crowd with that gay friendliness so characteristic of Kathmandu.

As we approached the Square the throng became even denser, so for the sake of my ribs it seemed prudent to escape and I found a seat, on an elephant-god's pedestal, from which to see the ceremonial entry into the temple courtyard. Here I was surrounded by laughing, teasing, curious children—some of them quite old friends—who were flying balloons and eating sticky sweetmeats and whose ambitions to climb all over me had to be checked by an explanation that I was not in my normal state of resilience. Soon the big bronze bell in the centre of the Square began to toll—with a sweet, mellow solemnity incongruously reminiscent of a European church bell—but though this was meant to herald the appearance of the procession there was neither sight nor sound of the goddesses half-an-hour later. It was now getting dusk and, as I feared for my ribs when walking home through rough, unlighted laneways, I reluctantly said good-bye to the children and left. Then, a few moments later, I passed the fourteen goddesses reclining on the verandah of a very scruffy tea-house, with their masks and wigs on their laps and cigarettes in their hands, while tea was being brewed to sustain them for the last lap to the temple.

# 9

## *Purifying Spirits*

*11 October. Pokhara.*

On arriving back here four days ago I experienced a very strong 'coming home' feeling: and since then it has been doubly difficult to accept the fact that soon I will be leaving for ever. I had expected to suffer the usual pangs when parting from the Tibetans, but only now do I fully realise the strength of my affection for Pokhara Valley in general and Pardi village in particular.

Tashi gave me a deliriously warm welcome and importantly led the way home from the camp—though after my long absence I had been prepared to find her allegiance at least partially transferred back to Ngawang Pema and his family, whose guest she had been. From her point of view my return was most inopportune because yesterday, incredible as it may seem, the precocious little hussy came on heat. Granted everyone and everything matures quickly in this climate, but for a few inches of puppyhood to come on heat at the age of five months and ten days really is taking precocity to extremes. Naturally I wasn't prepared (nor, presumably, was Tashi) so I'm very much afraid that the worst has happened. Yesterday afternoon she came in, after one of her gambols with the local hounds, looking slightly distraught—but at the time I attributed this to some tiff with a buddy and thought nothing of it. Yet now that the penny has dropped I suspect that she had just then lost her virginity and was registering a seemly degree of emotional upheaval. This afternoon, when she was taken for a frustrating walk on a chain, I had to use a stick in defence of her probably extinct virtue. One hates to thwart young love, yet altogether apart from the silly little thing's immaturity the legal implications of this situation are quite petrifying. It is difficult enough to import 'a domestic pet of the canine species' into Ireland in an unmarried state—but the imagination boggles as it has never boggled before at the prospect of importing said domestic pet plus innumerable progeny; and they would be innumerable if Tashi's fertility were to match her precocity, just as they would be too adorable to leave behind if they took after their mamma.

Now the nights are really cold here—and the days indescribably beautiful, with clear skies over the Annapurna range—so Tashi insists on coming into my sleeping-bag. At first I protested, thinking that she would suffocate, but she refused to take 'no' for an answer; and obviously she had had it all worked out beforehand, because on admission she immediately burrowed down to the end and curled up at my feet. Whereupon I decided that this was really quite a good idea, since she forms a hot-bottle that never gets cold.

*19 October.*

All last night it rained heavily and the downpour continued until 3 p.m. today, like a revival of the monsoon. The locals say that this is freakish in October, though from mid-November onwards the valley does have occasional severe hailstorms.

Now that the so-called war is over tourists are again coming to Nepal, and almost every day during this past week a special plane has flown from Kathmandu to spew out on our airstrip a rigidly regimented group of 'Round-the-Worlders'. These groups of course comprise the bravest tourist spirits—the ones who have taken a deep breath and, against their friends' advice, decided to risk two or three hours in Pokhara, bringing hygienically packed lunches with them and drinking very little at breakfast-time because—'My dear, we were *warned!* There simply *aren't* any toilets in the place!' It is most unkind to laugh at such groups—but impossible not to do so, when they emerge from their planes wearing that same expression of bemused weariness, thinly veiled by a spurious joy at the excitement of 'exploring', which I have so often seen on the faces of similar groups being spewed out of luxury coaches in my own 'beauty-spot' home-town; and inevitably a regiment of Round-the-Worlders looks even funnier in Pokhara than it does in Ireland. I feel delightfully integrated with my neighbours when we stand in a row near the airstrip, being hypnotised by the latest Paris or New York fashions which, seen from a Central Nepal angle, appear even more grotesque than they actually are.

Usually the regiment is commanded by a buxom blonde 'guidette' (a monstrous word with which I have lately become reluctantly familiar) who wears 'sensible' shoes and strides ahead clanging an arty bronze bell—'typical of Old Nepal'—to keep her troops in line. Unhappily few of the females follow her good example in footwear and crises become monotonous as the high-heelers get their deserts on our rocky tracks.

A few days ago one high-heeler caused me hours of tormenting curiosity. Her regiment was passing my house, at the non-U end of the bazaar, when she noticed me sitting on my doorstep doing nothing—a satisfying occupation now known to too few Europeans. At once she stopped to stare, as though I were a singularly repellent phenomenon on par with regional odours; then she called after a friend—'Betty, *look!* Do you suppose she *lives* there?' And ever since I have been consumed by a desire to know the content of Betty's inaudible reply.

Yesterday a regiment of Round-the-Worlders was cut off from its base and trapped in Pokhara overnight by the abrupt change in the weather. I didn't have the sadistic pleasure of visiting our bug-infested doss-houses while the abandoned troops were quartering there, and my imagination is unequal to visualising their reactions to the 'service'. But this afternoon I did observe them—unwashed, unfed, and unslept—getting into formation on the airstrip in readiness for the rescue operation: and I must say they looked ripe for rescuing. One could see them cowering before the advancing spectre of dysentery—if they hadn't already brain-washed themselves into developing it—and their chic ensembles had taken it hard. That regiment will remember Pokhara long after the Taj has been forgotten.

### 3 November.

A few days ago I gave my landlord a week's notice, and ever since there has been a 'purifying' campaign in progress in my room. This is being conducted with characteristic Asian disregard for privacy; at any hour of the day a bearded sadhu, laden with joss-sticks, sacred water, flowers, fruit and Sanskrit texts, may come scrambling up my ladder to seat himself in the middle of the floor—completely ignoring my presence—and perform interminable rituals to cleanse this room of the pollution caused by its untouchable resident. Despite his pretence that I do not exist—which may be part of the rite—I have by now become quite attached to 'my' sadhu, whose expression is less grim and predatory than that of the average Brahmin priest. The main part of the ceremony consists of long chantings, interrupted at set intervals by the strewing of flowers in the four corners of the room and the placing of a piece of fruit and a small coin on the table right under my astonished nose. At first I wondered if these were presents to me—but apparently not, for they are removed at the end of each session, though the flowers remain to wither in the corners. (This lavish use of fruit, flowers and vegetables is to me one of the most pleasing features of Hindu rituals in Nepal; it gives them a simple beauty and grace quite absent from any of the Buddhist rituals that one sees practised in the camp.)

I have to admit that the general lack of privacy here does become slightly trying after a time. Of course one could simply keep one's door bolted: yet to do this would be much more than a physical locking-out of the neighbours, and seclusion could never compensate for the damage inflicted on one's relationship with the village. Unfortunately compromise is impossible on such issues: one must either totally accept or reject local customs.

The weather has been appalling for the past fortnight, and as this is rice-harvesting time these rains are likely to bring considerable hardship to Pokhara. They are also hindering the recently begun seasonal house-building activities, which are now giving a great atmosphere of bustle to the whole valley. Men are constantly passing to and fro, leading creaking bullock-carts piled with rocks and stones; and women and children are to be seen everywhere carrying colossal loads of grass for the roofs, or of clay for the walls, or forming teams of three or four to transport bamboo poles for the supports. It's all so simple—one day there is a vacant plot of land and a week later a family is moving into a solid, attractive new home. Of course in the interval even the four-year-olds have been working virtually day and night it's enchanting to see them trotting sturdily along behind their parents, carrying miniature *dokars* of grass—the N.S.P.C.C. might not approve, but these children look happily proud to be so involved in this important family undertaking. Usually the houses are not completed until their owners have moved in. Then the women plaster the walls and floors with red mud while the men are carving and attaching the wooden doors and shutters, and building an outside stairway of stone or timber, if the ground floor is to be used as a stable.

This afternoon the camp held a farewell party for me, and this was indeed a melancholy occasion. It rained greyly all the time, which seemed appropriate, but the Tiblets insisted on dancing in my honour under the dismal sky, and everyone ate prodigious quantities of delicious *moo-moo*, which had been boiled in oil and syrup, and drank endless bowls of salted tea mixed with real yak-butter.


*5 November. Kathmandu.*

I have now proved conclusively that one pain does indeed cancel out another; today I awoke with such an unprecedented hangover that this afternoon's dreaded departure from Pok-hara meant nothing as compared with the activities of that personal Goddess of Destruction who seemed to be residing in my head.

In the course of a not abstemious life I have only once before had a hangover—at the age of twenty, after drinking a half-bottle of the cheapest Spanish brandy—but obviously it was the mingling of *chang* and *rakshi* that did the damage. Kessang and the Khamba community of Pokhara had invited me to a 6 p.m. Tibetan farewell party at The Annapurna, and a Pardi Gurkha friend had invited me to a 9 p.m. Nepalese farewell party at a Thakkholi eating-house in the village—and having gone to both parties and drunk multi-racially I can't reasonably complain about the consequences.

The weather surpassed itself yesterday; at 4.30 p.m., after a day of heavy rain, Pokhara was subjected to a cloudburst that made the worst of the monsoon downpours look merely damp. This lasted for a whole terrifying hour, before stopping abruptly, as though a dam had been closed. Then we set out for The Annapurna, and Tashi had to be carried all the way; at no point on the track was the furiously tearing water below my waist and at one stage it rose to neck-level and I had to swim to higher ground, gripping Tashi's scruff with one hand. Perhaps after all it was fortunate that I spent the evening pickled in alcohol: otherwise I might have awakened with pneumonia instead of a hangover.

When Tibetans give a party it is nothing less than a banquet. At first, because of the party to come, I tried to back-pedal when offered solid refreshment, but everything was so delicious that self-control became impossible—and would in any case have been impolite when such an effort had been made for the occasion. By the time I stood up from the meal at 8.30 I could scarcely walk; and some of my fellow guests were quite frankly dozing off with their heads on the table.

The Thakkholi eating-house was scrupulously clean, as Thakkholi homes almost always are, and the ochre walls and floor glowed warmly by the light of twisting flames that came leaping out of a hole in the ground in one corner—rather as though we were on the edge of a baby volcano. There were ten of us officially present for the meal—but innumerable others drifted in and out of the background shadows—and we all sat cross-legged in a circle, on little squares of Tibetan carpeting. Luckily the main meal was not served until eleven o'clock, though we were nibbling incessantly at various tit-bits as we swilled the rawest of raw *rakshi*, ordered specially by my host from his village. He claimed that it was the most potent alcohol obtainable in Nepal (where no alcohol is exactly impotent) and today I am prepared to endorse this.

All the food was served on brilliantly burnished brass dishes of varying sizes—from minute ones for the hors-d'œuvres to circular trays for the rice—and our 'nibblings' in fact amounted to quite a meal. We began with tiny strips of perfectly braised wild-goat meat—among the tastiest savouries I have ever eaten —followed by fried sardine-like fish from the lake, followed by two hard-boiled eggs apiece, followed by one fried egg, followed by an omelette containing intolerably hot chopped peppers that compelled me to spit it out with more haste than good manners. And all the time we sipped steadily at *rakshi*, more *rakshi* and still more *rakshi* until I felt as though a bonfire were burning in my guts—but by then I had passed the point of no return.

The main course consisted of a gigantic mound of rice, with curried vegetables and dahl. As it was being served the local prostitute wandered in, hoping for a customer at the end of our revels; but she could see at a glance that after this party no one would be in a fit state to patronise her, so she immediately dropped her professional manner and settled down merely to be sociable. I have always thought her the best-looking woman in the village; she has fine-cut Aryan features, fair skin, and glossy, jet hair. By fire-light she seemed quite beautiful—until one noticed that brittle unhappiness and unwomanliness which disfigures even the loveliest of her sisters in every country of the world. From her nose hung an enormous circular gold ornament, which compelled her to smoke her countless cigarettes through the corner of her mouth, and her clothes were ragged and filthy—though of such good material that one suspected them of having been acquired as payment for favours received. One could see that this addition to the party displeased the Thakkholi proprietress—though it was only when her own attractive sixteen-year-old daughter began to talk to the gate-crasher that an indirect protest was made by sharply ordering the girl to bed.

I cannot pretend to know at what time the party ended; but when two swaying neighbours escorted me home and pushed me up the ladder I was quite unable to distinguish one end of my sleeping-bag from the other—so I merely collapsed on top of it.

The next few hours were not restful; in the midst of sundry nightmares I awoke once and for some moments remained firmly convinced that I was no longer a human being but one of Jupiter's satellites—a singularly disquieting delusion, possibly exclusive to *rakshi*. And today my condition resembled a serious illness rather than a hangover—indeed I have never had any illness from natural causes that felt even half so serious.

Pokhara airstrip chose the occasion to break all its own records for 'erraticism'. Though I had been requested to report at 9.30

for a 10 a.m. flight our plane did not depart until 4.30 p.m. However, I was indifferent to this; it could not have mattered less to me where I was, or for how long, or why. I sat in The Annapurna, wrapped in a cocoon of malaise and misery, with my fellow-revellers—none of them looking too robust—and we drank cup after cup of heavily salted black coffee, which is reputed to counteract the worst effect of *rakshi* poisoning, and our long silences were broken only by staccato comments on how very dreadful we felt.

Today was a Public Holiday in Pokhara; I think someone told me that the valley was celebrating the wedding of the two banks of the Seti River. This sounds improbable enough to be a figment of my *rakshi*-ridden imagination—but even more improbable things *do* occur in Nepal. In any case, whatever the cause of the celebrations they were very elaborate, and on two occasions freight-planes returning from Bhairawa had to circle the valley for ten or twelve minutes while slow processions of hundreds of women crossed the airstrip. Everyone was dressed in their most brilliant clothes, and there was much singing and dancing and blowing of conches, and carrying of effigies of the Seti on flower-laden platforms. For hours these noisy, colourful processions wound around the valley and it seemed to me that the populace was in a most tiresome and unnecessarily frivolous mood. All that gay laughter, song and music penetrated to my brain as a series of demoniacal shrieks, and the blur of colourful clothes sent sharp arrows of pain darting across my forehead.

When I at last dragged myself on to the plane I seemed to be laden with white scarves from the Tibetans and flower-garlands from the Nepalese—but perhaps my condition was creating this compensatory illusion of popularity.

I began to feel a little less unhuman during the plane journey and on arrival a couple of stiff Courvoisiers speeded the cure; in the circumstances this could hardly be described as 'a hair of the dog', but the principle was perhaps the same.

And now I'm going early to bed.

# 10

# *On Foot to Langtang*

I have spent the past few days trying to forget the Pokhara Tibetans and organising a fortnight's exploratory trek to the Langtang area due north of Kathmandu—though perhaps 'organising' is too strong a word for my sort of pre-trek arrangements.

Trekking parties here vary enormously according to the status, pernicketiness and physical fitness (or unfitness) of their members. The most elaborate are the comical Royal Progresses of Ambassadors, who travel accompanied by scores of porters, a team manager to control them, a cook, a kitchen-boy, a guide, an interpreter, personal servants, quantities of imported food, cases of alcohol and every conceivable piece of equipment from a mobile lavatory to a folding wardrobe. The next and largest group are the lesser Embassy officials and Foreign Aid men, who travel in moderately luxurious parties numbering their porters by the dozen and foregoing lavatories and wardrobes— but bringing tents, tables, chairs, beds, larders and cellars; and then there are the hoi-polloi, who are too poor—or too sensible— to do anything but rough it.

I had planned to go alone on my own short trek, but Rudi Weissmuller, a Swiss friend who is familiar with the area, told me that this would be unfair on the locals because during winter they have no surplus food to sell to travellers; he also pointed out that I would be permanently lost without a guide, and advised me to go to the notorious Globe Restaurant to look for a Sherpa who would be willing to act as both porter and guide.

Had I not by now been semi-integrated in the Nepal province of Tibland it would have been difficult to find such a combination; the Sherpas are being a little spoiled by the Big Time Expeditions and are no longer very enthusiastic about ambling in the foothills with ordinary mortals. However, through Tibetan friends I contacted Mingmar, a twenty-four-year-old native of Namche Bazaar who agreed to come with me for eight shillings a day—by Sherpa standards a sensationally low wage.

A month ago I applied to the Singha Durbar for a trekking permit, but inevitably I have spent most of my time during the past few days prising it out of the relevant Government Department. In addition to losing my application form these carica-tures of bureaucrats had also lost my passport, so I just hung around the office waiting . . . and waiting . . . and waiting . . . until at last I became a Public Nuisance. Then someone be-stirred himself to excavate a mound of documents (doubtless losing several other passports in the process), and a battered green booklet inscribed EIRE eventually appeared. This was at once seized on by me—to the great distress of the clerk, who insisted that it belonged to a Czech stocking-manufacturer—and in due course the permit was grudgingly issued by a more senior clerk, who reprimanded me for not having made my application until the last moment.

This morning I again met Mingmar and gave him money to buy rice, salt, tea and a saucepan. He seemed considerably agitated by the scantiness of these provisions—not on his own behalf, but on mine—nor was he much consoled to hear that I myself was bringing twelve tins of sardines, twelve packets of dried soup, a tin of coffee, two mugs, two spoons and a knife. This was still not the sort of provisioning and equipment he expected of even the humblest Western trekker, and despite my assurance that I perversely enjoy hardship he remained con-vinced that I would fold up *en route* for lack of comfort.

Yesterday I spent an unforgettable afternoon wandering around Patan—beyond a doubt my favourite part of the valley. To me there is by now something very special about this dis-integrating yet still lovely city; familiarity with the most obscure of its filthy little alleys and a positive sense of friendship towards its time-worn, grotesquely carved animal-gods has changed my original excited admiration to a warm affection.

The rice-harvesting is at its height this week and as I strolled around the narrow streets, feeling the local magic rising like a tide to engulf me, the air was hazily golden with threshing dust.

Now Patan is to be seen in the rôle of a big farming-village and even in the Durbar Square, where a prim group of guided tourists was pretending not to notice the temple-god's penes, I had to pick my way carefully between mounds of glowing grain and stacks of straw. Most people quit all other work at harvest-time and return home to help—a delightfully sane arrange-ment of priorities which does nothing to speed the modernisa-tion of Nepal. While the men cut the crop in the fields the women attend to the threshing, and outside every house along every street the family's rice supply for the next year was being heaped. Normally the surplus is sold to bazaar merchants, but unhappily there will be little surplus this year, for Kathmandu has also had vile weather during the last fortnight.

Perhaps there won't be time for me to visit Patan again, but I could have no lovelier a final memory than yesterday's, when the streets were one vast sun-burnished granary, with crimson skirts swirling above golden grain, and sheaves of shining straw being balanced on raven heads, and the untidy music of swinging jewellery sounding faintly as lithe bodies displayed a timeless art.

*10 November. Trisuli.*

A typical Nepalese day, with lots more waiting. Mingmar and I had arranged to meet at 6 a.m., on a certain bridge; but we each went to a wrong one—unfortunately not the same wrong one—and by the time we had got ourselves sorted out it was 9 a.m.

Trisuli is a valley north-west of Kathmandu where the Indian Aid Mission is now working on a colossal hydro-electric project. A rough forty-mile track has been hacked out across the moun-tains and every day an incredible number of heavy, battered trucks carry machinery, piping and cement to the work-site. To my annoyance Mingmar decided that we would do the first stage of our trek—in what he most misleadingly described as 'comfort'—by taking a truck to Trisuli. I argued that my con-ception of a Himalayan trek did not include rides in motor vehicles; but it is against modern Sherpa principles to walk one yard further than is absolutely necessary, so I soon gave in and we set out for Balaju, the suburb of Kathmandu from which the Trisuli track begins.

This is the industrial area of the valley, where foreign aid has already done its worst and produced incongruous little factories, schools and blocks of 'workers' flats—not to mention a deep-freeze plant with a notice advising foreigners to book space for storing their PERCIABLE goods; even in the context it took me a few moments to decipher that one.

We waited here by the roadside for over an hour, during which I became more and more restive. It is easy to wait patiently when a situation is beyond one's control, but to sit around pointlessly when one could be happily walking into the hills is very galling indeed. Yet Sherpas are as obstinate as Tibetans, and it would have been impossible to convince Mingmar that some people do enjoy walking.

When a cement truck finally appeared we joined the twenty other passengers after a prolonged haggle about fares; obviously, though his own purse was not affected, it was a point of honour with Mingmar to secure the lowest possible rate from the Sikh driver. We then drove a few hundred yards up the village street, which is being newly paved, but soon our way was blocked by an ancient steam-roller that looked as though it had been abducted from some Museum of Early Machinery. This fascinating object, having expired on the narrowest section of the embryonic road, was now resisting all attempts to push, tow or otherwise move it out of the way. Occasionally a scowling young Indian with set jaw appeared from somewhere, shinned up to the driver's seat and struggled violently with whatever it is that makes ancient steam-rollers roll; but nothing ever happened.

Meanwhile our driver was having trouble with the police, who could not make up their minds whether we should proceed to Trisuli (steam-rollers permitting) immediately or at 5 o'clock this afternoon. (It was not clear to me why the police were in control of our apparently innocent movements: but I have long since ceased to be surprised by the quirks of Nepalese officialdom.) No less than three times all twenty-two passengers and their luggage were moved out of the truck, and back into the truck, as the police vacillated. One feels that Lewis Carroll must have secretly visited Nepal; a strong 'Alice' atmosphere now enveloped the whole scene, and to Mingmar's alarm I succumbed to an uncontrollable giggling fit when, for the third time, we were ordered back into the truck.

At this point an Indian Senior Engineer arrived at the scene of the break-down and did something so drastic that the steam-roller gave a scream of terror, emitted unbelievable clouds of steam and moved at terrifying speed down the steep hill, grazing the side of our truck as it passed. Fortunately this development coincided with a police mood favouring our immediate depart-ure, so off we went at full speed—10 m.p.h.—up the hill over the half-made road.

One suspects Sikh drivers of fiddling their loads so that they can make a good profit on carrying passengers and our covered truck was only one quarter full of cement sacks; but, as these constitute a most unpleasant cargo with which to travel, I soon climbed out on to the roof of the cab and hung on there, obtain-ing splendid though terrifying views for most of the forty-six mile, six-hour journey.

This track makes the Rajpath look like the M.1 and, as we crawled along, I reflected yet again on the unlikelihood of Nepal ever having a conventional net-work of roads, or of China ever wanting to annex a country that could be of no possible use, either agriculturally or industrially, to anyone. There is only one Himalayan range in the world, much of which happens to be right here in Nepal, and even the ingenuity of mid-twentieth century technologists can do very little about it. The Chinese have just spent four million pounds on building their sixty-five mile dirt track 'strategic highway' from Kathmandu to Kodari —on the Tibetan frontier—and no doubt they regard this final link in the Lhasa–India road as being worth every penny of these four millions; but the building, and even more the main-taining of commercial roads throughout landsliding Nepal is never likely to be considered economic by any government.

As we left Balaju I was brooding morbidly on yesterday's American jet crash, in relation to our flight home; but before we had travelled far on this track I could only think how very slim my chances were of ever again boarding an aeroplane. The snag is that when sitting in a corner of the box on a cab-roof one's seat is projecting beyond the wheels—which are only a matter of inches from the often crumbling verge—so at hair-pin bends one imagines repeatedly that the lumbering vehicle is about to go over the edge. Recently I have been congratulating myself on having an improved head for heights but, though it is true that I no longer even notice 1,000-foot drops, and am only mildly impressed by 2,000-foot drops, I do still take fright on finding myself poised over 4,000-foot abysses while being driven by a slightly inebriated Sikh. Yet when I had adjusted to the singularity of this road—which is not to be compared with anything I have ever seen elsewhere—it became paradoxically soothing to go swinging around mountain after mountain, hour after hour; but the jolting was hellish, and tonight my whole body feels as though it had been put through a mangle. Such journeys are not the best sort of preparation for strenuous treks.

The soil in this area appears to be much poorer than around Pokhara. The main crops are millet and maize, but three-quarters of the land is an uncultivable—though gloriously beautiful—mixture of rock and forest.

During the day several trucks and two jeepfuls of Indian engineers came towards us *en route* for Kathmandu, and during the complicated manœuvrings that have to be executed before vehicles can pass each other here our lorry went axle-deep into soft mud at the cliff side of the track. Obviously there was going to be a long delay, while the more able-bodied passengers freed the vehicle with spades borrowed from local peasants, so I suggested to Mingmar that we should walk the remaining ten miles to Trisuli Bazaar: but the idea was spurned. I then briefly considered going on alone; however, Nepal being Nepal, the truck could suddenly take a fancy to return to Kathmandu with Mingmar and most of my kit on board—or some other inconceivable catastrophe might occur to prevent us from ever meeting again in this life.

I noticed that the four Tibetans among the passengers were the most willing and energetic helpers; they showed no resentment of the Sikh's peremptory instructions, which so antagonised the local farmers that they were understandably reluctant to lend their spades and finally charged for the loan.

Within the past decade there has been some deterioration in Indo-Nepalese relations, and by now, having studied at close quarters quite a number of individual Nepalese–Indian relationships, I feel that India must accept rather more than half the blame for this. Admittedly the Nepalese have the usual excessive—though attractive—pride of mountain peoples and are very quick to resent, or even imagine, minor slights; but it is unnecessary for them to over-exercise their imagination in this context for the Indians usually treat them with breathtaking tactlessness. As citizens of a country to which the British introduced railways, hospitals, electricity and postal services the Indians now affect extreme contempt for a city like Kathmandu—forgetting that Delhi might be similarly undeveloped had foreigners never meddled with Indian affairs. In a place like Pokhara the condescension of the resident Indians is beyond *my* endurance, let alone that of the Nepalese. Were it not so infuriating it would be funny to see how expertly these men reproduce the attitudes of the worst type of British sahib in India; and frequently too there is venom in their voices, for they seem to be compulsively avenging themselves on the Nepalese for the unforgotten horde of trivial insults directed at their own countrymen in the past.

However, it is probable that in any case the Nepalese would have been hostile to India at this present point in history, because of our common human inability to accept assistance graciously. During the past six months a number of Nepalese have sulkily told me that had India not been given so many dollars by America she could not possibly have given so many rupees to Nepal—which makes one wonder just how much furtive animosity is provoked in materially poor countries by the lavishness of Western financial aid.

Our truck mishap had occurred when we were almost down to river level, and now long streams of late sunshine were making the savage clefts in the hills—relics of monsoon landslides—glow redly amidst the dark green of the forests and the pale golden-green of ripening millet. At this season there is no great urgency here about work in the fields, and as time passed a small crowd gathered around the truck to enjoy our little crisis. One woman was accompanied by her self-possessed five-year-old son who, feeling a bit peckish, had a long drink from his mother's breast—and then stood up, wiped his mouth, took a cigarette from the pocket of his tattered shift and strolled over to me to request a match. One hears that mothers should not smoke while breast-feeding their children: but apparently it is quite in order for Nepalese children to smoke while being breast-fed.

After seventy minutes of hard work the truck was at last liberated and we drove down to the valley floor where, at 1,700 feet, the air seemed thickly warm. Then, having crossed the river by a startlingly posh new bridge, we arrived at Trisuli Bazaar just as darkness fell and are spending the night in a ramshackle eating-house that calls itself an hotel—having evidently 'got notions', as we say in Ireland, since so many Indians came to work here. This small town is built on a steep slope directly above the river, and all the streets are smelly flights of steps. As usual in Nepal the men seem to spend most of their evening hours gambling intently, and it was difficult to get the hotelkeeper away from his cards for long enough to lead us to the top of a dark, narrow stairway. We have a most luxuriously furnished room to ourselves—with no less than three straw mattresses on the floor; but these are probably the headquarters of an army of bed-bugs so I have urged Mingmar to sleep on all three and am hoping that the army will concentrate on his impervious body. My own sleeping-bag has been laid in the centre of the mud floor, as far away as possible from the presumably infested walls.

*11 November. In a Shack on a Ridge.*

After an undisturbed nine-hour sleep we woke at six o'clock and fifteen minutes later were on the track, Mingmar carrying sixty pounds (a light load for a Sherpa) and I myself carrying thirty pounds (a heavy load for an effete Westerner). Mingmar's load could be much lighter were his standards not modelled absurdly on those of the expeditions he has worked for; in addition to his flea-bag he is carrying an inflatable rubber mattress and a thick blanket, which together must weigh at least twenty-five pounds.

The Trisuli Valley would be very lovely had the Indian Aid project not already desecrated it with the roar of machinery, and with hillocks of cement and stacks of piping. Now monstrous bulldozers and angular cranes are bullying the river into submission, and one is frightened by the speed with which men can despoil beauty. I was glad when after two hours' brisk walking we had passed those scenes and recrossed the river to where our track began its climb. Here a hamlet of wooden houses stood just above the river and, though it was a little early for trekkers' brunch, Mingmar decided that we should eat now as we would come to no other settlement before dusk.

By the time we had finished our meal and set off up the first mountain (alias ridge) the sun was quite fierce and Mingmar was muttering impolite things about the heat. On being questioned he admitted that he was wearing woollen ankle-length underpants and nylon skiing pants under his denim jeans, plus a woolly vest, a flannel shirt and a sweater under his down-padded wind-cheater. As I was too hot in a thin cotton shirt and shorts the mere thought of this apparel weakened me and eventually I talked him out of two-thirds of his garments—leaving him still grossly over-dressed and considerably increasing his load. This Sherpa predilection for excessive clothing amounts to a mania; having acquired these status symbols from various expeditions they cannot bear not to wear them everywhere and all the time.

Today we were climbing most of the way, going north above the Kyirung River. Our track was never forced right down to river-level, though it often descended a few thousand feet to avoid the more intractable precipices and then climbed steeply again to its average level of about 5,000 feet; but at no stage was it as gruelling as the Pokhara–Siglis route.

Yet simply to say that we were going up and down hills all day gives a misleading impression of monotony; around every corner of the winding track one saw a new loveliness, or an already familiar and striking vista from a completely different angle. Sheer mountains rose beyond the narrow Kyirung gorge and we passed from thick forests to barren stretches of rock-littered moor, and from sunny, grassy glades, half-encircled by high grey cliffs, to cool, dim tunnels overhung by giant shrubs and filled with the tumult of waterfalls—while everywhere were patches of pungent herbs, and a glory of wild flowers splashing the mountainside with oranges, blues, reds, yellows, whites and pinks.

This region is virtually a no-man's-land between the Hindu-dominated area to the south and the almost exclusively Buddhist area to the north, and I felt ridiculously moved on coming to my first ancient wayside *chorten*—a sight which indicated that now I'm as close to Tibet, spiritually and geographically, as any ordinary traveller can be in this sad decade. These stone *chortens*, usually built in the middle of paths, are symbols of Nirvana; when walking around them Buddhists always keep them on their right and it is one of the signs of a Bön-po that he keeps them on his left. This was a very old *chorten*, with grass and weeds flourishing in the crevices between the stones; one could almost have passed by without noticing it, yet its very inconspicuousness seemed to symbolise most fittingly the often imperfectly understood but ever present Buddhist influence that guides all Tibetan peoples.

I arrived at this solitary hovel on the crest of a ridge forty minutes ahead of Mingmar, who is in rather poor shape today because of a nasty boil on his right cheek. Western travellers do not often trek around here, yet the seven members of the household accepted my arrival without showing a trace of curiosity, disapproval or welcome: their apathy took me back to that appalling train-journey through Bihar.

This hut is built of rock-slabs, with a plank roof anchored by stones, and the squalor makes it seem more like a nineteenth-century convict's cell than a home. I am not easily shaken by Asian standards of living, which frequently are not nearly as low, within their own climatic and cultural context, as affluent Western travellers imagine them to be; yet this degree of poverty is devastating by any standards. These people grow a little millet on the unsympathetic mountainside, but it is pitifully inadequate for their annual needs and tonight they had a supper of stewed nettles (known to them as stinging-grass), flavoured with chillies and washed down with *rakshi*. Seeing this fare Mingmar and I simultaneously suggested to each other that we should cook a double ration of rice, and on being offered the extra food they seized fistfuls of it from our saucepan and ate it ravenously.

There are two rooms here—an outer one leading on to the

verandah and containing two plank beds, and an inner one with a fire in the middle of the floor, around which everyone crowds when darkness has fallen. Mercifully fuel is no problem and cheerfully-leaping flames do something to alleviate the general misery. When any object is being sought beyond the radius of the firelight a blazing brand is used as a candle, and crimson embers replace tobacco in the family hookah, which is passed silently from person to person; but the acrid wood-smoke (one of the causes of glaucoma) is very hard on the eyes and I can hardly see to write this.

In the darkness of the outer room a youngish woman is lying alone beneath a filthy blanket, moaning and coughing. Obviously she is in the last stages of T.B., yet the rest of the family seem dully indifferent to her distress. A little while ago I gave her some aspirin, just to show an interest; she was pathetically grateful and now says she feels a little better, but the moaning and the rasping cough continue.

I've tried to find out which tribe these people belong to, but they don't seem to know themselves; Mingmar says that their dialect is almost incomprehensible to him, though definitely derived from the Tibeto–Burmese rather than the Sanskrit language-group. Their features are more Mongolian than Aryan and, as none of the universal signs of Hinduism are apparent in the hovel, I assume them to be nominally Buddhist—though at this stage of dehumanisation it is unlikely that religion plays much part in their life.

As I write the complicated shutters that serve instead of a door are being lifted into place and securely barred with long wooden poles; so now I must spread my flea-bag on the second plank-bed before the firelight has entirely faded.

## 12 November. Thangjet.

We were on our way by 6 a.m., having slept from 8.30 p.m. —if you can call it sleeping, between the biting of bugs and what sounded like the death-throes of that unfortunate woman.

From outside the hovel, before we continued down the ridge, we caught our last glimpse of the broad Trisuli Valley, far away beyond all the hills we crossed yesterday; and now the valley was so covered in cloud that it seemed like a sea of milk, whose motionless waves were clinging to the bases of many mountains.

Five hours later we stopped for brunch at a tiny hamlet of filthy stone farmhouses. Here was the same absence of food—too acute to be called a mere shortage—and at least every second person, including the children, had goitre. The skin diseases were not as bad as one would expect them to be but significant coughs were prevalent, and eye infections very common. The shattering poverty of this region almost counteracts the splendour of the surroundings; yet Langtang has always been among the most backward areas of Nepal, so it would be unfair to generalise from what one observes here. The people are mainly Tamangs, who speak a dialect of Tibetan, and Dr David Snellgrove estimates that they moved across the main Himalayan range before the sixth century A.D.

Like all Nepal's hill-people they have suffered from consistent governmental neglect, and even now, when some feeble effort towards responsible government is being made in other areas, as despised 'Bhotias' they are not receiving their fair share of attention. Also few Gurkha soldiers are recruited from this district, so army pay-packets don't help the economy.

My Swiss relief-map of Nepal puts Thangjet west of the Kyirung River but, with all due respect to Messrs Kummerly and Frey, it happens to be east of it—or else I'm too addled to know where the sun is setting. (However, even such distinguished geographical publishers can readily be forgiven for losing their grip when producing a map of Nepal.) At first I thought it probable that a more prepossessing Thangjet existed beyond the Kyirung and that this was merely Little-Thangjet-Across-The-River: but the locals deny that any other similarly named place exists nearer than Tange in Thakkholi.

This is my first Tibetan-style village and on seeing the neglected *mani*-wall and the decrepit arched gateway I again experienced the bitter-sweet thrill of nearness to the unattainable. Today we passed several more *chortens* and a few very tall prayer-flag poles—suddenly recalling the existence of gods and men in the midst of the mountains' isolation. And now, when I look up from my writing, I can see a large, tumbledown *chorten* in the middle of the village 'street', with white prayer flags fluttering beside it in the cold evening wind. It gives me a special pleasure to see these flags flying against their natural background, instead of merely indicating refugee settlements; yet here one has the sad feeling that a long separation from the mainstream of Tibetan Buddhism has reduced local religion to a rather perfunctory following of superstitious customs.

We arrived at Thangjet just before 3 p.m. after a much tougher walk than yesterday's, and when Mingmar decided to call a halt, though the next village was only three hours away, I mutinously suggested that we should go on. In reply he pointed to a mountain north of another river and said, 'Look at our track.' Obediently I looked—and stopped feeling mutinous. Thangjet is at 8,000 feet and to get to the next village we must descend 5,000 feet to river-level, before climbing to 9,000 feet, at which point the track rounds the flank of the opposite mountain—and for all I know continues to climb.

Thangjet consists of about a hundred and fifty slate-roofed houses, and, being one of the main halts on the Langtang–Kathmandu route, it sports an astonishingly clean doss-house, run by a cheerful Thakkholi woman. The place is a lean-to rather than a building, with an inner wall of stones, loosely piled together as in Connemara, an outer wall and roof of bamboo-matting and no gable-walls. The result, at this height in mid-November, adds up to a Cold Night; but luckily Rudi Weiss-muller insisted on lending me a windcheater, which I will wear with my slacks as pyjamas.

There was a treat for supper—boiled buffalo-milk poured over my rice instead of the usual soup. This establishment is also a tea-house—the hallmark of Thangjet's sophistication!—and when darkness had fallen some half-dozen men, wrapped in ragged blankets, came to sit around the fire and drink glasses of tea. As they spoke in Tibetan I could follow some of the conversation, which was all about yetis. Our hostess and Mingmar denied that any such things exist, but the locals and our fellow lodger (a Tibetan trader) believed in them very firmly and only disagreed about the yeti's nature: some maintained that it was an animal, while others insisted that it was an evil Spirit incarnate. Two of the villagers claimed to have seen small yetis, about the size of a five-year-old child, and at this stage I offered, through Mingmar, my own opinion that the yeti is indeed an animal, unknown to zoologists, which lives at exceptionally high altitudes and very sensibly declines to be captured.

At present I am sitting in unparalleled comfort on the Tibetan trader's wool-sack, which measures five feet by three—though the significance of this statistic cannot be appreciated by anyone without first-hand knowledge of these Nepalese tracks. John Morris has written '. . . but I must emphasise that the paths in the hills of Nepal cannot in any way be compared with even the roughest tracks in the more remote parts of Europe: they are merely the result of people having walked over the same route for many generations.' Indeed they are—and 'path' would be too flowery a description for much of the route we covered today. I now see that quite apart from carrying food Mingmar *is* essential as a guide. No doubt one could find the way eventually, but this afternoon we were climbing over fantastic wastes of colossal, wobbling, jagged rocks, through which my eyes could detect no vestige of a track; and the most disconcerting thing about this terrain is that when one is heading for a northern destination the *right* path often goes south and the *wrong* path north.

I am being fascinated this evening by the passers-by, who walk up and down the rocky, steep street carrying long branches of blazing wood at arm's length—street lighting, Thangjet style!

*13 November. Shablung.*

The gods were against us today, and an individual who calls himself 'The Police' has forbidden us to go north-east from here into the Langtang Valley. It's another of these Nepalese muddles—or is it? According to this unsavoury bit of humanity —whose uniform consists of cotton underpants and a torn Western shirt and who is the only Brahmin in the village—my permit says that we can go to Gosainkund Lekh, but not any further north. The document, being written in Nepali, is of course unintelligible to Mingmar and me—so we can't argue. Admittedly it is very possible that within the Singha Durbar a request for a Langtang permit would elicit a Gosainkund Lekh permit, either through stupidity or for political reasons, and 'The Police' may now be luxuriating quite justifiably in this rare opportunity to exercise his authority against a Westerner; but it is equally possible that he sees here a glorious chance to land a fat bribe. However, unfortunately for him I am quite happy to turn south-east in the morning instead of north-east: the real frustration is not being able to go due north, where Tibet lies less than five hours' walk away.

Among the more dramatic contrasts of this trek are the frequent swift transitions from season to season. When we left Thangjet at dawn it was winter: sharp air stung our faces, the early light was metallic and the fields were colourless and quiescent. Yet by three o'clock it was high summer in Shablung and we sat arguing with 'The Police' under a deep blue sky, among blossom-laden almond-trees which seemed like pink clouds that had drifted to the cliff edge. Here long grass grew lush beneath flowering shrubs, above a flashing green river, and the air was soft with warm content. We had enjoyed an autumn zone too, during our long descent, seeing shining red, black and brown berries and nuts, and walking through the crispness of crimson, orange and russet leaves.

After our very tough climb on leaving Thangjet we had been glad to stop for an early brunch at a four-shack Tamang hamlet half-way down a mountainside. Here the poverty was grim enough, yet the people seemed alert—indeed, almost gay—and they showed both a normal curiosity and a shy friendliness.

The population of these stone-walled, grass- or plank-roofed shacks was thirty-six and there was a prodigious number of charming children who seemed surprisingly fit, apart from the inevitable eye-infections. I asked if coughs were common here but apparently they are not. The health of these settlements is largely controlled by chance; if one tubercular trader spends a night in a house he can infect the whole community.

While Mingmar was cooking I watched part of the millet harvest being threshed. On a level, hard-earth terrace in front of one of the shacks an elderly man was rhythmically pounding the grain with a thick six-foot pole; beside him fluttered tall prayer-flags, beyond him was an abrupt drop of 3,000 feet and in the background shone the snow-peaks of Tibet. When the grain had been sufficiently pounded the womenfolk collected it in large, oval wicker baskets and, having taken it to another terrace, spread it out on round wicker trays and tossed it so adroitly that all the chaff quickly flew off. This looked easy, yet when I tried to do it half the grain fell to the ground and half the chaff remained on the tray—to the delight of the onlookers.

While we were eating Mingmar added to my cartographical confusion by declaring that the east-west river which we had just crossed is the Kyirung. Logically the Kyirung should be the north-south river which this torrent joins below Thangjet, which we have been following up from Trisuli and which rises some thirty miles north of the Tibetan frontier town of Kyirung. I note that Messrs Kummerly and Frey have cautiously re-frained from naming this river above its confluence (where we stopped for brunch the first day) with what I had perhaps mis-takenly assumed to be the young Trisuli, which rises a few miles north-west of Helmu. The whole thing is rather intriguing—and personally I like vague maps that leave one free to speculate.

No less intriguing in its way is the amount of rice consumed daily by Mingmar. Though lean, and hardly five foot tall, he gets through three-quarters of a pound of the stodge at each meal. Two ounces go to make the average rice pudding so you can imagine what twelve ounces looks like when cooked and heaped on a big brass platter. I myself would be immobilised for a week after one such repast—but Mingmar cannot under-stand how I walk so far and so fast on a mere ladleful of rice and a small tin of sardines. Neither can he understand my impulse to leap into glacial torrents whenever possible. Admittedly these waters *are* cold, but it is a supremely satisfying sensation to immerse one's sweaty, weary body beneath a white rush of iciness—and then to emerge, tingling, into warm sunshine.

Shablung is only about 3,000 feet high, yet it has an even stronger Tibetan flavour than Thangjet. It is not marked on my map, nor is the considerable torrent that flows from the north-east and here joins the Kyirung—or the Trisuli, as the case may be. The village stands on a little plateau just north of this tribu-tary, which is spanned by a wood and rope suspension bridge, and it is in the shadow of the next high ridge. The Kyirung is crossed by a rope pulley-bridge, on which men hang by the arms high above the water, and beyond it there is a long strip of cultivable land along the lower slopes of the opposite ridge; so the people are relatively prosperous, though the inherent Tibetan filthiness keeps the appearance of squalor well up to local stand- ards. Millet and maize are the main crops, and herds of cattle, goats and sheep graze on the higher pastures. Shablung also has a school house, of which the villagers are inordinately proud; but naturally it is not now staffed, nor likely to be in the fore- seeable future.

To outsiders there is an exhilarating atmosphere of siege about all these isolated settlements. They are at the furthest possible remove from the industrial areas of Europe where scraps of countryside, disfigured by pylons and wire-fencing, are only grudgingly tolerated by those to whom financial profit comes first. Here in the Himalayas it is Man who is just tolerated, in meagre communities at infrequent intervals, where the moun- tains relent enough for him to survive by the exercise of heroic labours—and also by the exercise of much more intelligence than is recognised by those theorising agricultural advisers who come East in droves, laden with university degrees, and who would be dead within a month if left to fend for themselves on a potentially fertile Himalayan mountainside.

Tonight we are staying with a delightful family whose home, like all the others in Shablung, is roughly constructed of stone, with a plank roof. Animals are housed on the ground floor and from the street one ascends a shaky step-ladder to a five-foot high doorway which leads to a single room, some twenty-five feet by twenty, with a large stone fireplace sunk into the uneven wooden floor at one end. Over this projects from the wall a smoke-blackened canopy of bamboo-matting laid over wooden slats—something I have never seen elsewhere; it is about five feet above the fire and appears to be used as a hot-press-cum- larder. These houses all have decorated wooden façades which vary considerably in artistry, though even the best of them are more crudely executed than the famous Newari carvings.

At the moment I am sitting in the little window-embrasure making the most of the fast-fading daylight and being attacked by a vanguard of bed-bugs who are too greedy to wait for darkness. From the rafters above hang three bows and a quiverful of arrows, and my unashamedly romantic soul rejoices at the idea of staying with people who still regularly use bows and arrows to shoot wild goat. This household consists of parents— Dawa and Tashi—who are in their early forties, and nine children; the eldest is aged eighteen and the youngest six months, which seems to indicate careful if not restrictive family-planning. All have survived, which must be rather unusual in these parts, but at present the three eldest are away tending flocks on the high pastures, from which they will soon be descending for the winter.

Now Mingmar has lit one of our candles and I have moved to sit on the floor. Beyond the fire Tashi is lying on a pile of piebald dzo-skins, naked from the waist up, feeding the baby. Her muscular torso is copper coloured in the flame-light and shoulder-length, lousy black hair draggles round her face as she beams at the infant while it happily sucks. Meanwhile the other children are tumbling in the shadowy background, like a litter of exuberant puppies, and Dawa is chopping with his kukri at a hunk of fresh mutton—making my mouth water at the prospect of *meat* for supper.

The manifold uses of the kukri fascinate me. One can do anything with it, from beheading an ox or felling a tree to sharpening a pencil or peeling a potato—not to mention killing men on all the battlefields of the world. The nonchalance with which these heavy, razor-sharp weapons are handled by small children is quite terrifying; if they made the slightest miscalculation they could very easily slice off one of their own limbs.

This evening I myself found use for the kukri as a surgical instrument. Mingmar has been unwell all day, the boil on his face having grown to carbuncle proportions, so I lanced it with the sterilised tip of Dawa's kukri and squeezed out an awe-inspiring amount of pus. It must have been causing him agony and making him feel as weak as a kitten—but like a good Sherpa he never complained. When the operation was over we were each given a mug of thick brown *chang*, made from millet instead of the more usual rice or barley. It tasted sour and was full of vaguely alarming foreign bodies; but the alcohol content was gratifyingly high and I did not say 'no' to either the second or third rounds.

Earlier this evening the Nyingmapa village lama came to greet me. He is a tall and very handsome man of about thirty-five, whose swinging maroon robes well become him; but he seemed a good deal more interested in trade than in theology and I doubt if he contributes much to the spiritual life of the community.

*14 November. A Gompa on a Mountain.*

This is the first evening that we have arrived at our destination exhausted rather than pleasantly tired; we left Shablung at 6 a.m. and by 5 p.m. had climbed more than 10,000 feet.

On recrossing the suspension bridge outside Shablung we went back towards Thangjet, and in my innocence this slightly puzzled me, as I couldn't remember seeing any track branching off to the east. Here flat, narrow, maize fields lay on our left and I was enchanted to see a troop of giant silver langurs having their breakfast among the crop. These monkeys do a lot of damage and are always stoned on sight by non-Hindu farmers, so they fled when we appeared, moving most gracefully with long, loping strides.

Leaving the maize fields behind, the track curved around an almost sheer mountain until Shablung could no longer be seen, and as I was walking ahead a whistle from Mingmar recalled me. I found him pointing towards one particular section of the mountain for no apparent reason, and he said 'Here we go up'; which we did, for the next ten hours.

Before long I realised that the rough track from Trisuli in fact represents a Nepalese main road. This hardly discernible path, which Mingmar had never used before, was so steep that for the first hour we were not really walking, but pulling our-selves up through long thick grass (there were no trees and few shrubs), using our hands as much as our feet. Soon Mingmar had been left far behind and I was alone, feeling like a lizard on a pyramid and rather proud of my newly-acquired ability to follow the illogic of an almost non-existent track. Often I stopped to rest and look round, and unhopefully I took a few photographs, knowing full well that my unique incompatibility with cameras made the effort a waste of money. Moreover, this incompatibility was now being aggravated by an aversion to the falsification of mountain photography. In such surroundings even the most expertly-wielded camera cannot help but lie, and once the reality has been seen the preservation of fragments seems futile. Also it distresses me to break up visually the wholeness of a Himalayan landscape in an effort to see it as a series of 'good pictures'. So I soon freed myself from my camera and surrendered to the purity of the light, the foaming strength of the already distant river, the heaving complex of mountains on every side and the tantalising cleft that leads to Tibet, drawing one's eye to that ultimate glory of snow-peaks blazing coldly along the near horizon.

Soon I began to wonder why *any* path existed here, since it seemed unlikely that even Nepalese humans would settle on such a slope; but then suddenly I found myself scrambling on to a wide, level ledge, where a crop of unripe barley was overlooked by two solid stone farmhouses.

As I walked across this ledge—luxuriating in a movement that was not upward—I fancied something fairy-tale-like about these austere, improbable, grey dwellings. It seemed as if they must be inhabited by witches, whose broomsticks could provide a helicopter service to Shablung; but in reality the settlement consisted of twelve delightful Tamangs, including a young monk from the Gosainkund Lekh Monastery who was visiting the home which he had left at the age of nine. Only this youth had ever seen a Westerner; yet even before Mingmar arrived, to give a lucid explanation of my presence, everyone had welcomed me warmly, though wonderingly.

The origins and patterns of such settlements fascinate me— where the people came from, why they chose to live in so remote a region, where their sons find wives and their daughters husbands, and how far afield they go on trading trips. I asked all these questions, through Mingmar, but got no satisfactory answers to the first two. Questions about *why* people had settled on this plateau they clearly regarded as absurd; there was land to be cultivated, and water and fuel near by, so it was an obvious place for humans to live—and apparently it was not as isolated as passers-by might imagine. During the summer people from Langtang go to and fro to the yak pastures higher up, and both

Thangjet and Shablung are, after all, quite near. In reply to my other questions I was told that marriages are not arranged, the young people choosing their own mates from these neighbouring villages or from the summer settlements of herds-people. Barley is their only saleable commodity and most of this goes to the Langtang folk, who are glad to have an easily accessible supply to supplement the potatoes and radishes that they grow for themselves beside the yak pastures. In exchange they give yak-butter, tea and salt, and for the rest this little community is self-supporting, producing its own *tsampa*, *chang*, potatoes, radishes, chillies and goat cheese, and weaving its own blankets and garments from goats' wool.

These people clearly felt no allegiance to any government, north or south. The surrounding mountains were their nation and their world, and no outside event could be said to affect them much; yet the Dalai Lama's flight to India and the subsequent Communist persecution of religion in Tibet had undoubtedly made some faint impression on their minds. I tried to find out—without implanting any disturbing ideas—if they feared a Chinese take-over of Nepal, but obviously the possibility did not worry them; either they had never considered it or they felt—probably rightly—that such a development would not make the slightest difference to them on their remote little ledge.

While Mingmar was cooking I sat smoking in the sun, and when I threw away the butt four waiting children dived for this precious prize which was won by a little girl who somehow coaxed two more puffs out of it. The adults then gathered to look wistfully at my packet of 'Panama'—a luxury Indian brand costing 8d for twenty. No one actually asked for a cigarette, but when I handed the packet round every face glowed with delight.

After our meal Mingmar and the monk held a long discussion about the track, and as we set off Mingmar informed me that from here onwards there was only a yak-path. I said that this sounded satisfactory, since yak presumably create a more distinct trail than humans; but according to Mingmar such infrequently used paths soon fade away, especially among dead leaves.

An easy twenty-minute climb brought us to the edge of a forest, where all signs of our path vanished, and after a moment's hesitation Mingmar admitted that he had no idea whether we should now continue upwards or go around the mountain. He only knew that our destination was on the other side of the ridge—and as the ridge in question stretched away vastly to north and south this degree of knowledge was not very helpful. Eventually he decided that we should try rounding the south flank and for the next half-hour we wandered along on the level, sometimes imagining that we had found the yak path, but soon realising that all these faint trails had been made by wood-gatherers from the settlement. Then suddenly we came to a sheer 5,000-foot drop into a side valley and at the sight of this abyss Mingmar shrewdly remarked that we were going in the wrong direction—so we promptly turned back.

Personally I was not at all averse to these haphazard wanderings. Here the trees were wide spaced—many had been felled—and in the brilliant midday sunshine the shrubs and ferns of the undergrowth filled this high silent world with rich autumn glows. We passed several open glades where amidst tawny, tangled grasses I saw the gleam of wild raspberries, strawberries, cranberries and blackberries—and stopped to eat them in fistfuls, with a view to stocking up on Vitamin C.

There was a strange familiarity about this scene 10,000 feet up in the Himalayan foothills. If one did not look beyond the immediate cosiness of the warm, mellow woodland one could imagine oneself in an Irish wood on a sunny October day—though however sunny that October day might be one would still need to wear more than the shirt and shorts that were adequate here in mid-November.

When we got back to where our path had vanished Mingmar took off his rucksack, announcing that he was going to look quickly in various directions for some trace of a yak-trail—and soon he came trotting triumphantly back, having found unmistakable signs of the creatures' progress. This path climbed very steeply, around the northern flank of the ridge, and in general it was visible only to Mingmar's eyes; had I been alone I would have denied its existence.

Here the forest was a twilit cavern of immensely tall and very ancient trees which repelled the sun and created an atmosphere of chill gloom. Many of these monsters had been blasted by lightning or uprooted by gales and we were slowed by having to scramble under or climb over the rotting, giant trunks that so often lay across our route. Soon my faith in this track was wavering and I suspiciously asked Mingmar how yaks were supposed to negotiate such obstacles. He replied that they jumped over them and, never having seen a yak in action, I felt in no position to argue; but it seemed to me that for this purpose a Grand National winner would be more appropriate than a yak.

The ground here was thickly covered with soft, slippery, black leaf-mould, and before long there was crackling ice underfoot, for we were climbing steadily. Now it was growing colder every moment and I staged the reverse of a strip-tease show, stopping repeatedly to put on socks, slacks, a vest, a sweater, a windcheater, a balaclava and gloves.

At about 12,000 feet the forest began to thin and then the path levelled out and became plain for all to see, curving past a herdsman's wooden hut and leading to a windswept, sunlit yak pasture. Now freshly covered snow-peaks were visible directly ahead—no more than a mile away as eagles fly—and I rejoiced at our emergence into this brilliant world of blue, gold and white.

Already I was feeling the lack of oxygen (no doubt because I smoke too much) and was finding it difficult, when climbing, to keep pace with Mingmar. After a ten-minute walk across the plateau we came to a fork in the track, where one branch continued around the mountain and another climbed steeply towards the summit. Some instinct (or perhaps it was only my hammering heart) told me that the *gompa* path went around, not up; but Mingmar, pointing to three *chortens* on the summit path, said 'up!'. So up we went, to the 13,400 summit, where there was no sign of any *gompa* and the icy wind almost stripped the skin off our faces. Moving a little way down I sat in the shelter of a yak-house and said rather breathlessly, 'I suppose we may call *this* a mountain-top?'—but Mingmar replied firmly that it was no more than a high hill-top; apparently in these parts only permanently snow-covered peaks qualify as mountains.

By now the sun was about to disappear behind the ridge

beyond the Kyirung and we still didn't know where the *gompa* was: but I was too exhilarated by the magnificence of the scene to worry. Apart from the snow-peaks our hill-top was the highest point in the area and, despite its relative insignificance, I felt a surge of triumph while surveying the countless lower ridges that surrounded us on every side like the immobile breakers of some fantastic ocean.

Then, wandering over to the eastern edge of the plateau, I saw the shining roof of the little *gompa* some 1,000 feet below us—approached by that track which went around instead of up. Now I was glad that we had taken the wrong fork, but poor Mingmar almost wept on realising that our final climb had been unnecessary. No track led directly down, and were we to follow our original path darkness would fall long before we reached shelter—so we decided to attempt a descent in as straight a line as possible.

The *gompa* had looked quite close from the summit but it took us over an hour to reach it, and that descent was almost as exhausting as the upward climb. At first the slope was densely covered with an odd sort of bushy undergrowth, about five feet high, which had extraordinarily springy and progress-resistant branches; yet without these the way would have been even more difficult—they provided something secure to clutch at when we were in danger of hurtling to eternity on the steepest stretches.

When the gradient eased we entered a weird forest of dead trees, some very tall, some mere broken stumps. All the branches had been lopped off, and at first I assumed that a half-hearted forest-fire had recently swept the hillside; but a closer scrutiny revealed no trace of burning so I can only suppose that some obscure disease attacked this forest long ago. Whatever the cause, the effect was extraordinarily sinister in the twilight, and it would not have greatly surprised me had we come upon Dante and Virgil standing on the brink of an abyss watching souls being tortured.

The young monk had told us that the five Nyingmapa lamas who spent each summer in the *gompa* had recently left, so we expected to find the place deserted—but to my astonished horror we discovered three small children in a stone hut beside the temple. They are aged about eight, six and three and they haven't seen their mother for over a fortnight; nor do they expect her back until next week. Yet this strange, solitary existence, in a region to which very few travellers come between October and April, doesn't seem to disturb them in the least. They know nothing of the world beyond their mountainside and would probably be more frightened by a street-scene in Kathmandu than they are by these long, cold, dark nights spent huddled together in a heap of dried bracken. Named Tsiring Droma, Dorje and Tashi Droma they are typical little Tiblets, black with dirt and full of the joys of life—though understandably a little in awe as yet of their Western visitor.

However, despite the apparent contentment of these diminutive waifs I can't help feeling that their mother must be unnatural by any standards. When alone they have nothing to eat but raw white turnips, which grow on a small patch of fertile soil near the *gompa*, and in this region hungry snow-leopards have been known to kill children during the winter. (As I write the Babes-on-the-Mountain are ravenously devouring some of our rice and Knorr's tomato-soup.)

This hut measures about 20′ × 8′ and the low ceiling-beams don't allow me to stand upright. Both they and the thick stone walls have been so tarred by many years of wood-smoke that they now look as though newly painted with shiny black varnish. Since I sat down here in a corner by the huge mud stove—on which the lamas' cooking is done—a faint, steady, dripping noise has been puzzling me and I have just now realised that it is coming from a huge earthenware jar in which *arak* (the Tibetan poteen) is being distilled for the edification of Their Reverences next summer.

Normally, while their mother is away, these children sleep in a little empty yak-house at the edge of this level shelf of ground, where the rats are less troublesome than in the hut. When alone they are unable to light a fire, having neither matches nor flint (which deprivation seems the only vestige of commonsense shown by the missing mother), and now they are delightedly spreading malodorous dzo-skins on the floor in front of the stove. Already it's freezing hard, and the sky is trembling beautifully with the brilliance of the stars.

*15 November. The Gompa.*

Yesterday evening I suspected that diarrhœa was on the way and by this morning my prognosis had been proved correct. I would have attributed this to mountain-sickness were Mingmar not similarly afflicted, which indicates a dysentery bacillus acquired *en route*—probably in the course of our potations at Shablung. I was out four times during the night, which in this weather is enough to give one chilblains on the behind, and by dawn I had got to the stage of scarcely being able to lift my head. Poor Mingmar was no better and we both had massive doses of sulphaguanidine tablets for breakfast, and at three-hourly intervals during the day; as a result we are now rapidly recovering, though neither of us could look at food this evening. (Not that there's much to look at.) We spent all day lying in hot sun—sheltered from the wind by three *chortens* that stand beside the yak-house—overlooking a tremendously deep valley that lies between our mountain and the dazzling snow-peaks opposite. Occasionally we stirred to help each other to our feet for the next instalment, and every few hours Mingmar staggered to the hut to brew the tea which our dehydrated bodies craved.

Last night it froze so hard that our water was solid ice this morning; the *gompa's* water supply comes from a stream some miles away and is cleverly brought here through a line of hollow tree-trunks, finally trickling from the last of these 'pipes' into a large brass jar.

The Babes-on-the-Mountain really are adorable—I'd love to kidnap them. Tsiring Droma, the elder girl, today spent hours sitting near us slicing white turnips, which she then spread out on a bamboo mat so that the sun would dry and preserve them for use later in the winter. The rest of her time was spent with Dorje, the boy, practising the writing of Tibetan—a startlingly erudite pastime explained by the fact that these are the off-spring of the lamas, who share one wife or concubine between them and who evidently take quite seriously the educational—if not the material—welfare of their family. Both children show great reverence for their tattered school books, which are pages from the ancient tomes of Buddhist scripture stored in the *gompa*. A deep respect for every object connected with their religion is ingrained in all Tibetans, however illiterate or un-couth they may be, and this respect is also extended to the religious objects of other faiths—an example of true civilization which adherents of other faiths could profitably emulate.

On the last lap of our trek to the summit yesterday we saw—to my surprise—innumerable pheasants, but around here the only birds visible are a pair of ravens, who spent much of the day perched on top of the prayer-flag poles, croaking com-panionably.

There was a most dramatic sunset this evening—ribbons of scarlet above distant, deep blue mountains, and higher a width of clear pale green, and higher still tenuous sheets of orange vapour swiftly spreading across half the sky. But Mingmar did not share my enthusiasm for this display, saying it presaged a blizzard tomorrow.

### 16 November. The Gompa.

How right Mingmar was in his weather forecast! We reckon we're lucky to have got back here safely this evening.

Both of us were in good form on awakening and we break-fasted then, having eaten nothing yesterday. When we left here at half-past seven the sky was cloudless and the snow-keen air intoxicating; but already Mingmar was studying the wind and being gloomy in consequence.

About a mile from the *gompa* I saw my first leopard-trap—a crude contrivance of wooden stakes built around a deep pit and looking as though it would delude none but the most seriously retarded leopard. Yet Mingmar assured me that this model is very successful.

We were now on the main Thangjet—Gosainkund Lekh track, beside which the Gompa is built, and for about an hour we walked around the mountain just below the tree line, passing many herdsmen's huts and yak-houses. Then we came to a wide expanse of moorland, sloping up to a minor glacier, and here began an easy hour's climb towards the 15,800-foot pass. Today I found myself well adjusted to the altitude, and I irritated Mingmar by frequently taking off my knapsack and scampering up the low ridge on our left to revel in an unimpeded view of the Langtang range, now thrillingly close. Because of these detours it was almost eleven o'clock as we approached the steep, final lap of the upward path, which here was barely distinguishable beneath new snow. And now we had our initial warning— a grey veil suddenly wisping around the snow-peaks to the south-east. At once Mingmar hesitated, looking rather uneasy; but then—to my surprise—he decided that we should at least cross the pass and survey the weather-scene on the far side, where it might possibly be clearer. However, his optimism was not justified. As we the reached top so did the blizzard and we were almost lifted off the ground by an icy blast. Five minutes earlier the sun had been shining, yet now we were deep in that odd, muffled gloom which seems to belong neither to night nor day, and the thick flurry of flakes was reducing visibility to a few yards. When we quickly turned back our fresh footprints had already been obliterated, and within fifteen minutes we were very thoroughly lost. There seemed no real cause for alarm, with five hours of daylight remaining and the tree line quite close; yet to be blundering around so unsurely in this sort of terrain does put one slightly on edge, and I was relieved when we suddenly emerged into sunshine on an unfamiliar plateau.

Hereabouts a hill is not simply a hill, but a succession of similar-looking ridges, and it's only too easy to go half-way down the wrong ridge before realising one's mistake. This we did twice, while searching for the main track, and by the time we had found it both of us were feeling the weakening effect of yesterday's intestinal contretemps; so I then produced my emergency ration of rasins, which we chewed while ambling leisurely downwards, our chilled bodies luxuriating in the warm sunshine.

The children were delighted to see us again and their pleasure quite made up for the disappointment of not being able to continue towards Gosainkund Lekh. Less than half-an-hour after our return the sky again clouded over and as I write it is snowing heavily outside—a cosy sight, as the five of us crouch around a blazing pyramid of logs, eagerly awaiting our rice and soup and boiled turnips; but it would have been pretty grim for the Babes-on-the-Mountain had they been alone this evening.

Mingmar has decided that our best plan for tomorrow is a return along the main track to Thangjet, where we will rejoin our original route. Having followed it about half-way back to Trisuli we can then branch off to the east and explore that high pocket of Sherpa settlements which lies towards Helmu, returning to Kathmandu down the valley of the Indramati River.

*17 November. Back at the Shack on the Ridge.*

The woman who was so ill here last week died a few days ago, leaving four little children motherless; but as they all look and sound tubercular they may not be long following her.

Today's nine-hour walk provided superb contrasts. When we left the *gompa* at 7.30 a.m., having given the children a final hot meal, snow lay a foot deep on the track—yet three hours later we were walking through groves of bamboo and banana-trees. I long to give some not entirely inadequate description of the glory and variety of that 8,000-foot descent, during which we saw many deer and pheasants but not one other human being; yet perhaps it's best to know when you're beaten.

Such a continuous descent on a very rough path is much more exhausting than any but the steepest climbs. This morning the nimble Mingmar was always far ahead of me, and he remarked that the majority of Westerners do find these descents very difficult, since we lack that inherent sure-footedness which enable the locals to skim so efficiently down stairways of insecure boulders.

From river-level a 4,000-foot climb took us to Thangjet, where we stopped for brunch. Since our last visit the tea-house has been enriched by a sack of sugar, but as it cost sixpence per teaspoonful we did not indulge.

This afternoon we saw a group of about twenty men and boys transporting newly-cut bamboo poles from the forest to their village—a distance of some five miles. Each load consisted of thirty eight-foot poles, divided into two bundles which were harnessed to the shoulders with long strands of tough jungle-grass. I could hardly believe my eyes when the first four men came racing at top speed down the precipice above our track dragging these unwieldy loads—which made an oddly musical clatter as the ends swept swiftly over the rough ground. At the junction with the main track the men had to do a sharp turn but even then they never slackened speed; and on approaching one of the many shaky, narrow, plank bridges that here span racing torrents they accelerated even more, so that their loads would have no time to slip over the edge and pull them into the water. Rarely have I seen a more impressive display of nerve, skill and strength; these men aroused the sort of admiration that one feels when watching a good toreador in action against a brave bull. Among the last to cross the bridge was a boy who looked about twelve but was probably at least sixteen. Perhaps this was his first bamboo expedition and he did not quite make it, one side of his load slipping off the planks. For a horrible moment it seemed that he must topple into the water; but he had kept his balance by some miracle and now he stood still, straining against the weight of the bamboo, while the man behind him struggled out of his own harness and rushed to pick up the hanging load. He then helped the boy to get safely over by walking behind him, holding both sides of the load clear of the bridge.

We followed the bamboo team for an hour, and their endurance, as they hauled these loads uphill, was even more impressive—if less spectacular—than their downhill sprints. Repeatedly one wonders just how these seemingly undernourished bodies manage to achieve physical feats that would be far beyond the powers of most well-fed Westerners.

*18 November. Serang Tholi.*

What a day! If we are not getting anywhere in particular we are certainly getting off the beaten track—and very nearly off every other track too! By now Mingmar has given up pretending to know exactly where we are, or where we will be by tomorrow night. He says that this whole expedition is 'a bad trek'; yet our erratic wanderings suit me very well indeed—I feel blissfully happy all day and every day.

We set off this morning at six o'clock and for the first two hours were following the main track back towards Trisuli. Then we turned east and, having twice lost the faint path, eventually

came to a small Tamang village where we stopped for a badly-
needed brunch; the morning's climb had been tough, and by
now I am beginning to suffer slightly from protein-deficiency.

This village, of some fifty houses, was almost deserted because
the millet harvest has just begun. After brunch Mingmar tried
to get some idea of where we should go next, but the only available informant was a deaf nonagenarian who insisted on direct-
ing us back to Trisuli; so we were left to the sluggish inspiration
of our own senses of direction.

By 3 p.m. we had descended to river-level, where we were
confronted by one of those nightmare tree-trunk 'bridges'
which demand the skill of a trapeze-walker. Admittedly this
specimen was only twenty feet long—but it did look terrifyingly
insecure, being casually held in place at either side by little
piles of loose rocks, while its width could barely accommodate
a single human foot. After one glance I funked it completely.
Forty feet below the water was churning violently through a
boulder-filled channel and even my trick of crossing such
bridges *à cheval* seemed inadvisable. Merely to see Mingmar
tripping lightly over almost made me ill and when he returned
to take my knapsack I also handed him my shirt, shorts and
shoes, informing him that I was going upstream to find some
point at which I could either wade or swim across. Then it was
his turn to feel ill; he went quite pale and said 'You'll drown!'
'Very likely,' I agreed. 'Yet somehow I prefer drowning to
falling off that unspeakable contraption you call a bridge.'

It was easier than I had expected to find a fording point.
Some quarter-of-a-mile upstream—where the river was about
100 yards wide and ten feet deep—a little dam had been built,
and though the current was still strong here it seemed that by
swimming diagonally above the dam I could just about make
it to the other side. Fortunately my self-confidence when *in*
water equals my lack of self-confidence when *over* water; I
always enjoy a challenge from this element and poor Mingmar,
who had anxiously followed me upstream on the opposite bank,
was suffering most from tension as I dived into the icy, clear
green pool. By the half-way stage I had the measure of the
current and knew that there was not the slightest danger; yet
I didn't dare ease off for long enough to yell reassuringly to

Mingmar and until I stepped onto the rock beside him he remained convinced that I *must* drown.

After this refreshment by immersion I was in excellent form for the next lap—a long, long climb up the steepest cultivated slope we have yet seen, where there was no path and we simply pulled ourselves somehow from one narrow terrace of ripening millet to another.

Tonight we are staying in a Tamang hamlet at 7,500 feet, where the slate-roofed houses are built of ochre mud and stone as in the Hindu villages around Pokhara. At the moment the populace are almost pushing each other over a precipice in their efforts to see me; and Mingmar is hardly less of a curiosity, for we are now far from the main tracks and few of these people have ever before seen either a Western female or a Sherpa porter in all his sartorial glory.

The filth of this house is extreme and the stable seemed so much less filthy that I chose it as my bedroom and am now leaning against the warm flank of a reclining buffalo. One hopes that bed-bugs will be fewer here than indoors: and the cow-bugs that must inevitably frequent Nepalese cattle are not so likely to be interested in me.

*19 November. Senthong.*

Leaving Serang Tholi at dawn we climbed steadily to the summit of a 9,000 foot hill. Ordinarily the sun comes over the mountains to us, but today we went over a mountain to the sun and it was wonderful to step from cold early shadows into warm golden air, and to see the new, gentle light lying on a wild tumble of deserted mountains.

By ten o'clock we had negotiated two of these mountains, following a faint path that frequently vanished. Then we came to a tiny settlement, on the verge of another cultivated hillside, where we ran into caste trouble for the first time on this trek. When Mingmar inquired where he might cook our brunch we discovered that this was a very orthodox Chetri village in which we, as untouchable non-Hindus, would not be admitted to any house; but eventually we found a woman who consented to cook for us, provided we remained outside her compound.

The conscientious Mingmar was frantically worried at the idea of anyone but himself cooking for me, and he swore that after this meal I would get every disease in the book. However, I consolingly pointed out that my immunities are abnormally well-developed, by Western standards—and also that Chetris are cleaner, as well as more intolerant, than Tamangs. Yet I must admit that this village was loathsomely smelly, and our rice did look and taste as though cooked in a pretty sordid pot. None of the people we have stayed with (apart from the Thakkholi woman at Thangjet) ever practises the art of washing up—unless one counts the licking of platters at the end of a meal, which happens to be the labour-saving device that I too employ when living alone in my own home.

From half-past eleven we walked almost continuously for six hours—first down to river-level, next up and over an 8,800-footer, then two-thirds of the way down this 'hill' until we came to Senthong, where there are a few Tamang households among many Chetris. It is an odd sensation, when looking for lodgings, to go from door to door asking what the family religion is and receiving cold stares from the Hindus. The Tamangs here are very much poorer than the Chetris and are unmistakably the outcasts of the village; but equally unmistakably they are a far nicer group of people than their Hindu neighbours. I don't resent being shunned by orthodox Hindus, who can't reasonably be expected to fraternise with the likes of me, yet it is sad that Hinduism, despite the breadth of its basic philosophy, has in practice the effect of blighting many potentially valuable human contacts—whereas Tibetan Buddhism, however imperfectly understood by the masses, has the precisely opposite effect.

Tonight I have again chosen the cattle-shed as there simply isn't space for me inside this tiny house, which shelters a complex family of eighteen children and six adults. I discovered last night that cattle are noisy creatures with which to sleep because of their extraordinarily tumultuous digestive processes, which seem to go on all night like a thunderstorm.

*20 November. Likarka.*

This morning I was awakened at half-past four by the ancient, soothing rhythm of millet being ground between the stones of a hand-mill. It was still dark and quite cold, and for the next hour I lay drowsily warm in my flea-bag, looking up at the golden throb of the stars and listening to the little stirrings of the village. The rice harvest had everyone on the move early, and as Mingmar and I made our way down to river-level soon after dawn we passed families already threshing grain on the wider terraces of the paddy fields. Here bullocks are used for the threshing, but at Serang Tholi—where the people also have cattle—we had seen the operation done by hand, each separate sheaf being beaten vigorously on the ground until every grain was shaken loose.

Were I only allowed a single adjective to describe Nepal I would have to use 'varied'. No two villages are quite alike in language, dress, customs, attitudes, architecture or surroundings, and one could not possibly refer to 'a typical village' of this region. Doubtless the isolation imposed by the terrain on each settlement is responsible for this most pleasing diversity, which makes one realise anew how horribly our Western uniformity impoverishes life. And an equally rich variety is found in the landscape; at every turn one is confronted by new, tremendous vistas of unimaginable beauty as though Nature, when creating these mountains, had been exercising the subtle imaginative power of a great musician elaborating on a simple basic theme.

Today has been the most strenuous of the entire trek. This morning's river was a wide seething torrent, spanned some 80 feet above the water by a swaying, decrepit suspension bridge; but luckily the hand-rails were sufficiently intact for me to feel no fear of the crossing, and at 7.15 a.m. we began the upward climb. From river-level—3,400 feet—until we had crossed an 11,800-foot pass there was no respite on level ground, and even Mingmar had to admit that he felt 'very tired' at the top—a sensational confession.

We had stopped soon after nine o'clock for an hour's brunch-break at a three-house Tamang settlement, and these were the last dwellings seen until we crossed the pass at midday and descended some 1,500 feet to this region of scattered Sherpa houses.

After the savagely steep climb up it was a relief to find ourselves looking down from the top of the pass over an easy green slope. Here huge grey boulders were strewn on the grass, patches of unmelted snow gleamed in shady spots, and flocks of long-haired, sturdy goats grazed in the care of a little boy who lay alone on a slab of rock, thoughtfully playing a flute. From this point the circular valley—some fifteen miles in circumference—appeared to be quite shallow, though later we saw the ravine in the centre through which a river flows away to the south. Immediately above us, to the north, a jagged mountain was only thinly wooded with giant pines, but about a mile beyond the sunny expanse of pasture dense forests darkened the sides of the valley. And here I felt more than usually aware of that special tranquillity always experienced at these heights—a depth of peace impossible to describe or explain, but reaching to every fibre of one's being.

Our destination was a little settlement already visible on the far side of the valley and it looked so deceptively close that now we dawdled along, relishing our walk down the easy incline. Half-an-hour's ambling brought us to a sheltered hollow where we saw two Sherpa dwellings, with freshly-printed prayer-flags flying between them. There was a well here, beside the path, and pausing to drink from it I noticed something that almost paralysed me with astonishment—wrapping-paper off a bar of Lifebuoy soap. I beckoned to Mingmar, and we stood staring at this baffling manifestation of 'civilisation' as though we were the first men on the moon and had found an empty match-box there before us. Then, continuing towards the houses, we came upon two gorgeous silk saris spread on the grass to dry—and next we saw a most beautiful young creature, wearing a pink sari and golden slippers, with attractive bazaar jewellery in her glossy hair and on her slender neck and arms. This vision was leaning against a low stone wall, talking to an older woman with a weather-roughened face whose muscular body was clad in the filthiest of rags and who obviously had never washed in her life.

Mingmar and I did not even attempt to conceal our curiosity; having greeted the women we too sat on the wall, and in reply to questions were told that three years ago the girl had gone to Bombay to be trained as a nurse and was now home on a month's leave. 'Careers for Girls' are of course unheard of in these parts and it was inexplicable to me that this youngster should have had sufficient education to undergo a nurse's training. Evidently there was a story here, but neither mother nor daughter was very communicative and we could find out nothing more.

I wondered how the girl's relatives were reacting to the appearance in their midst of such unprecedented elegance and sophistication. Would they feel proud of her, or uneasy, or a little scornful of her fussiness and daintiness? Certainly the girl herself, by so scrupulously maintaining 'Bombay standards' against the heaviest of odds, was affirming her belief in the superiority of her new mode of life. She was most affectionate towards her mother, yet she did look rather strained, and it seemed likely that the immediate impact of the return had been disquieting and that she was secretly and guiltily looking forward to her departure.

Meeting this girl helped me to understand why Asian villagers who have had a medical training are so reluctant to return to those areas where help is most needed. For them the sheer novelty of both the material and mental opportunities of urban life is overwhelming, and in such a totally new world they become new people, continually discovering unsuspected potentialities within themselves. Some people accuse them of allowing improved conditions to 'go to their heads'; yet this seems an unfair description of the natural excitement caused by widening horizons. The comparative values of what is lost and what gained by migration to a city is not relevant to this argument. These young people are usually conscious only of gaining, and at this stage of individual development are as self-centred as babies, reaching out with both hands for all the advantages of education and unaware that their own good fortune imposes on them a responsibility to help their fellows. It seems unrealistic to demand, from this generation of newly-educated Asians, the self-discipline that would enable them willingly to relinquish their brave new world. Such a sacrifice would require a much riper fruit of education than any that they can be expected to bear; and this is one of the main obstacles that for years to come will hinder Health Programmes in Asia—however generously the West may finance them.

Before leaving this curiously pathetic mother and daughter we had asked about the path through the forest; yet within an hour of entering the twilight beneath the trees we were more lost than one could believe possible. I had expected quite a clear track between the two settlements, but if any such exists we never found it. For over two hours we went scrambling up and down precipitous slopes, through thick, thorny undergrowth, and repeatedly we were thwarted by impassable ravines. At half-past four we knew that less than ninety minutes of daylight remained and now Mingmar was getting really frightened; he had begun to pray non-stop, using that odd Buddhist hum which sounds rather comical until one has become familiar with it. Neither of us had any idea of the way back, so we decided to continue the struggle forward—and then suddenly we came on something that had once been a track, though now it is in a dangerous state of disrepair. Having nervously followed it through two deep dark ravines—even Mingmar was nervous, to my immense gratification—we emerged at last on to another wide stretch of level turf; and twenty minutes later, after crossing several fields of buck-wheat, barley and potatoes, we were relaxing with this charming Sherpa family.

Their house is similar to the one we stayed in at Shablung, though the living-room is twice as big and very much cleaner. Dry maize-cobs hang from the rafters and handsomely carved cupboards line the wall that faces the low door and two tiny windows. If one can judge by the array of silver votive bowls, and silver-bound wooden tea-cups, the family must be quite rich by local standards. Against the wall in one corner leans a four-foot-high copper-banded bamboo churn for making buttered tea, and in a little room leading off this is the family chapel, where eleven tiny butter-lamps flicker cosily beneath a grimy but very lovely *thanka* representing the Compassionate Aspect of the Lord Buddha.

This family consists of a grandmother, her son, his wife and five adorable children who stopped being shy of me in record time. As I write, sitting on the floor near the fire, the two younger ones are standing beside me, leaning on my shoulders and intently watching that strange procedure which covers clean paper with a nasty mess of squiggles.

As soon as we arrived here I sat in the window-embrasure to enjoy one of the most beautiful sunsets I have ever seen. This house—at 10,400 feet—faces due west, and I was overlooking range after range of dusk-blue mountains, beyond which the ghostly snows of the distant Dhauligiri massif were just visible against a crimson horizon. Above this sunset flare was a blue-green ocean of space, in which the golden boat of Venus sailed alone; and higher still the zenith was tinged pinkish brown. Truly this was a most noble scene, so still with peace and so vital with beauty in the ebbing of the day.

On a more mundane level the evening was scarcely less memorable, because we had potatoes and milk for supper. Perhaps only a compatriot could appreciate the gastronomic ecstasy into which an Irishwoman can fall when served with potatoes after living on rice for a fortnight. Yet Mingmar seemed equally thrilled; though he can eat rice in such abundance, potatoes are the staple food of the Sherpas in their home district. He successfully consumed thirty-three large specimens and was quite concerned when, after twelve monsters, I reluctantly declined a third helping for sheer lack of space. Indeed this four-house-settlement is a veritable food-paradise; we have been able to buy five eggs, which we will hard-boil and take with us to-morrow as both our rice and sardine supplies are getting low.

*21 November. A Farm on a Hilltop.*

I am willing to concede that this *is* only a hill-top, since we are now down to 6,000 feet. The hill in question is a spur of one of the giant mountains that overshadow this valley on both sides, and after the silence of the heights it's quite disconcerting this evening to hear the roar of the nearby river.

Oddly enough it was Mingmar who felt poorly today, after yesterday's marathon. This morning's easy ten-mile walk was mainly downhill and we stopped frequently; yet he made

heavy weather of the few inevitable climbs, and when we
arrived here at half-past two he suggested that an early halt
might be good for *me!* Perhaps he over-indulged in *chang* last
night, forgetting our dire experience after the Shablung binge.

Soon after leaving Likarka at 6.30 a.m. we crossed the steep
wooded ridge that rises sharply behind the settlement and that
loveliest of valleys was out of sight. About an hour later I saw
my first herd of dzo—and was vaguely disappointed to find they
look exactly like cows with very bushy tails. They were being
guarded by a pair of enormous, ferocious-looking Tibetan
mastiffs who almost foamed at the mouth as I wandered through
the herd taking photographs. Mingmar says that these dogs are
trained to kill intruding humans; during the day they are
usually tied to wooden stakes with short, heavy chains and they
wear large, clangorous iron bells around their necks. But at
night they roam free and are far more dangerous than wild
animals; I know several Tibetans whose faces have been horribly disfigured by their attacks. Today I felt decidedly apprehensive when we had to pass a herd in charge of an untied dog;
but the enraged creature was restrained by two tiny children
who flung their arms around his neck and told him to be quiet.
I didn't really expect him to obey—yet immediately he subsided and began to wag his tail at the children, ignoring us as
we sidled past.

Soon afterwards we met a youth returning to Likarka from
his first trading expedition to Kathmandu. He had received a
Rs. 100 note in payment for wool, but being illiterate and having
never before handled big money he was not at all sure what this
signified. When he stopped us to ask for a definition Mingmar
said that such a large note would be useless in this area, so I
changed it for twenty Rs. 5/- notes, to the boy's delight; he
evidently imagined that his father would be much better pleased
by twenty notes than by one! He then showed us what had once
been a very good Swiss watch; it had been sold him in Kathmandu for—he thought!—Rs. 50/- and was still ticking, but
the minute-hand had come off the day before—doubtless
because he had been playing too vigorously with the winder.
(He had of course no notion how to read the time.) I advised
him to leave it alone until he next visited Kathmandu; but then

there ensued a lengthy discussion between him and Mingmar on the advisability of exchanging watches. Mingmar's would have been the better of the two even had the boy's been perfect; yet the Sherpa trading urge is so strong that apparently a losing deal is preferable to no deal at all and finally Mingmar accepted the broken watch, plus Rs. 25/-, in exchange for his own Omega.

Half-an-hour later we stopped again at one of those 'dairies' fairly common in this area, where small herds of dzo are looked after by cheerful shepherdesses who make Tibetan-type cheese and butter. I intend bringing home a piece of the cheese, which has to be seen to be believed. It is harder than any rock except granite and is said to be still edible three centuries after it has been made—if one knows the technique required for eating granite-hard substances.

This 'dairy' was a little bamboo-matting hut on a grassy slope encircled by the forest and here we each enjoyed a long drink of butter-milk, and a platter of whey fried in butter and pleasantly tainted by the smoke of the wood-fire. Several very young dzo calves stood near by and completely captivated me. At this age they have their father's thick coat and are bundles of furry huggableness, with huge melting eyes and affectionate licks for all and sundry.

Several other brief delays were caused by Mingmar stopping at every farmhouse *en route* to enquire if there was any butter for sale; his mother died a year ago and now he wants to make *tormas* and burn lamps in honour of the anniversary. His trader father had two wives, one living in Namche Bazaar and the other in Lhasa. When he died Mingmar was only four and was brought up by both his mother and his step-mother, who themselves traded extensively between Tibet and India. Lhamo, his twenty-two year old sister, now looks after the family trading concerns and Pemba, his elder half-brother, runs one of the Tibetan hotels in Kathmandu—assisted by his own mother. This morning Mingmar bought two pounds of Tibetan cheese for her, as he always brings back a present of her favourite delicacy when he has been away on trek. So between butter for his dead mother and cheese for his live step-mother our progress was considerably slowed.

Obviously his sister Lhamo is Mingmar's favourite; he repeatedly refers to her with affection and pride, saying what a clever business-woman she is and how much he is looking forward to seeing her, after a year's separation, when she comes from Lhasa to Kathmandu next month, en route for Calcutta. These Sherpas certainly get around—and they seem to need no passport for all their travels between Tibet, Nepal and India. Of course, Lhamo now flies from Kathmandu to Calcutta, and for all I know travels by truck in Tibet. She has two husbands so far—one who looks after the family farm near Namche Bazaar and one in Kathmandu, who also has another wife permanently resident there to comfort him while the tycoon Lhamo attends to her International Business. No wonder Sherpa relationships are not easy to sort out!

Our last and longest delay came soon after midday, when we paused to watch a religious ceremony being conducted outside a stone hut on a ledge. For some time before reaching this ledge we could hear the wonderful melody of drum, bell, cymbals and conch-shell—music that made me feel very homesick for the Pokhara camp, and that sounded even more stirring against its natural background. I tried to find out what the ceremony was all about, but even if Mingmar knew he clearly did not want to discuss it with an outsider; so I stopped probing and contented myself with imprudently drinking four wooden bowlfuls of the best *chang* I have ever tasted.

The elderly lama conducting the ceremony was dressed in black instead of the usual maroon robes, and his young monk assistant wore layman's clothes. Both sat cross-legged on the ground, with their backs to the hut wall, and the Scriptures were laid before the lama on a low wooden table. His Reverence held a bell in his right hand and a *dorje* in his left—the *dorje* being frequently abandoned when he needed another swig of *chang*, which he favoured instead of the buttered-tea consumed endlessly during ceremonies by the more orthodox lamas. At right angles to the wall stood a painting of the Lord Buddha with the usual *tormas* and butter-lamps laid before it, and in front of this was a hanging drum, some three feet in circumference, which a tall, slim youth, clad in the local kilt, beat regularly in time to the chanting. About thirty people sat nearby in a semi-circle, laughing, chatting, drinking *chang* and eating cold sliced potatoes. The atmosphere was gay and friendly, and we were made to feel so welcome that we remained with the little group for over half-an-hour, each of us giving an offering to the lama before we left.

The young mother of the Sherpa family with whom we are staying tonight recently spent three years as a coolie on the roads in Assam, and Mingmar told me that it is common for the people of this area to emigrate temporarily to India and work in road gangs with the Tibetan refugees. Then, having saved up more money than they could ever earn in Nepal—and increased it on the way home by astute trading in Kalimpong—they return to settle down here. I attempted to discover whether they are officially accepted into the road gangs as Nepalese citizens, or whether they masquerade as Tibetan refugees; but my questions on this subject were plainly regarded as indelicate so I did not pursue the enquiry.

Tonight Mingmar at last knows where we are and says we will be back at base by midday on 24 November. The track from here to Kathmandu is familiar to him, which seems sad; it has been sheer bliss wandering lost-like from mountain to mountain.

*22 November. A Hovel on a Mountain-top.*

This is the *most* squalid lodging we have encountered on the whole trek; it is even filthier than the children's hut beside the Gompa. The small room is windowless and now that darkness has fallen a bullock, four goats, seven hens and a cock are sharing the apartment with a family of six, plus Mingmar and me. Here we are again above 9,000 feet and the night-air is so cold that the door has been shut fast, allowing no outlet for the billowing wood smoke, which is making me cough incessantly and having the usual excruciating effect on my eyes; but as compensation these gentle, cheerful Tamangs are exceptionally likeable, and their anxiety to make me comfortable is all the more touching because of the irredeemable discomfort of their home.

Today's walk was another marathon, and by brunch-time I

knew why Mingmar had not been keen on going further yesterday afternoon. We started the day's adventures at 7 a.m. with
quite a hazardous fording of a fiercely-fast, waist-deep, icy
river. Here Mingmar was the terrified one—for a change—and
as we waded across together he clung to me so frantically that
he very nearly unbalanced us both. We needed every ounce of
our strength to keep upright against the force of the water and
it was so extremely difficult to retain a foothold on the large,
constantly shifting stones that I didn't really think we could
make it without a ducking.

At times the water had been up to our armpits and now we
were painfully cold; but that was soon cured by a ninety-
minute climb up a precipitous, slippery and very narrow path
through dense scrub. Here it was my turn to be terrified; the
snag was that I couldn't see the crumbling path through the
thick grass and undergrowth—but I could see very plainly the
drop on the right, though I didn't dare look down for long
enough to estimate its depth.

By about half-past nine we had left this unwholesome path
behind and gone downhill again towards the river. We stopped
for brunch at a stinking, fly-infested hovel near the junction with
the main Kathmandu–Gosainkund Lekh track; and an hour
later we were on this highway, sharing it with groups of heavily-
laden Tibetans, Tamangs and Chetris and feeling already half-
way back to the bustle of metropolitan life.

For the next four hours we continued gradually but steadily
downhill, following the river. At times the path led over stretches
of colossal boulders, or through bright widths of fine silver sand,
and once we crossed a dilapidated suspension bridge that
swayed uncertainly 150 feet above the water. One feels slightly
impatient about the neglect of these plank bridges; with so
much forest on every side there can be no shortage of raw
material for their repair.

At three o'clock we reached a village which boasted the first
shop seen since our departure from Trisuli. Here we asked for
tea, since our own supply expired a few days ago, but the shop
stocked only ancient, flyblown, Indian sweets and unsmokable
cigarettes and mildewed biscuits—of which we bought two
packets for consumption on the spot.

Next we again climbed steeply for three hours—up and up and up, with the shining snow-peaks to the north becoming lovelier every moment. Here the lower, richer slopes are cultivated by Chetris or Newaris and the upper, more barren slopes by Tamangs. The whole region seems very densely populated —and smelly in proportion—when compared with the lonely mountains now behind us. One of the incidental joys of lonely mountains is the absence of that overpowering stench of human excrement which is always present in the more populous parts of Nepal.

These insect-plagued lodgings are beginning to prey slightly on my nerves—and it's not difficult to foresee that tonight is going to be a bug-classic. Since leaving Trisuli I've not had one unbroken night's rest and, though the locals do not suffer to the same extent, I hear them scratching and muttering in their sleep every night. So the bugs must do real damage to health by making sound sleep impossible.

### 23 November. Kathmandu.

We achieved yet another marathon today, which got us here ahead of schedule—and what a welcome I received from Tashi! Like most Tibetans she is very soft-spoken so she didn't bark or yelp, the only audible sign of rejoicing being that peculiar, rapid sniffling noise with which she always greets my returns; but for the first few moments it seemed that she would wriggle out of her skin with joy, or that her over-wagged tail would come adrift—it's nice to be so important to somebody.

This morning I saw my first total eclipse of the sun, which lasted from about 8.15 until 9.30—and in honour of which today is yet another public holiday throughout Nepal.

We left our hovel before dawn, since last night even Mingmar was unable to sleep for bugs, and by eight o'clock we had reached the top of a 9,000-foot hill, after an easy climb through crisp, early air. From here we were overlooking a long, deep, narrow valley, and our path now continued almost level for some two miles, before plunging abruptly down to a small village by the river.

As we were scrambling down from the ridge-top to join this

path I noticed something very odd about the quality of the light, and simultaneously I registered an unnatural drop in the temperature. Overtaking Mingmar I said, 'What on earth is happening? The light's gone funny, and it's so *cold!*' To this obtuse question a native English-speaker might have been forgiven for replying that nothing was happening *on earth*; but Mingmar merely said, 'The moon is having a meal.' I stared at him for a moment, wondering if he were going dotty—and then I realised that the dottiness was on my side, for when he pointed to the sun I saw that about a quarter of its surface had already been obscured by the 'hungry' moon.

What an appropriate place this was for experiencing the eerieness of a solar eclipse! As we walked along that path, so high above the valley, we could hear conches being blown wildly and cymbals and drums being beaten frenziedly, while all the lamas and priests of the little villages far below shouted and wailed and screamed in their contest with those evil spirits who, by attacking the sun, were threatening the whole of human existence. This extraordinary panic of sounds, combined with the 'evening' twitter of bewildered birds and the unique, greenish half-light, evidently aroused within me some deep racial memory, and for an instant, at the precise moment of total eclipse and estrangement from our whole source of life, I felt as my own that primitive fear which was then dominating the whole of Nepal.

# Epilogue

The last days are always sad. One's return is uncertain, but it is wretchedly certain that should one ever return 'all will be changed, changed utterly' in such places as Kathmandu and Pokhara.

Some changes would of course be welcome, especially in relation to the refugees. Their numbers are comparatively few in Nepal and, perhaps because of the scale of the problem, it is easier there than elsewhere to see clearly the fundamental problems inherent in every refugee situation. A consideration of these problems during my time in Pokhara led me to certain unpopular conclusions which have been reinforced, since my return to Europe, by discussions with other fieldworkers on leave from Asia and Africa. To the many generous and sympathetic supporters of Western charitable organisations our views may seem unfeeling, or even shocking. Yet they are based on observations made while sharing the daily life of the refugees— an experience which we hope does not impair our sensibility, though it may purge us of that dangerous sentimentality which so often bedevils the thinking of those who direct refugee aid operations by remote control.

The power of mass media to provoke emotional and ill-considered generosity was plainly shown by the public reaction to the Aberfan disaster, and one finds the same phenomenon, in a less extreme form, throughout the refugee world. Obviously the concern for refugees now felt in the West is stimulated partly by a sincere desire 'to help the less fortunate' and partly by an uneasy awareness that our own society is persistently over-indulging itself in a variety of ways. To give money to charitable organisations is one of the easiest possible methods of lulling one's social conscience, and as some of these organisations become more high-powered, and more ambitious to implement impressive projects abroad, situations can easily arise in which problems are aggravated because of the resources that have been accumulated to deal with them. Already, in certain areas, we are expiating our collective guilt at the expense of the refugees by absurdly prolonging the period during which a particular group is granted refugee status. Materially, and from a short term point of view, this may be a positive achievement; yet if one looks far enough ahead it is seen to be entirely negative, since excessive cosseting cannot fail to breed a community of parasites.

It should be obvious that our first duty is to help the refugees to help themselves, rather than merely to feed, clothe and nurse them. Immediately after their arrival in a strange land they obviously do need considerable material support, as well as sensible guidance on how best to adjust to their new environment. Yet the essence of a refugee tragedy is not disease, hunger or cold. It is the loss of the emotional security of belonging to a stable community in a certain country, and therefore, in exile, the refugee's most valuable possession is his self-respect—which should be used by us as a tool to help him re-establish his identity as a responsible individual. However, this self-respect is not very highly developed among certain types of refugees and can soon be destroyed by indiscriminate 'aid'. Undoubtedly, less material support from charitable organisations would mean an initial period of greater hardship for most refugee groups; but—supposing the practical advice and reassuring affection of field-workers to be still available—a reduction in aid would also provide a valuable challenge which, if it were met successfully, could rapidly restore the refugees' self-confidence and sense of security. By leaving them in a position where, to survive, they must quickly integrate as productive units in their new environment we would be doing them a far better service than by singling them out for special treatment over an indefinite period—and thus increasing both their own and their neighbours' awareness of the refugee as an 'alien'.

In many cases there are of course innumerable political and economic obstacles to their employment; but these obstacles are not lessened when charitable organisations concentrate hundreds of people in one area. There is some evidence to support the theory that if refugees were to disperse in small groups throughout their host countries—perhaps having received, as aid, a small capital sum per family—they could earn a living much more easily than either they or their Western benefactors are now prepared to admit. In a world where millions are starving unobtrusively in their own countries the refugee 'Big Business' seems to be getting perilously out of proportion. If a million Indians migrated to Burma or Malaya this year, in order to qualify for Red Cross vitamin pills and W.V.S. blankets and U.S. Surplus Food, one could hardly blame them.

During my last week at Kathmandu I sent many frantic cables to New Delhi and Dublin on Tashi's behalf. Her entry-permit from the Irish Department of Agriculture should have been awaiting me at the British Embassy on 23 November; but it wasn't, and our flight home had been booked weeks ago for 3 December, and as time passed I began to detect a certain affinity between the relevant civil servants in Dublin and my friends in the Singha Durbar.

Every morning Tashi accompanied me to the new Indian Aid Telephone and Telegraph Office where, while I drafted progressively less polite messages to Dublin, the clerks eyed her critically and discussed the particular brand of lunacy revealed by a desire to bring any such object back to Ireland. Then, after four days of impoverishing communications, I ended the campaign with a defiant flourish and cabled that a black-and-tan bitch from Nepal would land at Dublin Airport at 3.20 p.m. on 3 December—with or without her visa, which had been applied for in September.

Early on the morning of 29 November Sigrid drove us to Gaucher Airport and soon we were flying parallel to one of the most magnificent sights in the world—the Himalayas seen from the air on a clear winter's day. To east and west they stretched as far as the eye could see, a wild symphony of remote whiteness, beautiful and terrible beyond all imagining. Yet, curiously, this was as imperfect an experience as seeing a tiger in a zoo. Better one glimpse of one peak from the top of a pass that has been struggled against than the whole of this facile, faintly sacrilegious survey from the artificial comfort of an aeroplane.

In Delhi we stayed with friends for a few days—while Tashi

received and recovered from her inoculations—and this inter-
lude was no bad thing before a return to Europe. Inevitably it
is a shock to leave Nepal, whatever one's destination, and in
India I now seemed to be encountering the acme of sophistication, luxury, convenience and reliability. It was a dull world—
flat and predictable—for there is today rather less difference
between Delhi and Dublin than between Delhi and Kathmandu.

Only after landing in India did I realise how efficiently Nepal
insulates its guests against the twentieth century. Unless one
belongs to Kathmandu's International Set (which most successfully evades the real Nepal) one unconsciously withdraws,
within hours of crossing the frontier, from all the complications
of our world. At first a bland fatalism diminishes their importance and then, as one succumbs to the natural isolation of
the Kingdom—an isolation now less physical than mental—
their reality comes to mean no more than that of Outer Space.
Vietnam, war in Kashmir, famine in India, the pound doing
odd things in Britain—all quickly recede into the realm of 'What-
doesn't-matter-because-nothing-can-be-done-about-it'. Perhaps
it is callous to recline comfortably on this indifference. But the
fact that in our world millions of citizens are subjected daily to
selected details of crises in sixteen different directions seems
more likely to dement the citizens than to aid the crises. So
now it felt strange indeed to be again Outside, where no mountains of indifference enclose valleys of calm.

In Delhi Tashi showed characteristic Tibetan adaptability,
both to her new surroundings and her new friends—as she has
continued to do in all her subsequent travels and social contacts.
Since her migration to Europe she has been variously described
as a 'stocking that was left too long on the needle' and 'something out of the Natural History Museum—perhaps a baby
Dinosaur'. But though she will never make Crufts everybody
loves her and she loves everybody, which is what matters.

Before leaving Delhi I had bought the statutory 'nose-and paw-
proof' basket—but I had also cunningly taken Tashi to Air
India's central office and introduced her to the Authorities.
Nothing else was necessary; they completely agreed that it
would be superfluous to imprison any such object in a basket

between Delhi and London and, as there would be some empty seats on the plane, they arranged to have one beside me for the greater comfort of the object in question. So Tashi, born in a Tibetan nomad's tent in the heart of Nepal, now had the run of a Boeing 707.

At Beirut she expressed the need for a grassy spot—and promptly disappeared into the blackness of the night. However, we were already without hope of arriving punctually in London, having been delayed three hours in Bombay because of engine-trouble, so the Captain asked the passengers if they would be good enough to forgive another slight delay while Miss Murphy pursued her dog. Fortunately the pursuit did not take long and I soon staggered into the cabin clutching a trembling Tashi, who apparently hadn't much liked what she'd seen of the Lebanon.

At Prague I kept her on her chain, lest she might have anti-Communist prejudices; and at London, feeling bleakly traitorous, I roped her in her basket and handed her over to the waiting R.S.P.C.A. van which ferried her across to our Aer Lingus plane, where she was ruthlessly consigned to the terrors of the luggage-compartment, despite my pleas that she should be allowed to travel in her basket beside me.

At Dublin Airport I might have been a lion-tamer importing a troupe of man-eaters. Uniformed officials of obscure significance were falling over each other in their anxiety to ensure that the infinitesimal Tashi did not break loose and overnight turn the nation rabid. An absurdly large van stood waiting to transport the basket to the State Quarantine Kennels ten miles north of Dublin, and I was firmly refused permission to accompany Tashi on her journey into the unfamiliar cold wetness of an Irish winter night. However, the kennels are excellently run and, during her long imprisonment, Tashi remained in perfect condition, growing a little more and suffering none of the possible ill-effects of quarantine. On the day of her release she obeyed commands as promptly and took life as calmly as she had ever done—perhaps because I had visited her regularly, taking a book and sitting for a few hours on the straw in her kennel, while she untied my shoe-laces for Auld Lang Syne. She always greeted my visits with joy, but accepted my departures with composure—and at last came the day when she departed too, into the breezy green fields and bright June sunshine. Nor can the joy she then showed at racing free have been any greater than my own on seeing that little black body again unfurling its ridiculous brown tail in the wind.

A seven months' visit is too brief for the development of a real understanding of any country as alien and complex as Nepal; but it is quite long enough for the visitor to come to love what has been experienced of both the virtues and the faults of this improbable little Kingdom. I am often asked, 'Did you like Nepal?'—to which I usually reply, 'Yes' and leave it at that. But no one merely 'likes' Nepal; Nepal weaves a net out of splendour and pettiness, squalor and colour, wisdom and inno-cence, tranquillity and gaiety, complacence and discontent, in-dolence and energy, generosity and cunning, freedom and bondage—and in this bewildering mesh foreign hearts are trapped, often to their own dismay.

There is much to be censured in the Kingdom, and there are many institutions that do need reforming; but to reform them in the image and likeness of the West would be a subtle geno-cide, for there is much, too, that should be cherished, rather than thrown to the Lions of Progress. However, it is of no avail to think or write thus. The West has arrived in Nepal, bubbling over with good intentions (though the fire that keeps them bub-bling may be fed on expediency), and soon our insensitivity to simple elegance, to the proud work of individual craftsmen, and to all the fine strands that go to make up a traditional culture will have spread material ugliness and moral uncertainty like plagues through the land. Already our forward-looking, past-despising 'experts' are striving to help Nepal 'to make up for lost time' by discarding the sound values that lie, half-hidden but still active, beneath 'pagan superstition'—and that would provide a firmer foundation on which to build the new Nepal than our own mass-production code, which makes a virtue of unnecessary earning for the sake of unnecessary spending.

Perhaps nowhere in Asia is the contrast between a dignified, decaying past and a brash, effervescent present as violent as in Nepal; and one knows that here too, eventually, the present will have its shoddy triumph. Yet even when the Nepalese way of life has been annihilated the Himalayas will remain, occasionally being invaded by high-powered expeditions but preserving an inviolable beauty to the end of time.

# Index

it stood, I didn't have the luxury of schematics and intel. And I *had* to act.

The look in Sandra's eyes had been haunting. What the hell had she been thinking? Or maybe I was hyped-up to the point that I was exaggerating things, seeing emotions that weren't really there.

We'd worked hard to get here, and I wasn't going to ruin it now by running after them. The Circe wanted a reading from the famous oracle, nothing more. Sandra was far too famous and loved; harming her would cause a three-world uproar, and the Circe were too smart to bring in that kind of scrutiny. They had a good thing going, after all.

Putting the worries aside, I turned my focus to the left and right doors. They were unguarded, but it could be quite different on the other side. And there was a very good chance that each door was warded. I should be able to tell once I touched them.

If confronted, I'd just lie my way through. It'd be perfectly reasonable to claim I was looking for the restroom. Had to be one around there somewhere. Even sirens had to pee.

I chose the door on the left, which did not exude any crafting signatures like a ward, but it was locked. "Okay. Door on the right it is, then." Also locked.

Great. The only door that wasn't locked was the center one. Enough time had passed that the hallway should be clear—at least from the Circe. I grabbed the handle and pulled it back slowly to peek inside. A long hallway with smooth walls and floor stretched out before me. I squeezed inside and eased the door closed.

I was pretty sure the farther I went, the more confusing this place would get. *The Circe's own labyrinth*, I thought, coming to a fork in the hall. Muted voices echoed from somewhere down the left passageway, so I took the right.

About twenty steps in, warmth flooded the mark on my shoulder.

It was so unexpected that my mouth opened in a silent cry and I almost fell. Holy shit. Every nerve tingled. My heart skipped and then began to pound hard. I leaned on the wall.

*Jesus. Hank.*

He was here. He was alive. Hank was alive.

Leander had said Hank lived, but this validation, this knowing it, this *feeling* it filled me with relief.

He was here and close. All I had to do now was play a game of "Getting Warmer" to figure out where he was being held.

I straightened and made it two steps before I realized he had to feel it, too. His mark would've warmed just like mine. A grin spread across my face. Wherever he was, he knew I was coming.

*Something had changed, he sensed it.*

*His body was healed enough to begin the lashes again, yet the whip master hadn't returned. He must be close now to reaching the six hundred and forty-two lashes. Christ, it felt like he had endured six thousand.*

*Perhaps his sentence had been fulfilled, which didn't mean shit. He might be going mad, but he knew enough to know they'd never be done with him, never let him go, never let him die.*

*Fucking bitches.*

*He couldn't wait to kill them. He was going to bathe in their blood, decorate his cell with their entrails, and use their heads for footstools. He was going—*

*Warmth spread suddenly through his chest.*

*He lay there frozen, heart pounding, holding his breath for fear this strangely familiar pleasure would just as suddenly leave him.*

*No, he couldn't take it.*

*Whatever new kind of torture this was, he'd rather be whipped than to feel this goodness and hope.*

*He roared in pain because, goddammit, he wanted none of it! No reminders, no marks, no dreams, no flashes of memory, of a life that could never be his!*

*"Circeeeee!" he bellowed. "Face me, you spineless old hags!" He started laughing until his gut hurt from it.*

*Then, he clutched the mark over his chest and began digging it out, ripping the flesh with his nails, wanting it gone, off of him so it couldn't be used against him.*

The deep yell thundered down the hallway, making me freeze in my tracks. It was too distant, and so ringed in echoes that I couldn't understand the words, but the sound made goose bumps crawl along my flesh. It was a wounded, angry, maniacal sound.

Hank was down there somewhere. That was my partner, my friend, my . . . something. Didn't matter if I was out of my element. Didn't matter that I had no idea what I was walking into much less how to get back out. There was no conceivable way to formulate a plan until I knew where Hank was, the condition he was in, and how he was being contained; right now, nothing mattered except finding him.

I started running down the hallway, finally finding a door. I eased it open, ready to fight. But inside, it was empty. And then the smell hit me. Fresh blood. Dried blood. Urine. Sweat. Leather. I covered my mouth and nose with one hand, noticing the manacles chained to the far wall and the dark pool of blood on the floor beneath them. So much blood.

A rack of whips and barbs lined one wall.

But everything stilled inside me at the sight of the small, narrow door to the right of the rack. I was across the room in a second, grabbing the key ring on the wall with shaking hands and unlocking the door.

As the lock clicked and released, a deep voice beyond the door spoke.

"About time. I thought you forgot about me."

For a moment, I thought he was talking to me, but his next words corrected that assumption. "Shall we bet again on how many lashes it takes to kill me this time?"

*Oh God. Hank.*

I pushed the door and it swung wide, bouncing

gently against the wall. I froze in the doorway at the sight of him spread eagle, facedown, shackled to the floor by two ankle manacles and a collar around his neck, holding him down.

He was naked, and covered in blood and wounds. I'd never seen anything like this before on a living person, one who was still able to speak. I couldn't move. My throat went thick and fat tears slipped from my eyes. His back was ripped open in clawlike slashes from his neck all the way to the backs of his thighs. There was hardly a clear bit of flesh to be seen. His wounds ranged from fresh to every stage of healing, which told the horrifying tale that this had been done to him over and over again, new wounds on top of old ones.

"God," I said, barely above a whisper. "Hank."

I entered the room on shaky legs. His hands were free, one flung out and the other tucked under his chest, fresh blood pooling on the stones. His hair was bloodied and matted and he'd gone completely still and silent at my voice.

I knelt down beside him. "Hank? It's me, Charlie. I'm going to get you out of here. Everything is going to be okay." My voice came out startlingly calm for all the chaos going around inside me.

I got up, intent on freeing him, intent on finding the fucking key. My hands shook. Christ, they had him chained facedown on the fucking floor.

Hank started laughing. The low, raspy chuckle grew until his body shook.

*What—?*

Before I could process his reaction, hands slid beneath my armpits and jerked me out of the room. The cell door slammed closed and locked. Manacles were slapped around my wrists as I came to my senses and tried to break free.

The amulet protecting me from the siren lure was yanked from my neck.

Arethusa's face came into view and her smile gave me chills. "Stop struggling."

And I obeyed.

Her voice . . . . it was like a drug, an intoxicating, wonderful drug. *Poisonous,* a small voice inside my head said. But it was just a small voice, nothing compared to the rapture of the Circe's power.

"Well, this changes things, sisters."

"Oh, I do love a tragic romance. How marvelous!" Calliadne exclaimed.

I swayed.

"We must begin interrogations at once."

Somehow, even in the fog of hearing them speak, I wasn't surprised by Ephyra's comment; she did seem the most brutal of the three, but her voice was so beautiful, like an angel, I didn't care too much about what she said.

I was handed off to a male siren, barely noticing the rough handling as he pushed me out the door and down the hallway. I stumbled, disoriented by the Circe's power and grief-stricken for Hank. I couldn't seem to get my bearings and when the guard shoved me into a small room, I fell to my knees.

I wasn't sure how long I stayed that way on the floor, eyes wide open, tears leaking out, knees bleeding. The only thing I saw was Hank lying on the floor.

Eventually, the fog lifted and I moved off my sore knees and onto my rear.

*Okay, Charlie. Time to think.* I lifted my manacled hands and rubbed both hands down my face. *You can't change what you saw. You can only move forward.*

I'd made it this far. They hadn't killed me, hadn't even harmed me, which meant they were saving that bit of fun for later.

Whatever the Circe planned, the first thing I had to learn was how to brace myself against their voices. I had to put the force of my will and my power behind keeping their voices from overwhelming my thoughts. I had to be prepared before they spoke because if I wasn't they'd have me enthralled with the first syllable. My power was strong enough. It had to be. And though the Circe were far stronger than the siren who'd attacked me, I knew it was possible. I knew my power could, at the very least, lessen the impact of their power.

And I had to find out what had happened to Alessandra because if the Circe knew about me, then everything about the oracle's presence in Fiallan was in question. I hoped like hell she was currently lying her heart out, telling them I'd tricked her, that she had no idea who I really was.

And lastly, and in keeping with my mantra, I had to kill the Circe.

"No problem. One step at a time, right?" I let out a hefty sigh and scooted so my back rested against the wall.

I wanted to laugh at the absurdity of it all, at the hopelessness, and it made me remember Hank laughing. He'd sounded . . . like he'd gone insane.

# 12

He wasn't surprised by much these days, but the Circe coming back into his cell was an unwelcomed surprise. His neck was freed and he was lifted to face them, held up by two sirens on either side of him.

Dizziness made the Circe's faces blend into one and then separate into six. Funny, that.

Except he was hungry and being upright made his stomach turn like one of those fun house rides at Stone Mountain. Fuck. He was going to hurl.

His body lurched and he dry heaved at their feet. There was nothing to come out but spit and bile; he couldn't remember the last time he'd eaten.

The Circe stepped back. He laughed at them.

"Niérian is much stronger than we thought."

"Perhaps better used in other ways, sisters."

"This human will be our leverage. We must know her secrets."

*"Shall we torture her first?"*

*"Surely she will break much quicker than a son of Elekti-Kairos."*

*"Surely." One of the bitches grabbed his face. "What is she to you, Malakim?"*

*"Release me, witch, and after I dismember you and strangle you with your own guts, I'll have mercy and throw your remains into the sea." He grinned at her, wanting her to fight him, wanting to lash out, even if it killed him. He wanted her death so badly, he could taste it.*

*She smiled at him. A beautiful smile. Evil to the core. Her grip tightened and then she looked down at his chest where he had clawed the marking. "You are linked to this human."*

*"Yes, but how are you linked?" another one said, which made him frown in confusion.*

*"He doesn't remember."*

*He hated that they spoke of him like this, so plainly, as though he did not exist. He struggled against the guards. "He is right here, morons."*

*For that he received a punch in the stomach by one of the guards, followed by an uppercut to the jaw. Without support, his legs were too weak to hold him and he collapsed onto the floor. Onto his back. He screamed in pain and rolled to his side, the shock of it stealing his breath, and then the kick to his back sent him to blackness.*

*He came to on his back, his entire body humming with pain; three faces stared down at him, chanting in the most beautiful melody and tone he had ever heard. Each reached down and touched him with their pointer finger. One on the forehead, one on the left temple, and the other on the right temple.*

*Bright light blinded him. And then he saw flashes. Of the woman in his dreams. But these visions, they conflicted with the ones he'd had before. Of her sitting on a couch . . .*

*"Do you love him?" someone, a female, asked her.*

*"No."*

*Then other visions, bits and pieces of her, laughing at him, thinking him dim-witted and slow. Using him to get what she wanted. He heard himself groan. He didn't like these things. These confusing things that somehow had the power to hurt him.*

*"Who wouldn't want a siren in their bed?" the Circe's voice echoed inside of his head. "You are but a trophy, a thing to be used, so she can say she had you."*

*"She doesn't love you."*

*"She doesn't respect you."*

*"She believes you to be lesser than siren, not raised as a siren, not taught as a siren, not educated or sophisticated."*

*And it was all true. He had fled Fiallan as an adult male with not even the most basic knowledge about how to live or care for himself. He'd had to learn it all from a hermit in the woods of Gorsedd.*

*The conflict inside of him pushed like a living thing at his chest until he demanded they stop.*

*"Do as we say, Niérian, and you shall reclaim the honor your treachery stole from your family. Do as we say and the name of Elekti-Kairos will be exonerated with honor and your estate reclaimed."*

*"Fuck you," he said, knowing they lied.*

*"Do as we say,"* the voice whispered softly against his ear, *"and we will release you from the NecroNaMoria. Your soul will find peace, Niérian. Peace."*

*Peace was more than a word, an idea, or state of being. It was a place. Something he'd seen for himself, felt for himself, a glimpse of true heaven, true paradise for his broken soul. His will cracked, just a small fissure, but a crack that spread. All he had to do was agree.*

*But then, he could always kill the bitches instead and release the spell that way. If only he had the strength within him. He was one siren against three of the most powerful siren witches in history, and they'd made sure his body was weak and drained.*

*"Remember what it feels like, siren,"* the beautiful voices whispered as one, one so powerful the temptation-laced words made him shudder. *"Your soul free from the confines of your body. Aren't you tired, Niérian? Of the pain, the regret, the longing and guilt? We offer you freedom, the infinite beauty, the absence of all but peace . . . Stillness. Serenity. Silence."*

*And that's when he caved, when he couldn't fight it anymore because he had tasted paradise so many times his heart and his soul wept for it. Those brief encounters with freedom haunted him, destroyed him. Tears slipped from the corners of his eyes and his throat tightened, but not before he said, "Agreed."*

*"You'll do anything we ask of you?"*

*He glared at them, all the hate he felt burning his eyes. "Yes. Anything."*

"Hello! Anyone out there?" I kicked the door, glared lasers at it, and then kicked it some more. If I had my boots I could really make some noise. As it was, my bare feet only made the hinges rattle. "Come on!" I yelled. "You have a prisoner in here in case you fucking forgot!"

If it wasn't for Sachâth hounding my every power move, I'd use my freakish fireball of an arm and burn my way free. But then passing out in the hallway where I'd be found and confined again wouldn't really do me any good.

"Ugh!" Hours of waiting. Hours of wondering. If they were going to interrogate me, then: "Get it over with already!" I wanted a fight, to avenge Hank, to give the Circe a taste of their own medicine, but they weren't going to oblige. I kicked the door again and marched back to the wall to sit down. I drew my knees to my chest and pulled the fabric of the white gown around my legs.

I closed my eyes. *Okay, chill. Find your Happy Place.*

Of course, my Happy Place was Emma, which was a bad idea. I was too charged, too emotional. I really should have a backup Happy Place where things were good and warm and—my stomach growled—and satisfying. Ooh. Like Aeva buns. The Happy Imp Bakery where all things were fluffy, white, and delicious.

I rested my forehead on my folded arms and imagined myself lounging on white clouds, eating an Aeva bun, savoring every bite, every sugary flavor . . . Finally, I felt exhaustion easing its way into my body and mind.

• • •

Note to self: using food to induce a calm state of mind while imprisoned is not the brightest idea in the world—I woke to an aching ass, stiff neck, and a *really* pissed off stomach.

My feet were freezing cold, but at least the ends of the gown had dried. I got up and brushed off my gown, then worked out my stiff joints.

The door to my cell opened. I glared at the siren guard, all my earlier ire resurfacing. I did not plan to be a good prisoner or make it easy for my captors; it was the principle of the thing. "It's about fucking time."

He grabbed my arm to pull me to the door, but instead swung me in an arc so that I slammed into the wall next to the open door. "Oops, sorry," he said, and then jerked me through the door and into the hallway.

*Asshole.*

But I did note, as we went down the passageway, that his voice didn't have much effect on me. The Circe were another matter, of course, but I'd been caught off guard before. This time I'd be better prepared.

I was taken into the main chamber, the massive cavern where the sea flowed in and out, the sound echoing off the walls. Some of the white blossoms we had placed in the water during the Panopéic rites remained in the calmer pools. The Circe were gathered behind the altar, their attention fixed on the altar's surface.

The urge to be sarcastic and disrespectful almost had me saying *Yo, bitches.* But I said nothing and parked a glower on my face as I was led forward.

They looked up in unison and I decided the whole triplet thing was getting old. I glanced down and saw what they'd been hovering over. *Oh great.* A certain stone tablet, yea big, with rounded corners and symbols just as Leander had described.

There was my ticket to free my sister and the others from their *ash* addiction.

Ephyra stepped around the altar and grabbed my right arm, holding it out to examine the writing as I concentrated on bracing myself against her voice. "It is the same," she said. Her fingers dug into my skin. My arm was still sore from the night before and it felt as though she was digging into a bad bruise, but her voice was so pretty . . .

*C'mon. Concentrate on your power!* I drew my energy into my core and envisioned it as a barrier against the Circe's voices.

Arethusa shoved the tablet at me. "What does this say?"

A wave of giddiness swamped me, but I held strong to the barrier I envisioned, finally finding my voice. "How should I know?" I tried to pull away but was held tight. "You're the old ones, not me."

"Yet you have the same writing on your arm."

"You must know what it means."

I jerked out of Ephyra's grip, rubbing the offended arm and taking a deep breath to steady myself against their thrall. "I don't. I have no idea what my markings say or what that tablet says. It's probably an ancient receipt for cows or something," I added just to irritate them.

"She lies," Ephyra said.

Calliadne touched my bare shoulder and walked around to my back, trailing her hand over my skin to the marking on my shoulder blade. Her touch made my skin crawl. *Barrier. Think Barrier. Don't let them in.* "And this, do you know what this means?" she asked.

I swallowed hard, using my anger to focus. "I'm guessing the answer doesn't really matter, does it?"

"Not really," Arethusa answered, her eyes narrowing. "All we need to know lies with another. With Niérian, as he bears the same mark on his chest."

"His *name* is Hank."

"No. His name is Niérian," Ephyra said, challenging me with a lift of her chin.

Fury leapt hot and ready to the surface, rising in me with every word I spoke. "Well, if you wanted him to keep his given name so badly then maybe you shouldn't have lied to him, labeled him a traitor, killed his entire family, and then tortured him to death, you stupid bitch!"

Her slap was so quick I didn't see it coming. There was enough power behind it to send me airborne. I landed in a heap on the cavern floor, so angry that the initial landing didn't hurt as much as it should have. I saw stars, though, and the side of my face felt numb.

That whole *don't kill the Circe* thing? Fucking dissolved. Disappeared. Gone. I stood, rage tearing around inside me like a tornado.

Rational Charlie reminded me I couldn't let loose the power gathering inside me. As much as I wanted to, I couldn't bring Sachâth here in front of them.

"Her arm, sisters, it's glowing."

I glanced down and covered my arm with my hand, not that it helped. The markings glowed blue from my hand to my shoulder. *Shit, shit, shit. Calm down. Must calm down. Think of the bakery.* But that only made me see red because I was starving, and that was another strike against them.

I never had the chance to calm myself because they approached me like I was some kind of interesting bug. A specimen. They began jabbing at me, pushing me to lose control; they wanted to see what would happen.

"Stop it!" I yelled, hearing the panic in my voice as I backed away until my foot slipped in the water. I struggled to retain my balance, going deeper into the water until it covered my calves. "You don't know what you're doing!"

Before I could blink, I was grabbed by the neck, hauled out of the water, and shoved against the altar. The tablet was stuck in my face. "Read it, then."

"I can't!" I cried.

"Try," they all said at the same time. With my defenses down, there was no barrier, yet I was brimming with divine power. When I looked at the words . . . I knew them. I began reading, not knowing what I was saying. I was just a vessel, a conduit from the words in front of me to a language that was eerily similar to the way Sachâth had spoken to me and Ahkneri had spoken in my dreams.

I spoke the words and then collapsed onto the altar, but was given little mercy as I was grabbed once again and shaken. "But what does it mean?"

"I don't know," I answered tiredly.

"Liar! You just read them! You know!"

I straightened, my endurance at an end, feeling drunk and reckless off their voices. I held my hands wide in a gesture that said I really didn't care whether she believed me or not. "I don't. Get over it, Ephyra. Now feed me because I'm hungry."

That really got under her skin, as I knew it would. A vein popped out on her perfect forehead and a growl erupted in her throat, which turned into a screech as she came at me. Arethusa stepped in front of her and said very evenly, "We have much to discuss. Let us convene with the oracle once more."

That got my attention. "Alessandra isn't part of this. She doesn't take sides. She didn't know—"

"Oh, but the oracle knows everything." Ephyra smirked. "She's ours now. Just like Panopé, just like Niérian, just like the Malakim, just like the king."

"Full of yourself, aren't you?" I shot back, but her words were burned into my brain and I had a very keen sense that something terrible had happened to Alessandra. I turned my attention to Calliadne, who seemed like the nicest of the three, if such a thing were possible. "What did you do to her? I swear . . . Please . . . just . . . don't hurt her."

A dimple formed in Calliadne's cheek as she considered my plea, met the eyes of her sisters, and then shrugged. "See for yourself if you'd like."

"Perhaps granting you this wish will encourage you to grant us what we wish," Arethusa said.

They led me down the passageway to the chamber with the three doors, through the center one and then instead of going right toward the cells, they turned left, the same way they'd gone earlier with Sandra.

As we walked, I tried to prepare myself. She was probably just in a cell, or shackled to a comfortable couch or something. Who'd hurt the oracle? She was one of the most famous people alive. They wouldn't do something so foolish as to harm her.

I'd all but convinced myself of that when the Circe opened a beautifully carved door leading into an equally beautiful room that resembled the palace in style, art, and architecture. There was power in this room. Old power. In the center was a circular hole, a huge chasm in the ground, and in the middle, in a smaller ring, was a rock jutting up from the depths of the chasm. On the rock was a statue, a female figure rising out of the waves reaching for the sky. She looked like glass, water somehow made solid, but not. A gold, glittery sheen sparkled in the glass and from her hands a shower of radiant gold light spilled upward and disappeared into a round disk in the ceiling that also glowed.

As we drew closer, I saw that the chasm went all the way around the statue. A small bridge connected the main floor with the statue; the chasm was too wide to jump.

The drone that came off the statue and the shower of pearly gold was enormous, like a heartbeat filled with energy and power, much like the spheres and the henge in the Grove.

We kept our distance, moving around the centerpiece and into the next room, which was smaller than the vast main chamber. The room was round with niches built into the walls. Some niches were empty, some held pedestals with relics, objects, and statues.

We went up two wide steps at the end of the room and into another yet smaller round room. "Ah, here we are."

My instincts screamed at me not to look. I knew this wasn't right, them bringing me here to see, the feeling in the room. But I had to look for Alessandra's sake because whatever they had done to her I had to know, so I could figure out how to save her.

But as my eyes found her, I realized with a sickening turn that saving her would be impossible.

# 13

"Hungry *now*, human?" Ephyra whispered as she breezed past me to park herself next to the pedestal in the center of room.

I struggled to stay standing. To stay conscious. Horror warred with such overwhelming grief that I could do nothing but stand there in shock and stare at my friend's head perched on the pedestal like some goddamned trophy.

*Oh God, Sandra. No.*

I slapped my hands over my open mouth so I wouldn't scream or vomit, but tears flowed instantly from my eyes and down over my hands.

Her eyes were shut. Her skin gray, lips purplish blue . . . Her beautiful black hair fell around the pedestal like a curtain. A crack drew my attention. In the back corner of the room a griffin fed on her headless body. "Oh God." I stumbled back, dazed, sickened, falling and then scrambling up, crawling away, but getting trapped in the folds of the gown. Tears streamed down my face as I sobbed and gasped for air.

*Keep crawling. Just get away. Oh God, Sandra. Sandra . . .*

I was vaguely aware that someone pulled me up. A siren guard. I could barely see for the tears clouding my vision. The Circe stood behind Alessandra's head. I turned away but rough hands grabbed my face and forced me to look. A groan burst from me. Hadn't I seen enough?

"Let us consult the oracle, shall we?" Arethusa said.

"And see the human's future for ourselves."

They chanted a short phrase together. Dread slid down my spine and all the blood in my body felt like it had drained out of me, leaving me with nothing but the cold.

Alessandra's eyes popped open.

I jumped and felt the siren guard jerk in surprise. Her eyes were vacant, but they were her eyes, the same earthy green, the same ones that had sparked with life and laughter. *Goddammit!*

Her mouth dropped open and a voice came out, and I knew this was crafting at its worst and most powerful.

*"One sleeps. One wakes. One weeps. One takes."*

She stopped and blinked. A frown wrinkled her

brow. *"Charlie?"* Her voice was lost, like a child in the dark, unseeing. Her eyes blinked, looking around wildly, but not finding me.

"I'm here, Sandra," I said in a strangled voice.

Her gaze snapped in my direction, though it seemed to look right through me. *"I lied, Charlie. I have always been able to see my fate."* A stunned whoosh left my lungs. *"Charlie . . . the answer, the . . ."* She gaped like a fish out of water, the instinct to breathe still with her. *"Accept yourself to make the shadow whole . . . together, together . . . but not by your hand,"* she warned, *". . . and death will come to death . . ."*

My heart hurt; the tight, aching squeeze unrelenting. I couldn't watch her gasping for air she didn't need, would never need again. Her words blazed a path into my memory and would haunt me forever. I squeezed my eyelids shut and forced away the image of her and the sounds of the griffin in the background, turning in the guard's hands as much as I could.

Then I was being led away, past the statue and down the hallway to my cell.

It seemed like ages ago that I wanted desperately to leave it, and now I wanted nothing more than to go inside, shut the door, curl up on the floor, and just lose myself in silence.

Sandra was gone.

As I lay there curled on my side, my back tucked

against the wall, I wished time would reverse. So many instances played through my memory, times where if I'd just done something differently, she'd still be alive.

I stayed in that cycle, constantly replaying events, unable to stop until I exhausted my mind.

If Sandra was with me, she'd laugh and tell me I couldn't escape Fate. One way or another, no matter what path I chose or decisions I made, I'd always come right back around to whatever significant event Fate had in store for me.

And she *knew*. That's what was killing me inside. She knew! She'd walked right into that passageway *knowing* what would happen. And still she went. The image of her looking back at me, all the emotion, the flash of fear in her eyes, it all made sense now. Now, when it was too late.

Her convictions and beliefs were infuriating. How could she have given up her life like that? She hadn't even tried to prevent it. *Damn it, Sandra! Fuck your stupid Fate!*

And yet her bravery, to walk the path of her beliefs, to have such faith . . . It put me to shame.

And it all hurt, it hurt so much . . .

I cried until my face was dry and hot and my head pounded. No matter how hard I tried, I couldn't sleep or rest my thoughts. After a time, I sat up, wiped my face with the end of the gown, and just stared at the bland stone walls in disbelief.

Eventually, her prophetic words seeped into the

numbness, and I let them roll around, repeating, listening, trying to make sense of what she'd said.

Far be it from me to guess the mind of an oracle, but it sure as hell sounded like Alessandra had been talking about Sachâth.

*To make the shadow whole. Death will come to death.*

Sachâth was one of my biggest obstacles. In order for me to have any kind of power at all, I had to defeat it. And I didn't have the answer on how to do that. Sandra knew, and the more I thought about it, the more I believed she was trying to give me the answer—how to kill Sachâth. But I had no clue what *not by my hand* and *together, together* meant.

My head fell back against the wall, wishing she was around to tell me.


The Circe had apparently decided to change tactics, because the next time the door opened, I was taken to a chamber where I bathed, put on a clean gown—this one also gathered over one shoulder—and was adorned with a circlet of gold placed around my left bicep.

The bath and the nice dress didn't mean squat to me, but the food was extremely meaningful as was the use of a restroom. I sat at a table in a room off the bath and ate quickly, taking advantage of the reprieve.

After their little show-and-tell, the Circe were probably certain I'd cooperate and translate the tablet. And, if they felt this new tactic of "nice game" wasn't working, they'd play the "torture game."

I had no choice but to play along until I could figure out my next move.

Once I was done eating, I didn't wait. I got up and walked to the main door I'd been brought through to the guard who stood there. "I'm done. I'm sure you have orders to take me to the Circe, so let's get this over with."

He regarded me thoughtfully, then turned and opened the door, ushering me into the hallway.

The Circe had allowed me to see Sandra in order to intimidate me, horrify me, and make me think twice about refusing them. It was a clear message on the lengths they'd go to get what they wanted. Well, it had worked. I *was* horrified, but not intimidated—okay, maybe I was, but that wasn't going to stop me from ending their reign. I took exception to murderous, power hungry witches who tortured and killed my friends, and I wouldn't rest until Sandra, Hank, and the countless other victims of the Circe were avenged.

And my determination to do just that was stronger than their intimidation.

Ahkneri had been called an instrument of retribution and vengeance, her sword, Anguish by Fire. Holding Urzenemelech had done something freakish to my arm, had somehow imbued it with the same kind of power as the sword—at least with the siren in my room it had seemed that way.

*Okay, Sandra. You want me to accept myself? Consider it done. I'm about to become your avenging angel.*

Unfortunately, my rousing internal pep talk only lasted the thirty seconds it took for the guard to lead me into another room.

I'd expected to go to the Circe's inner sanctum, not a few steps down the hall. I knew immediately that the game had changed once again. Trying to brace myself for whatever they had planned, I went past the guard and into the unfamiliar chamber.

The door shut behind me.

And there was Hank.

And all the breath left my lungs, replaced by a cool acrobatic wind that tumbled through my chest and down into my belly. My feet seemed to grow roots into the floor and it felt like the entire room—not just me—held its breath.

It felt like years had passed since I last saw him. The size of him, the way he filled a room, struck me anew. He had healed significantly. The fact that he was standing on his own two feet was a very good sign.

He'd been bathed and dressed in clean clothing. His wavy blond hair was longer, more bohemian than ever, and his beard was gone, revealing a strikingly beautiful face, one whose lips usually curved like the devil and whose eyes glinted with shameless confidence.

But those eyes now stared at me flat and hard, like cold, dark sapphires.

I stayed frozen, suddenly unsure, heart pounding.

His aura was blank and there was a void, an absence of self where there should've been . . . something.

"Uh, surprise . . ." I said lamely, searching for more words. "This is not exactly the way I pictured rescuing you . . ."

He didn't respond, just stared at me, his fists clenched at his sides. I wanted to edge back toward the door.

"So, um, you look better, Hank."

"My *name* is Niérian," he said, and I was blessed with the most gorgeous voice in all three worlds. Rich, deep, rough, potent . . .

Until his words sank in and lit a fire under my skin. He showed not even a flicker of emotion at seeing me. Nothing.

This wasn't the Hank I'd expected to find.

All the blame for this sudden transformation was squarely on the Circe's shoulders, not his. They'd done something to him, had messed with his mind, had tortured him so badly . . . hell, I'd stand there, too, and act however they wanted me to act in order to get out of that cell and away from the barbed whips.

My main concern was whether or not he truly *believed* in what he said, that he was now Niérian, and if the Circe had pushed him to a point of no return . . .

Knowing Hank like I did, there were only a few

ways to knock him off balance and get through to him. I could come on to him, or I could piss him off. Quite frankly neither one appealed to me for various reasons, but I decided to go with pissing him off, since I had more practice in that department and knew how to push those buttons a lot quicker than the others.

After what he'd endured, I found it pretty distasteful to do what I was about to do, but there was no guarantee when I'd see him again. This might be the only opportunity I had to shake him up and get through to him.

I folded my arms over my chest and cocked an eyebrow at him, hating my next words. "Don't tell me they got to you. What? A couple spankings and you're the Circe's new groupie? Didn't expect you to roll over and kiss ass."

His eyes narrowed. He didn't seem to like that at all.

*Oh yeah, big boy, I'm going to get under your skin, and this is just the beginning.*


*Chaos reigned inside of him.*

*Joy. Betrayal. Lust. Anger. Possessiveness.*

*Images flashed inside his weary mind, and he couldn't separate out what was real or what was fiction.*

*When she first walked into the room, his heart lurched and he was consumed with the need to reach for her. But then the other images came and he wasn't so sure. Those things she thought of him, those things she said, they cut him in a way that made him empty and hopeless.*

*She used him, lied to him.*

*And now she dared to stand there with her arms crossed and disdain on her face? She dared speak to him with such loathing and disrespect?*

*Before he knew it, he had her by the throat, shoved against the wall. "I would gladly go by whatever name the Circe chose as long as I get what I want in the end."*

*Her brown eyes flashed fire. She choked out: "And what is it you want, Hank? The Circe are using you, poisoning your mind—"*

*"No different than you."*

*"Oh, that's great," she shot back, struggling to speak. "Okay, so . . . poisoning your mind against me. I thought you were . . . smarter than that."*

*His grip on her throat increased and then eased until he simply cradled her neck in his hand. His eyelids slid closed. Gods, he was tired. His mark was too warm, too uncomfortable. She was too warm, too comfortable, and, despite his will, his body leaned into hers until his forehead rested against her own. She smelled familiar. Good. Exotic. Untamed.*

*Full tilt, balls to the wall, the chief called her.*

*Niérian shook his head.*

*He didn't need or want any more thoughts or memories, any more regrets. Yes, he'd had another life, pretended to be this Hank for a while, but none of it mattered now. And she was better off knowing she couldn't save him.*

*Why she'd even want to after all the conflicting things he'd remembered of her . . . No, if he tried to solve that puzzle, his head would explode.*

"It doesn't matter," he ground out. "Just tell them how to read the tablet." *His other hand lifted as though it had a mind of its own, tunneling into her hair, threading his fingers through its softness, and then toying with the ends. It wasn't the color he thought it should be, but maybe he was wrong.*

*Gods, how he hated this woman! Tying him in knots like this, making him want her, even as she schemed against him and laughed at him. He couldn't take it, couldn't take her.* "Please. If you have any care for me at all, tell them . . . and set me free."

*Her breath was shaky.* "What are you saying? They'll let you go if I translate the tablet?"

*Freedom to her meant something far different than what it meant to him. And even though he knew it was wrong, he didn't correct her assumption.* "Yes. They swore it, and once sworn are bound by their words."

*He could feel her mind working, calculating, already wondering if she could figure out how to translate the text in order to free him. He hated himself. If she knew the truth, that his freedom meant his much desired death, she would not be so eager to help him.*

"I'll figure it out," *she was saying.* "I'll tap into my power. I'll try again. Maybe it just takes practice and then maybe I can read what it says."

*He moved his hand from her throat and with his other hand, he cradled her face.* "Stop, Charlie. Just . . . stop."

*Her big eyes turned up at him, glassy, confused, and hurt. Her hands curled around his forearms. "Tell me what to do." A tear slipped from her eye. "Tell me how to help you."*

*"Set me free."*

## 14

*Set me free.*

Those words had no sooner been uttered than the door opened and a guard removed me from the room. Hank hadn't even looked at me; he simply stepped away, turned his back, and that was it.

The short minutes we had were intense, confusing, and hurtful. I wanted to help him, to read that damned tablet and secure his freedom. The Circe had used him to convince me to do just that, had obviously screwed with his mind, but why did it feel so . . . final? I couldn't shake the feeling that something else was wrong, and quite frankly, it felt like I'd been hit by a rogue wave and was still sputtering up salt water on the shore.

"You can tell the Circe I'm ready to cooperate," I told the guard before entering my cell.

I was left alone for all of ten minutes before being retrieved again and taken to the massive cave opening to the sea. Hank was there, which surprised me. He stood rigid, a stone sentinel staring out at the water with flat, cold eyes. The neck manacle was back, chaining him to the wall behind him. *They're that afraid of him,* I thought.

I approached the altar and picked up the stone tablet. It looked so innocuous and yet the small piece of clay was the key to my sister's freedom and Hank's freedom. To hell with Leander and his doom-and-gloom diagnosis about the NecroNaMoria. Hank *would* recover. And the first step to recovery was freedom from the Circe.

*If* I could translate it.

Of course, passing along the knowledge written on the tablet to the Circe was one hell of a gamble, but I'd come this far. Sandra was gone, kind of, and I wasn't going to fail or abandon my partner; he'd had enough of that in his life already. I'd come here to find him and return him home. That goal hadn't changed.

And, besides, if the words did end up making sense to me, who said I had to tell them the truth? This was simply an exercise in buying time.

I mustered my determination and turned my attention to the tablet. The symbols and slashes did, in fact, resemble the markings on my arm. But just looking at them didn't tell me a damned thing. "If I'm able to translate this," I said, eyeing all three and pulling up my shield against their voices, "you'll free him."

"Of course," Arethusa said.

"We have already sworn this to him."

"Our word, once given, cannot be broken."

"And if I can't translate it, then what?" I asked.

Electricity snapped in the air. Metal and magic sparked against stone. I turned slowly to see a male siren striding across the floor, dragging a whip behind him. A metal, spiked barb was tied to the end of the whip and it glowed with some kind of arcane energy.

My gut tightened. I flicked a glance to Hank, it all making sense now why he'd been brought here. "That whip touches his back and I won't translate a word."

"You will translate it."

"The tablet's meaning has eluded us from the beginning."

"We'd all but forgotten about it until you came along."

"And now we know"—Ephyra glanced at my right arm—"there is power in the symbols."

"The deity has brought you to us."

"A gift of power, surely."

I frowned. "Like you don't have enough already?" Three pairs of eyes stared back at me blankly, as though the idea of it was incomprehensible. "Right," I muttered, returning my focus to the tablet, holding it in both hands, and closing my eyes.

With Sachâth threatening any power move, and life being in virtual overdrive the last few months, I hadn't really practiced calling up my power at will.

Sure, it rose like gangbusters with my emotions, but standing here like this, with the whip sparking, the Circe's eyes on me, and a translation to make instead of a fight . . . my power didn't rise quickly, let's just put it that way.

But with enough concentration . . . there. There it was . . . pooling slowly in my center. A quiet kind of event. I heard the Circe whispering in that strange singsong way of theirs, which was a little distracting.

Finally, I felt the familiar tingle, the hot and cold, the hum that bled into every part of my body. I looked at the tablet, seeing the symbols through a filter of energy. The language flowed into my mind, and I could speak the writing as naturally as breathing . . . but no matter how hard I tried, I couldn't make the connection between this ancient language and my own.

*Damn it all to hell.* I kept trying, but it was a lost cause.

I finally gave up, releasing the mental hold I had, and felt the energy drain away into a dormant state. Weariness replaced the void. "I'm sorry," I said, breathing heavily. "I can say the words—I just don't know that they mean."

I swallowed the lump in my throat, hesitant to look at Hank, and my fear spiking. I'd failed to do the one thing needed to set him free. When I did glance at him, he stood stock-still. *I'm sorry.*

My fingers curled into tight fists against the altar. "It's not his fault." I tried to reason with them. I'd seen what that whip could do. "Please don't hurt him." If that barb struck his skin, all bets were off. I knew I'd lose it.

"You will try again," Ephyra demanded. She nodded to the whip master. He grabbed Hank and turned him around to face the wall.

I cursed Sachâth, cursed Fate for having given me great power and then tying my hands behind my back. What was the point? Frustrated, I grabbed the tablet with both hands and tried again . . .

And failed again. I glanced up at the Circe, intent on making them understand. "It's not—"

The whip cracked.

I flinched. The sound reverberated through the chamber. The barb sliced through Hank's shirt at the shoulder, leaving a long tear. At first there was nothing, a delayed reaction. And then the blood came.

Hank remained silent, but his body was taut, the muscles on his arms tight, the cords on his neck standing out. The whip sliced through the air with the backlash, creating a distinct sound, and the barb skittered across the stone, snapping and sparking as it came to rest.

Panic and fear ballooned, reawakening all the power I'd just drawn. My pulse began a frantic dance. I felt trapped, with no way out, no way to help Hank, no way to stop the whip or the Circe.

A hand on my arm pulled my attention back to the Circe. Arethusa had me and was leaning over, peering at the symbols on my arm, which had begun to glow brightly. I jerked against her. "Get *off* me."

Rage clouded my thinking. I wanted to kill her, right then and there. I was pretty sure I would, but Sachâth lurked in the back of my mind. While I might be able to kill one, the other two would have me at their mercy if Death came and knocked me out.

"We must learn more of this power, sisters," she said. "If not through the tablet, then through the human."

"Not going to happen," I ground out, pulling back, but she was stronger than she looked.

I tried to push my power back down, but Calliadne reached over the altar and grabbed my other arm. "Yes, let's see what happens."

"Stop it!" I managed to pull free and slugged Arethusa in the jaw. "You don't know what you're doing!" Their hands dug deeply into my arms. Power continued to fill me, fueled by my panic. Ephyra stepped in the center of her sisters and smirked. They were going to make me use it. I didn't see any way out of it, but I knew one thing: I sure as hell would take someone down with me. Collateral damage—they should've thought of that before they pushed me.

Ephyra placed one hand on Arethusa's shoulder and her other on Calliadne's, making a link between the four of us. Heat surged through both of my arms. I screamed, gasping as their power slid into me.

I squeezed my eyelids closed and gave myself up to the divine. It was so eager that it lashed out immediately. I heard myself scream again but was lost in the pain of their power being pushed back from my body.

My eyes popped open as a strange sort of calm took over. My hand curled around Arethusa's arm and I directed everything I had into that hand, into doing exactly what she had done to me, but a thousandfold. From my shoulder to my fingertip, my arm burned cold and hot and deadly.

"You wanted my power?" Light breached my fingertips. "Here. I hope you choke on it."

And then it arced out of me with the force of a rocket, burning electric as it went into Arethusa, and shoving me backward. I hit the ground and saw stars, but quickly scrambled to my feet to defend myself.

A high-pitched keening erupted in the chamber, rebounding off the walls, and making me cover my ears. After several seconds, the volume dropped enough to allow me to raise my head.

*Holy shit.*

A bluish white light—*what came from me*—ate its way slowly through Arethusa's chest. Direct hit. Her sisters were pulling at her, chanting, using their power to try and save her, and screaming.

God, the screaming.

Hank faced the wall, had a fistful of chain, and was trying to pull it free of the stone, using one foot braced on the wall for better leverage.

*I have to help him. Before Sachâth gets here. Before I'm completely screwed.*

I made for Hank, but Ephyra's head snapped up. The light in her eyes was maniacal. I got two steps before she threw out her hand and shouted one word. *Stop*.

Instantly I was rooted to the floor, held there by her word. I pushed against it, knowing my power was greater than hers, knowing I had to figure out how to fucking gather it again and use it. Through the adrenaline haze and the sound of my own wild pulse pounding through my ears like a ritual drum, images and language scattered across my brain. Ancient things. Words that echoed in my head.

My skin tingled with power, and I latched on to that sensation. Growing it, fanning the embers left over from before. I wasn't as empty as I thought.

I gave everything I had to push through the force of Ephyra's word. A scream built from somewhere deep inside of me, burgeoning, growing, trembling along with the rest of me as I gave all my strength and power. The sound burst from me and I fell forward onto my hands and knees, gasping.

Oh shit. I'd done it.

Startled, I glanced up and met the shocked eyes of the two Circe. Arethusa was gone, burned up. Dead. And I had just broken through Ephyra's power word.

The siren with the whip gaped from the Circe to me, unable to move or process what he was seeing.

And then the entire chamber shook. Small rocks came loose from the cave ceiling high above, pinging the floor and splashing into the pools. A whine like an inbound missile filled the space and the sonic boom rocked me onto my ass just as the wall around Hank's chain cracked and shattered with his strength.

*Too late. Death has come,* I thought, scrambling to my feet just as shadows crept quickly into the cave like a coming storm, gathering me up.

*He was free.*

*Bitches would pay.*

*One already had. Arethusa was dead. And the two who were about to die faced him along with the whip master who had moved behind them. Only it was too late; he was already there, snatching Calliadne by the throat, spinning her in his arms so that her back was against him, bracing his elbow on her shoulder, and grabbing her head, twisting her neck until he heard the sickening, satisfying crunch of her spine snapping in two.*

*A second, two at the most. And it was done.*

*With a gathering of strength and a growl, he wrenched her head from her body. Blood, warm and thick, ran over his hands and forearms as the rest of her slid down to a pile at his feet—the only thing now lying between him and his next target.*

*Ephyra's face had drained of all color. He lifted the head of her sister, holding it out to her, making her see what he was capable of, what he was good at.*

*And then he started laughing. It was too easy. And he'd wanted them to suffer as he had suffered.*

*He tossed the head aside, staring at the last remaining*

*Circe, his bloodlust nowhere near fulfilled—he was just get-ting warmed up.*

*"Run," he told her, letting her see the intention in his eyes, the gleam of anticipation that he felt all the way to his toes.*

*Her eyes flashed fire. The whip master grabbed her arm. She snatched the tablet and they fled.*

*The hunt was on.*

*Calm settled over him. He walked toward the passageway where Ephyra had disappeared, stopping for a moment to look over his shoulder at the gray shadows swirling above, holding Charlie immobile in their grip. Then he continued walking.*

*Nothing mattered now but the kill.*

*Nothing.*

Pressure squeezed my neck, but I wouldn't exactly describe it as a hand. All around me darkness floated. Directly in front of me, it began to condense, slowly forming a dark, featureless face with ghostly eyes.

That had never happened before.

I tried to swallow but couldn't. I could barely move enough to look down, far below me, to the altar. Hank stood there, paused at the passageway, staring over his shoulder. Staring at me.

And then he turned and walked away.

He just walked away.

Sachâth spoke then, and I nearly wet my gown, the voice reverberating through me so heavy and power-ful that everything went a little squirrely. It sounded like a hundred voices all speaking at once. It made the

Circe look like amateurs, and I was glad I couldn't understand the words.

I struggled, tried to grab at the pressure on my neck, but there was nothing solid to hit or kick or grab on to. Pressure built in my face. My pulse went into overdrive, and I knew I couldn't keep this up for much longer.

The blackness around the white eyes began to form into finer features—still dark and difficult to see, but there was a real face there, coming together until finally it resembled a female, but still wrapped in shadow. I stopped struggling. All around the face, the shadows moved and swirled like tentacles. One whipped toward me, striking me on the cheek, drawing blood, blood that was taken to the dark mouth and tasted.

Its brow furrowed deep and angry and frustrated. The pressure on my neck increased. It leaned in and spoke in a very pissed off voice before throwing me down and retreating into a swirl of vanishing gray.

I braced for impact, for my body to break against stone.

But I slapped against water instead, hitting one of the pools, and drawing in a shocked gasp that filled my lungs with seawater. I sank to the glittering bottom as everything went black.


*Emma.*

Her face appeared so clearly in the blackness. But

it was different, *she* was different. Older. Gorgeous. The sun was like a halo behind her, making the red in her brown hair turn to fire and gold. It was down, long, like mine used to be, and it moved in the breeze, and she laughed, dimples slicing into smooth cheeks, eyes brimming with happiness and serenity, a confidence that wasn't there now. Wasn't there yet.

Love. Profound love. So perfect and pure, it made my soul hurt. It pierced my heart and demanded I acknowledge its significance.

The golden light behind Emma's form shimmered, growing until it blinded everything and in this light another form took shape. Female shape, hair moving as though underwater and glinting like sunlight on the sea. I felt a smile, more than I saw one. Felt kindness and acceptance.

I saw myself reaching out, but didn't feel the movement, only knowing that I was supposed to open my hand. It was enveloped in golden warmth. Two pearls were pressed into my palm. They were the size of marbles, and heavy. The inscription on the jewels glowed.

I gazed in dreamlike wonder at what rested in my hand. I remembered the dancers at the banquet, the story . . . I knew what I held.

*Yes,* a voice entered my mind, a beautiful voice filled with kindness and love and power. And I knew this could only be Panopé, the Witch of the Sea, the mother to the siren race. But how? Laughter filled my head, sweet and ethereal, and I wondered if I was gone.

*No, you're not dead, human. The only way I could reach you was here, in the sea. The Circe have imprisoned me.*

Imprisoned?

*They have kept my power locked in their sanctum. They had so much promise. They took the gift of my vision and twisted it, became too powerful, too unworthy . . .*

I glanced down at the Source Words in my hand. *The Adonai never stole them.* It was my voice. *You took them back.*

*It was long before the Circe were born, but yes. My children were not ready for them.*

*And now they are?* And why was she giving them to me? I wasn't a siren. I wasn't preprogrammed to read or wield the words inscribed on the pearls. And why two of them?

*They are but two of the three words I took back. And there is one who is ready to wield them.* Hank? But . . .

*To wield words of Creation and Destruction one must understand the weight of that power, the sacrifice, and the responsibility. The corruption power can bring. Only now is he ready for such gifts.*

*But how?* I found myself asking. He could only wield one of them . . . right?

*When the families of Elekti and Kairos combined through marriage, the children inherited the innate power to wield not one but two Source Words. Destruction, originally intended for the Elekti, and Creation, intended for Kairos. Niérian was one of only a few children born to this marriage before the Circe struck and destroyed the house forever. Give him the jewels. With them, the Circe's power*

*will end as it should have ended long ago and I will be free.*
*We all will be free.*

I hesitated. Unsure of why, but knowing that no one gave something for nothing. It just didn't work that way. And if it did . . .

*There is always a cost. I give Niérian a curse as much as a gift, but it is his choice, if he chooses to bear it or not. Now, you must leave the water. Leave now.*

# 15

I came awake, hacking and heaving salt water. My upper half was splayed on the stone floor of the cave, my lower half still in the pool. I was freezing, shaking, and for a while too weak to pull myself the rest of the way out. When I finally did manage it, I collapsed.

Once my breathing returned to normal and some of the shaking stopped, I pushed up to a sitting position.

*Oh.*

Ten feet in front of me lay Calliadne's head. The physical response to that sight was instant, and my stomach scrunched up tightly. I winced, turning away only to see a thin red line going down the cracks and dips in the floor. I followed it back to the source where her body lay next to the altar. It was a gruesome sight, but even so I felt an enormous amount of satisfaction for Sandra. Next to the body was a pile of ash that had once been Arethusa.

Hank was gone. Ephyra was gone. The siren with the whip was gone. And so was the tablet.

The chamber was quiet except for the ever constant sound of the waves flowing into and out of the cave. And then it hit me. The sea. Panopé. *Holy shit.* Holding my breath, I opened my palm. They were there. They were real. The Source Words of Creation and Destruction lay nestled in the palm of my hand.

Heart pounding, I picked one up to examine the softly glowing inscription wrapped around in a spiral. God, it was beautiful and mesmerizing, and I felt a little like Frodo Baggins looking at the Ring of Power.

*You're losing it, Charlie.*

Sandra would've had a good laugh at me for that random thought. But Sandra would never laugh again. A hardness settled over me then, a tight, steely resolve. I pushed to my feet, wringing out as much of the gown as I could with one hand, and then headed for the passageway.

With every step I took, I grew weaker. Once I made it to the room with the three doors, I had to sit on the same bench that Sandra had pointed out before she died.

Blood was splattered on the wall across from me. One of the guards lay in a heap on the floor. Sirens could live for hundreds of years, as long as they didn't face a trauma too intense to heal from. Decapitation, fire, the heart being ripped from their body, or—like the siren on the ground—the skull being bashed into a stone wall until the brain was damaged and exposed.

If I thought Hank had sounded insane before, I knew now he was consumed. Some might take the opportunity to run away and escape. But others like Hank didn't think about their own lives—only about defeating the evil or die trying.

I turned away from the scene, knowing I should feel *something,* have some reaction to the blood and small clumps of brain matter stuck to the wall, but the sight barely even turned my stomach. The physical drain had crept into my mind and dulled everything, even my reaction to Hank's bloody rampage. But I had the Source Words. With them we had a fighting chance. I had to keep going.

That last surge of strength that always got me through, that always enabled me to shove everything else aside, felt so out of reach. Two of the Circe were dead. One by me, one by Hank. He was clearly on the warpath, but was his rage enough? Not if Ephyra made it back to the grid. If she drew upon the power of the Malakim, we were toast.

"I'm not done yet." I kept one hand on the wall to support myself as I stood. There was no fight left in me, but if I was going to crap out, then I'd do it after giving Hank the Source Words at least.

The hallway that led to the Circe's inner chamber was empty and quiet save for my movement and breathing. The Circe had been so sure of their power, so set in their ways and secrets that now their lack of protection worked against them.

The sanctum door was wide open. Two bodies lay over the threshold. I stepped over them, sliding in their blood. My feet were bare, the soles leaving bloody prints as I edged around the vast room.

Power pulsated strong and loud, mingling with the eerie echo of chanting. Ephyra stood in front of the strange glassy statue, which I realized was a cage imprisoning the deity and her power. The bridges were gone. The last Circe was completely out of reach, and was glowing with gold radiance.

Hank faced off with his tormentor, the siren with the whip, as Ephyra watched. They circled each other as I continued to edge my way around the room. The smaller room off the main chamber came into view and beyond it the pedestal with Sandra's head. I froze. Her eyes were open and glowing green. Her voice was the source of the eerie chanting, her mouth moving fast and possessed, spouting off strange lines and rhymes, increasing in magnitude. The power was so thick in the air that I wondered if it had set the oracle off.

The sound of the whip made me flinch. The siren arced it over his head and aimed for Hank. No longer shackled to a wall, Hank could move. And he was fast, just rolling out of the barb's touch. A crack filled the room and then the whip sailed again, this time Hank didn't dodge, but spun, and snatched the barb. It sliced his hand, but he held on, using his other hand to grab the leather and yank the whip from the siren.

The siren advanced, but Hank was ready. They met in a brief but brutal hand-to-hand, Hank never letting go of the whip and finally wrapping it around the siren's waist. With a hand on each end, Hank pulled, using all of his brute force. The whip tightened around the siren until it cut into him, severing him to the spine. Hank shoved him off the chasm ledge as his body broke in two pieces.

And Ephyra watched the entire thing. She never lifted a finger to help the siren, and she didn't seem surprised or upset that her last defender was dead.

Hank stood in front of her, chest heaving, gripping the handle of the whip. Ephyra looked strong and so sure of herself. She didn't need any guards, I realized. Whatever power was contained in that statue, she had tapped into it. That's why she glowed; that's why she looked smug. She was also holding the stone tablet in her hand.

I squeezed the jewels tightly in my fist, considering my options.

A chill crept up my spine. Her head turned toward me. I straightened. "Ah, so you survived," she said in a voice magnified and so powerful that my eardrums rang. Before I could cover them with my hands I was picked up and tossed with a word. I experienced two seconds of weightlessness before slamming into the far wall. My skull, which was already bruised and battered, hit hard and something cracked in my back.

I slid to the floor, the movement agonizing to my back, neck, and head. My lung wasn't working right. I was numb on the left side and knew I must've broken a rib, one that had punctured my lung. There was so much pain that I was too afraid to move. One tiny shift would intensify the hurt, and might make me pass out.

But I had to move, had to—

My vision swam. Heat radiated in me as my body tried to heal itself, but there just wasn't enough time. Using my forearms, I began dragging my broken body ever so slowly—ever so excruciatingly—over the floor. Keeping my head up was like trying to lift a bowling ball. Blood filled my mouth. I spit it onto the floor.

"Hurt much?" I heard Ephyra say, before I was jerked by an unseen force and swept along the floor. I screamed, holding tightly to the Source Words. *Don't pass out. Don't pass out. Not yet. Please, not yet . . .*

I didn't stop sliding until I came to the ledge, one hand dangling over and feeling the cool air rushing up from the depths below.

"You do the honors, Niérian. Whip her."

Had I been able to laugh I would have. Sick bitch. Hank stood over me with that evil whip in his hand. Sweat and blood covered him. His eyes were flat and his jaw was tight and grim. He shook all over and I realized that he was trying to disobey her.

"Do it," she commanded, using all of the power at her disposal. His aura was still blank, but now I could see faint grayish words and symbols around him.

His hand lifted and a frown began to crease his forehead. His breathing became even more pronounced, as though he fought his greatest battle right then and there.

"Remember our deal, Niérian," she said, her voice trembling with power. "The NecroNaMoria still binds your soul. Only I can release it. You have two choices. Honor your word and I'll lift the spell. Or try to kill me to end it. I know you'd rather kill me, but really . . . look at me. I have more power than you can ever imagine. My sisters' power is now my own." She glanced up at the energy flowing upward. "And the deity's and the Malakim's . . . You can't kill me. And when you fail, you will face the next thousand years wishing for a death I will not grant you. Your soul will never find freedom, never find that peace you're so desperate for." She glanced at me and smiled. "You follow this one order, and I will lift the NecroNaMoria."

Hank glanced to the chasm. Ephyra laughed. "Killing yourself won't release you. The spell does have certain safeguards. No, Niérian. You are mine. Mine until I release you. Whip her until she dies."

He looked wild, feral, and I knew he couldn't fight her. "And let's not forget," Ephyra added, "that she lies. She thinks you nothing more than a simpleton. She never really cared for you. Never loved you."

"That's not true." Blood spilled out with my words. "Hank, you know she's lying."

Ephyra laughed again. "Peace, Niérian. I offer you a swift death and a soul free to enter the Afterlife."

I blinked. "What?"

"Oh, didn't he tell you? He gets the death he longs for in return for following my orders."

That couldn't be right. Hank would never wish for death. He was a fighter to the end. And he sure as hell would never wish it if it meant harming someone else. Like me. "That true?" I asked him. "You'd rather die than fight?"

"If he continues to fight and loses, his soul is forever tied to his body, his bones . . . It is a hell, a torture you cannot possibly fathom, human," Ephyra answered for him. "He can't risk that. He knows he can't defeat me. So, what will it be, Niérian? Rest and peace, or everlasting torment?"

Our eyes met, mine and Hank's. There was no emotion there. They'd hurt him so badly that all he wanted was to die. I swallowed, wondering if he'd do it, if he'd kill me—part of me not blaming him if he tried.

The only way to free him and leave him alive was to take out Ephyra before she killed him. And from where I was lying, she sure as hell had the upper hand. I coughed up blood and a spasm of pain ripped through my side. Cold sweat broke out.

Unable to keep my head turned anymore, I let it fall back on my arm. I felt Hank over me, heard the spark of the whip as he withdrew it off the floor in a slow arc, heard the sigh as it went airborne.

My fists tightened around the jewels. Under Ephyra's spell, giving it to him now could be a monumental mistake. I didn't know what to do. But I did know if he did this, if he killed me, it would destroy whatever thread of sanity he had left.

And then the barb struck.

A shocked gasp robbed me of breath and filled me with a sting, a burn so harsh it felt like someone held me down and poured boiling water over my skin. Then I was crying out loud. How had he endured this?

The barb had torn my gown to my waist, baring my back. Then Hank's knee touched my side as he knelt beside me.

"What is this?" His question came out very low, guttural, angry as his fingertips brushed my mark. He was silent for a moment. "Truth mark," he whispered to himself, remembering.

All he had to do was ask, ask if the lies the Circe had told him were true. The mark prevented me from lying in response to a direct question. "Ask me," I forced out.

"Finish her," Ephyra commanded.

Before he could rise, I braced myself for the pain and rolled onto my back, just praying I would have enough time before I passed out.

I grabbed his left hand, as his right still held the whip, and pressed the pearls into his bloody palm. I wanted him to ask me to tell the truth. If he did, he'd know everything Ephyra said about me was a lie. But he didn't ask me, he just stared at me coldly and then opened his hand to look at what lay there. "They're

Source Words," I bit out, holding on to consciousness. "Yours. Your family's . . ."

He didn't respond. His hand closed over the pearls. There wasn't a flicker of anything, and I didn't know what else to do. I wanted to reach up and touch him. His hair, dark and wet with sweat hanging over his brow, his blood-streaked warrior's face, the small lines around his eyes that used to deepen when he grinned, the strength in every breath he took . . .

"Choose, Niérian."

"Ask me," I forced out. "Ask me the truth."

His voice was hard when he spoke. "I don't have to."

He stood and faced Ephyra, his left hand fisted, still holding the pearls. Tiny spider veins of gold appeared through the skin. He lifted his hand and opened his palm, eyes fixed on his prey.

The Circe's eyes went wide. So did mine.

The blood vessels in Hank's hand and wrist shimmered gold, the power of the words filling him, sweeping up his arm. It took my breath away, and I knew this was one of those images branded into my memory forever.

*He'd whipped her. The barb had rent the gown from her shoulder, exposing her back and the mark she bore. The mark like his. He knelt next to her. He knew what it was, and yet . . .*

*"Finish her." Ephyra's command shivered through him.*

*He went to place a hand on her broken body. Pushing her*

*off the ledge would be such a simple thing and then he'd find peace.*

*The serenity he'd glimpsed and longed for so many times called to him, beckoned him stronger than any siren lure.*

*Just do as asked and then it'd be his. Or he could kill Ephyra instead.*

*He wanted to scream with this war inside of him. This fucking indecision.*

*Niérian. Hank.*

*Who the fuck was he?*

*Did it even matter now?*

*And then she placed the words into his hand. His fist closed tighter over the pearls. The tighter he squeezed, the hotter they became.*

*"Choose, Niérian," he heard the voice of the Circe call to him amid the oracle's constant utterings and the ragged breathing of the woman next to him.*

*The indecision pulled on his mind, stretching it out like a rubber band as far as it would go and then snapping back, breaking, opening, flooding with something new. Warmth surged from the words, seeping down into his hand, spreading out and bringing with it understanding and knowledge. "Ask me," Charlie urged. "Ask me the truth."*

*"I don't have to."*

*He didn't need to ask her for the truth; he already knew it.*

*He didn't need to decide; his decision was already made.*

*It was crystal clear, and he'd rain destruction down on them all.*

*And then try like hell to survive it.*

*When he glanced up, he realized that only a heartbeat*

*had passed and the last Circe was waiting for him to fulfill his part of the bargain. He stood.*

*His hand was hot now. Shimmering golden power snaked through him. He opened his palm for the Circe to see. The pearls were gone. They'd sunk deep into his skin, into the essence of his being, leaving behind a round brand. The words that had been inscribed on the jewels were now within this mark, shimmering like the gold energy radiating from the Circe.*

*His mouth twitched, then widened in a deadly smile.*

*Time slowed. Realization appeared in her look and she threw out her hands, her mouth opening, a syllable coming out. Oh, she knew. She knew the choice he'd made.*

*But he was already speaking, already drawing that shimmering gold knowledge into his core, gathering the word he knew but didn't know, building and building and building.*

*Destruction rang out of him with utter clarity; he didn't care if it killed him because he was taking her with him. Either way he won. He saw her death before his word even reached her.*

*As her power flowed out to him, it was obliterated by his as it rode on an unseen wave toward her. Her eyes went wide. And then it reached her and blew her body apart.*

*One second there, the next . . . not.*

*An unsatisfying revenge.*

*Directly behind where the Circe's body had been, the wave connected with the statue.*

*A crack boomed, shaking the chamber.*

*Oh shit.*

*He reached down and grabbed Charlie, tossing her scream-*

*ing self over his shoulder. He heard another crack, this one from Charlie, and knew that something else had broken inside of her. He'd wounded her more, but then wounded was better than dead, and that's what they'd be if they didn't get the hell out of there.*

*He ran, but her voice stopped him. "Sandra," she slurred. "You have to get her. Please. I promised . . ."*

*"Fuck." He swung back around and raced for the oracle who was chanting wildly to the eerie sound of the statue cracking, like an arctic ice sheet about to give way.*

*He fisted the black hair, dragged the head off the pedestal, turned, and ran.*

*Over the dead sirens at the door, down the passageway . . . And then it shattered, the sound dropping him to his knees as he tried to balance the woman on his shoulder and not drop the head in his hand. He used his forearms to cover his ears, as something bigger and far more powerful erupted outward, blowing apart the chamber behind them like an atomic bomb.*

*He surged to his feet.*

*Out into the chamber that was open to the sea. The walls behind him blew. They were picked up by the force and sent hurtling toward the cave opening. The walls disintegrated. His body was pinged by debris, large portions of the wall, tiny pebbles like a million arrows slicing into his flesh.*

*And then they were out, blinded by light and then submerged in deep water.*

*He kicked his way to the surface and dragged them to one of the many rocks that jutted up into the bay of Fiallan. He pushed Charlie as high as he could, laid the head of the oracle* beside her, and hung on, his body pulled back and forth by the churning water.

His strength waned.

The cliff that made up the south side of the bay collapsed, rocks dropping into the sea, the great obelisk tower on top of it crumbling, too. And like dominoes the next two towers in the wall went down. The last one, which rose out of the cliffs on the other side of the bay, remained standing.

A massive wave barreled toward them. "Fucking hell." He drew in the last of his strength and hauled his ass onto the rock and then dragged them higher, to the very top while the wave crashed at their feet, spraying over them with force and moving on out to sea.

He lay, belly down over the jagged rock, breathing harder than he ever had before. Soaking wet, his body limp, and his exhausted mind in disbelief. The grid was down. The Circe were gone.

After a time, there came a strange, echoing "Thank you." It flowed through his exhausted mind with a warmth that he could only describe as a smile.

"The sea will heal you"—this time the echo was clear, the voice grief-strickenly beautiful—"and restore that which was needed in you to end the Circe's reign. You have done well, siren."

As she spoke, he saw images of the past and knew that in the sirens' time of need, during the war with the Adonai, that the deity had shown herself to the Circe and given them the means to protect the city while its strongest warriors were away fighting. The deity had offered her own power, a temporary gift. But the Circe had bound her, turning her own *power and that of the Malakim against her, binding her there where they used the power, drank from it, used it to rule, and to live far longer than they should have.*

*All this time, she had been trapped.*

*Until she was able to pass along the gift of the Source Words to him. And now they were his. He opened his palm to find the mark still there, like some round brand made from pearly white ink with the golden shimmering inscriptions written there. His words. His family's legacy finally achieved. He'd been made for this. Trusted.*

*"And the Malakim?" he asked, staring over the settling water to the crumbling towers.*

*"Three will survive. One has chosen to pass on to the Afterlife. The truth will be shown to the people."*

*He stared at the city that had betrayed him, the city that had stood by when his family had been killed. He felt no love for it, no love or understanding for its people. He was not one of them nor did he want to be. His path was set. His choice made.*

*"They would follow you," the voice said to him. "You could be king . . ."*

*The thought made him shudder.*

*He sure as shit wasn't going to devote his lifetime serving those who never once questioned the Circe, never once took a fucking stand. Besides, he already had a life, one he fully intended to embrace now that he was no longer a fugitive and the Circe were dead. "I'd rather be Hank."*

*"You would go back to Earth, to your old life?"*

*He thought for a long moment, not about his choice, but about the damage done to his psyche, his soul. He would never be the same, he knew that. He knew the road he faced, the way the pain would creep over everything he was and wanted to be. How the hollowness left from his soul continually leaving and returning would grow. He was fractured. Even though his soul was back and he was free from the NecroNaMoria, he no longer felt . . . whole.*

*"Stay with me and heal, Niérian. Give yourself time."*

*He let his forehead fall on his arm, tired, so fucking tired . . . "I would go home."*

*A soft sigh seemed to blow over him. "And so you shall, but healed from your wounds at least." She hesitated before adding softly, and with so much love that it burned his chest, "Your strength will see you through, Niérian. Your soul will heal in time. Until then . . . enjoy . . ."*

*He lifted his head, immediately knowing her intent. "No, I don't want—"*

*And with that the sea rose up and swallowed them.*

# 16

I woke to warmth and the smell of citrus, herbs, and salt water, realizing with a jolt that the excruciating pain I'd passed out to in the Circe's inner sanctum was gone. I was sore and stiff, but that was all. I'd healed.

Bright stones glittered into focus—hundreds of them inset to form a wave pattern in the white ceiling above me. They looked like jewels set in a ceiling of pearl.

Carefully, I moved onto my elbows and scanned the room to determine location and threat factor. I'd seen Ephyra blown into a billion bits, but that didn't mean shit. I'd seen stranger things re-form or come back from the dead . . .

Despite the grogginess, I sat up and swung my legs over the lounge. After the vertigo passed, I pushed to my feet, expecting to feel some measure of hurt. But the only thing I felt was cool silk falling down my legs.

*What the hell?*

I wore a slinky gown of the deepest blue. Where the light hit the material, it shimmered in a rainbow of colors. It was gathered at one shoulder and trimmed with light blue stones that felt cool to the touch. My feet were still bare, but clean, and thin bands of sparkling stones encased my ankles.

I ran my hand over my ribs, distinctly remembering a few being broken—at least one had punctured my lung—but only a bruised sensation remained. I touched the back of my head where I'd cracked my skull. Again, only a bruise. My hair was dry and clean, left down to fall in soft waves to my shoulders, and I saw as it fell forward that it was back to being my natural color. Both of my biceps were wrapped in jewel-encrusted bands of gold.

"I've fucking died and gone to Harry Winston's."

I sat back down in utter confusion, rubbing my face and feeling dried tears staining a trail from the corners of my eyes to my jaw, like I had been crying in my sleep. My heart hurt as everything came flooding back. Sandra.

And Hank . . .

My mark was warm.

My mark was warm! I shot to my feet. *Hank.* The room spun. Okay, maybe not the best idea to stand so quickly. I stayed still, waiting for things to settle down.

The temple, the clothes . . . it was enough to believe I was dreaming or having some sort of out-of-body experience. Or that I did, in fact, die. I felt real, though. Solid. Grounded. And the fact that my mark was warm meant wherever *this* was, Hank had come along for the ride, too.

I swore softly, wondering if it was over, if we were out of the constant barrage of threats and torture.

Warm, humid air breezed across my skin, drawing my attention to the right where columns framed a view of a blue horizon shot with streams of pink and orange. To the left was a gallery of six white columns. Thick spiral bands of inset jewels wrapped around each one from top to bottom. If only I had a pocket-knife . . .

I went toward the gallery of columns, keeping my eyes trained for movement, for an attack, going slowly because no matter how beautiful a place it didn't mean there wasn't evil underneath.

I stepped through the last set of columns and went down three wide steps into a courtyard of soft, spongy grass, dotted by delicate trees that reminded me of weeping willows, but their thin limbs were tipped with fragrant white blossoms. I stopped suddenly in the grass, wondering what I was doing, and why I moved from the temple. Maybe I should go back, let whatever or whoever had brought me here come to me.

But then that wasn't exactly my style.

A few feet ahead of me was another temple identical to the one I woke in except steam rose from the center. The sound of water lapped the sides, and a strong arm sliced up through the steam and disappeared.

I wiggled my toes in the grass and bit the inside of my cheek, suddenly unsure and self-conscious in the goddess attire. It was all hazy. I didn't remember getting here or where *here* was. And I definitely didn't like being kept in the dark.

I gathered the sides of the gown, went up the steps and into the temple.

Five seconds later, I stopped near the long side of the pool. All the determination to demand answers evaporated as I watched Hank, Niérian, Siren of Creation and Destruction, dip beneath the water. He came up for air at the far end. Water swirled around his hips and ran down his back as he stood. His back and one hip were terribly scarred, but the lines were faint and flat as though years of healing had occurred.

How long had we been asleep?

His arms lifted, biceps and back muscles flexing as he shoved his hair back from his face. Then, he stilled.

Arms still up, he turned and my stomach did a full three-sixty.

God, he was beautiful.

And there was so much more to him than just the beauty. It was everything I'd learned, everything on the inside, everything he had endured that added to the picture standing there all hard and lean, a fallen angel with a tormented soul and a devil's attitude.

His gaze was solemn and unreadable as it swept me from head to toe and back up again. He was so still and quiet in his regard, giving off a calm vibe that conflicted with the power and intensity radiating from him. I swallowed. His arms dropped. His hands floated idly on the water.

Fires burned in the two basins in the far corners, and bejeweled columns rose from each corner of the pool. I resisted the urge to do something with my hands, like wring them on the gown.

*God, please don't let this be a dream.*

*God, please let this be a dream.*

This didn't happen to me. I prided myself on control, on knowing what I wanted and going after it. Unless, apparently, that thing was Hank.

Heart pounding, I walked down the long side of the pool, in and out of shadow, the siren tracking me with his eyes and body. He was leaner from his time in Fiallan, but no less intimidating. And wet like that, with his hair swept back from his face, full mouth darkened red from the heat in the room, and spiky wet lashes . . .

One corner of his mouth quirked, slicing a faint dimple into the side of his cheek. I'd been waiting for that, I realized, the sardonic grin. Something that told me this was Hank, and not Niérian.

"Stop that," he said, slowly—and, sweet Jesus, the deep rumble of his voice drenched me in a wave of lust. "Or I'll take you up on it."

Those were words he'd used once upon a time in

another pool far, far away. I couldn't help but smile. I had a witty comeback on the tip of my tongue, but when I opened my mouth to deliver it, nothing came out. I didn't have anything to say. Warmth spread over my cheeks.

His grin grew into a blinding white smile. "Lost your train of thought, did you?"

Normally that would've gotten a rise out of me. But I just stood there like an idiot, my blood thumping thick and hard through my veins.

As we stared, the mood went heavy and significant and highly charged. I began to wonder if siren staring could cause a mini-orgasm, because I sure as hell was getting hotter by the minute. And, Hank, damn him, must've sensed it because he had to go and make things worse.

"Drop the gown and get in the pool, Charlie." His hot gaze swept over me. "But leave the jewelry."

Oh boy.

*The devil is back,* I thought, catching a topaz blue glint in his eyes. He just had to go tempting me, putting images in my head that left me reeling. Hell, all I could see for a second was the material sliding off my body, leaving me naked, the jewels around my ankles and biceps glittering.

This was the Hank I knew, the one who liked to confound me and rib me every chance he got. Like now. But was it real?

Dream or not, wherever the hell we were, I had a

decision to make. One that every ounce of my physical self screamed I make in the affirmative.

I walked around the corner to the short side of the pool where steep steps led into water. I gestured to the shenti loincloth he wore. "I see you haven't dropped trou."

He swam over, the water licking his chin, his eyes dancing. "Just wanted you to stay conscious until you got in the water."

I laughed at that, but quickly sobered up because he stood again. He moved closer to the steps, and I was transfixed by the water swirling around his navel.

"Charlie."

I blinked, dragging my attention back up. "Huh?" His eyes had gone diamond blue. "Where are we? What happened?" I croaked out.

"Panopé's realm. Her . . . *gift* to us. To heal. In peace. The Circe are dead. Time is slower here, much slower . . ." He gazed at the gown again and I was pretty sure he liked what he saw. "The gown, I imagine, is her attempt to play matchmaker."

"Ah." I meant to say more, but that was all that came.

He waited, wondering what I'd do. What choice I'd make.

The choice was clear, though. No point in denying that. So much had happened, so much pain and hurt and heartache, and I wanted to wash it all away, to make something better. With him.

The last time I'd seen Hank—the Hank that

I knew, not the Niérian whom the Circe had tortured—was back at the station when the sirens from Fiallan had shown up to apprehend him. And before that we'd been running for our lives in Charbydon.

We hadn't had a chance to just . . . be. And, hey, if time was slower here, we were out of danger, and Hank was standing there in the flesh, you'd better believe I was going to take advantage of it.

Okay, then. Decision made.

When I reached up to move the gown off my shoulder, a faint note of surprise swept across his expression and then was gone, replaced by a hunger that flashed raw and tense. There was a desperation in that brief flash, and it made my heart hurt. He needed this. I needed this. Something good to banish the pain and grief.

The gown fluttered to my feet.

Hank's eyes immediately went to my breasts. I smiled, feeling shy, but loving the fact that his response was so male, so normal. A groan rumbled in his chest and it was in that moment that I left any self-critical thoughts behind. He devoured me with his gaze, stopping to linger and torture himself over all the parts that had been hidden from him before. Then, finally, he met my gaze and rubbed a hand down his jaw.

I quirked my lips. "Lose your train of thought?"

He laughed and held out a hand. "Hell, no. My train of thought hasn't deviated since you walked into the temple."

Hot water closed over my skin as I stepped down.

Sliding my hand into his felt . . . right. And then suddenly my emotions shifted from anticipation to an overwhelming sense of relief and intense emotion. Hank dragged me off the step and into his arms.

He was okay. Alive. Not executed. Not a casualty. A survivor.

I wrapped my arms around his neck and just hugged him, my nakedness totally forgotten as all the fear and grief and pain flooded back. I pressed my face into the crook of his neck and just held on. My heart pounded. I couldn't speak if I'd tried.

He held me just as tightly.

We stayed like that for a long time. His heartbeat strong against mine. I wanted to tell him how glad I was that he was okay, that we'd made it. But there were no words.

Then he pushed me back, his expression stark and serious, haunted. "I know I got lost. I know what I did to you." And it was killing him inside, that he had struck me with the whip, had walked away from me when Sachâth had me. "And that is something . . ." He lifted his gaze to the ceiling, looking for the right words as his Adam's apple slid up and down. Then he seemed agitated, refocusing on me. "Why the hell did you drop the gown?"

I blinked. "What do you mean?" Embarrassment filled me. "You asked me to!" I said in accusation.

"I didn't think you'd do it." I tried to pull away

from him, but his arms were like steel. "But I'm eternally grateful you did as that image is now burned onto my brain for all time." His hand cupped my face. "You take my breath away, Charlie. You always have."

"Hank. Did you or did you not want me to lose the gown? And why are we even having this conversation?"

"Because I fucking hurt you, that's why."

And he needed absolution, maybe even retribution, some kind of punishment to assuage the guilt he felt. So I closed my eyes and kissed him as gently as I could on his warm, wet lips. *There. Absolved.*

My heart knocked hard in my chest. I pulled back a fraction, lips just touching, sharing breath, savoring the sensations of being this close, this intimate. He smelled clean and male. I kissed his cheek, his jaw, his neck, flicking out my tongue to taste him.

His fingers dug into my skin. Then we looked at each other. He tucked a strand of my hair behind my ear and then rested his forehead against mine as if pained. "I hate myself for saying this . . . I don't think there are condoms in Deity Land."

Sirens didn't carry disease nor did they contract or carry human diseases, but pregnancy between races was possible. "I'm on the pill, the latest and greatest . . . And I haven't been with anyone since the divorce." Heat filled my face, but I pressed on honestly. "I don't want to stop. Do you?"

He lifted his head. "You sure about this?" If I was even the slightest bit unsure, he'd back off. I nodded.

A slow, crooked grin built on his face. "Because you do realize . . . once you go siren, you never go back."

I laughed, joy filling out all the dark corners. "I can't believe you just said that."

"Your fault. You make me crazy." He gave me a squeeze and nuzzled my neck. "I like seeing you smile, hearing you laugh . . ."

I pulled back slightly and waited until he lifted his head, then I cupped his face and kissed him hard, speaking against his lips and grabbing him through the shenti. "It's not laughing I'm wanting to do, siren."

"Christ. You're killing me . . ." His tongue slid into my mouth, deep and hungry and so carnal, I nearly lost it right there.

He pushed me back, pinned me against the side of the pool with his size, and kissed the daylights out of me.

His hands roamed, rough and hot as his mouth moved to my neck. He hiked my leg over his hip and held it there. The shenti was gone—didn't know when that happened—and I felt him hot and hard against me. My pulse pounded so quick, I could barely speak. "Do it. Please." Him. Inside me. Now. I pulled him close, wanting to meld into him, become so close that there was no distinction, nothing separating us.

If he didn't do it now, I'd go over the edge without him. *Next time,* my frantic brain promised, *next time we'll go slower.*

He chuckled, and I realized I said that last part

out loud. Didn't care. I urged him, snuggling my hips closer, trying to—

And then he spoke.

His lips moved against my neck and his siren voice flowed out of him like warm honey, tugging on every pleasure nerve I possessed, magnifying . . . everything. At the same moment, he slid into me. One long stroke, all the way, and the world as I knew it shattered, replaced by one of mind-altering pleasure.

He didn't move until my spasms ceased and I came out of my stupor. He was still inside of me, hot and hard as a rock. I kissed the tense muscle in his jaw and said breathlessly, "Okay, now I'm ready. Go."

He groaned and thrust.

"I think you short-circuited some of my brain cells." Hank lay with a towel around his waist on the lounge near the pool, his eyes closed and his fingers linked over his bare stomach.

I lay similarly on a twin lounge next to his, so sated my body was a useless lump. "I think I overdosed on endorphins."

His deep, satisfied chuckle made me smile. "You did lose consciousness a couple times."

I laughed at the joke. But who knew? I might have. There were moments I . . . I couldn't even put into words, didn't even know a body could experience that *much*. I'd barely had enough strength left over to get out of the pool, dry off, and pull the gown over my head.

He rolled onto his side, propped himself up on his elbow, and rested his head on his hand. "I thought your cavewoman demands were . . . adorable."

Oh, yeah, Hank was back and giving me hell.

I slapped my hands over my face. "Oh my God."

"I was particularly fond of *Move. Now* and *Go*."

I glared over at him even though I couldn't stop grinning. "You know, I'm not even going to try to improve my sex talk," I said, "because you've got the market cornered in that department." I lifted my nose in the air and said airily, "I'll just work my magic . . . elsewhere."

"Explain," he said, deadpan, and then smiled widely.

God, if he didn't stop looking like that I was going to jump him. Again.

I was . . . happy. And it was more than simply getting my universe rocked multiple times. Hank and I, we got each other. We had the same offbeat sense of humor, the same love of the good fight. I trusted him. I knew he had my back. He always had.

I tried, I really tried to lie there and not let the worries creep in, but I couldn't help wondering how things would be once we got back home. If we could be partners, friends, *and* lovers. If it would alter our perception and our actions at work, under fire, under pressure.

If Emma would accept this new direction in our relationship.

"We'll figure it out," Hank said, sensing my shift in mood. "Whatever comes, we'll deal with it. As fast or slow as you want to take it, Charlie. I'm not going anywhere."

I sat up. "I'm sorry I left you at the station." I'd hated that moment, and I had to say that, to get it off my chest. When I'd had to choose between running after Bryn and fighting against the sirens who had come to take Hank back to Fiallan. I wanted him to know it hadn't been an easy decision.

He sat up, swung his legs over the lounge until our knees were touching. "I seem to recall telling you to go."

I frowned. "Yeah, but . . . still. It wasn't easy and you're my partner, leaving you was . . ."

"The right call." He leaned forward and kissed my forehead. "But I'm glad it matters. And I'm sorry for hurting you."

"I know what they did to you, Hank. I saw it. I knew about the NecroNaMoria before Ephyra mentioned it." I regarded him for a long time, studying his face, his expression, trying to see for myself that he was truly healed. "Is it gone, the spell? Did it end when she died?"

He toyed with my hand. "It's over." He smiled and shrugged, then plowed his fingers through his hair, releasing a deep sigh. "The Circe are gone, that's all that matters. They made me crazy for a while, fucked with my head, but I know what they did and I'll get over it." Which was putting it mildly, but I decided to leave it alone.

And what else could he do? I'd been through horrors I'd never forget, ones that still lingered in my psyche. Putting one foot in front of the other, as cliché as it sounded, was what had gotten me through. People who were there for me, who never pushed me to heal, but gave me time and let me know they were there, they cared.

I'd be that person for Hank and I wouldn't push.

He stood up and held out his hand. "Come on."

I slid my hand into his and together we walked toward the pool, where Hank retrieved his clothes and dressed. Just dropped towel and bared ass. *Nothing to be shy about,* I thought, smiling.

He sat to pull on his boots, regarding my gown. "You're keeping the gown." He glanced up, eyes sweeping the room, raising his voice. "And the jewels."

"Are you telling me this or Panopé?"

"Both." Done with his shoes, he stood, then reached behind the bench and lifted a sack.

I went still. "Please don't tell me that's Sandra."

"Okay. It's not Sandra."

"Hank!"

"Well, what did you expect me to do with her? Set her on the table? She's a *head,* Charlie. A *talking* head." A wave of weariness hit me and I sat down in a slump as Hank regarded me for a long moment. "What the hell was she doing in Fiallan?"

"She showed up at the terminal. She . . . helped me. Said that this was her path, that her fate was tied to ours." I thought of our time in Fiallan, before things went wrong, and felt the rise of grief again. My fingers twisted the gown. "I actually liked her. Can you believe that? She was a good person, Hank. Really good and . . ." I couldn't finish, couldn't go down that road, so I drew in a deep breath and went another way, one less painful. "She made me promise to bring her home, said Tuni would know what to do. Thank you," I said, "for going back for her."

After twisting the fabric some more, I continued. "The worst part about it is that she *knew*. She knew what would happen to her and still she went." I wasn't sure I'd ever totally understand why or get over the look on her face the last time I saw her alive.

Hank held out his hand, his voice gentle and understanding. "Come on, kiddo. Let's go home."

I let him pull me up. And just like that, I was gone, weightless. One second physical, the next, nothing but energy particles. Then I was whole again, my weight settling hard down into me.

# 17

We stood on the cliffs of Fiallan, facing the sea.

Far across the bay, the tower was gone, large blocks of it scattered or submerged into the sea below along with a good portion of the cliff itself.

Behind us was the left cliff tower, which still stood, its top blazing with the setting sun's light. If I had to guess by the amount of activity going on across the bay, only an hour or two had passed since the collapse.

The waves rolled in and out. The wind whipped at our clothes and hair, bringing with it the salty, wet air.

"Did you bring us here or did Panopé?"

"The goddess," he answered, staring at the destruction. "I have yet to master that power."

I squeezed his hand. "You okay?" This was his home, his people, his history . . .

He gave a faint shrug, his profile unreadable as he continued to gaze at the city.

"How could the Circe have trapped a deity?" I asked at length.

"Panopé gave them her power to help create the grid. It was supposed to be temporary, drawing on her powers and the Malakim to make the walls impenetrable. The Circe must've devised a way to keep Panopé there. They saw an opportunity and took it. Panopé waited, all this time, for someone to come along."

"Someone like you." I smiled and wiggled my eyebrows at him.

He snorted. "Yeah, who knew . . . ? Come on, we need to find a mage to get us out of here."

We left the cliffs behind and walked a winding path through the inner city, to the main gate. A few curious looks were thrown our way, my gown and jewels drawing the eye, but attention was focused on the chaos of the three towers falling, the recovery effort, the wounded . . .

"Why do you think she waited so long, though?" I said as we went. "I mean, every year during the rites, sirens walk through her waters. Why didn't she say anything?"

"Maybe she did. I don't know. Maybe she knew that if she did communicate, the Circe would immediately silence the person and the goddess from speaking again. Maybe she was waiting for the right moment, an enemy of the Circe. Who knows?"

Once we were in the outer city, Hank arranged for a mage to take us back to Ithonia. He bent down and unclasped one of the ankle bracelets and handed it to the mage, whose eyes turned to saucers. "Will this do?"

The mage stammered and managed a nod.

Hank turned to me. "He'll take you first, straight to the terminal in Ithonia, then he'll come back for me."

Part of me wanted to tell him to go first. I'd left him behind once, and didn't want to do it again. But I knew he'd brook no argument, so I nodded. The mage pocketed the anklet, took my elbow, and we were off.

I arrived at the terminal and waited for Hank to join me. He appeared in short order and then we headed toward the gate. Unfortunately, the gate agent from before wasn't there as I was hoping.

With no ID or papers, we had to be fingerprinted, run through the system, and then had to wait for temporary passes before being allowed through the gate and into the sphere. We also nearly came to blows with several gate officials about the head in the bag.

We spent three hours sitting in a windowless room, getting the basic interrogation tactics. Amateurs. I told it like it was. Sandra had given specific instructions to her guard in the event of her death. An agent had gone through the gate into Atlanta, contacted Tuni, her jinn bodyguard, and had returned with him to confirm the oracle's last will and wishes.

A jinn's presence in Ithonia, even at the gate, was a memorable event. Tuni was huge, with smooth gray skin, bald head, pierced ears, and a bolt through one eyebrow. His eyes were violet and intense, and he strode from the gate like some demon lord who had every right to be there.

He pretty much stopped everyone in their tracks.

I stood from the long bench against the wall near the gate agent's desk. I had no idea what kind of relationship Alessandra had with Tuni, but I did know he was her number one, and he took his job seriously. My anxiety rose the closer he got. I waited for his eyes to glow violet, but he strode by me without a glance and followed the agent into a room.

There was silence over the entire terminal as everyone in the know waited for the explosion, for Tuni to flip out when they gave him Sandra's head. But the only sound was the click of the door as it opened.

Tuni strode out with the sack. This time he stopped in front of me. His eyes swept over my gown and his brow lifted a fraction. He reached to his back pocket, pulled out a letter, and handed it to me. "She wanted you to have this."

I took the letter. "Tuni . . . I'm sorry . . ."

"Don't be. She knew what she was doing."

With that, he gave a curt nod to Hank and continued on. The entire terminal didn't release their collective breath until Tuni disappeared into the sphere.

Since Hank and I were both in the system with federal law enforcement status, and our story checked out—as much as it could be checked—we were eventually given clearance to leave.

From Hartsfield-Jackson, it was a taxi ride into the city, Sandra's letter still clutched tightly in my hand. Hank was quiet for most of the ride, staring out the window at the dark landscape of steel and concrete and lights. Coming back to Atlanta felt surreal after where I'd been, what I'd seen, the things I'd done . . .

"How did you know about the NecroNaMoria?" Hank asked quietly.

I started at the beginning and told him about walking through the city, trying to use my mark to get a lead on his location, finding his home, and my altercation with Leander. "He seemed to know a lot about you. Do you know him?"

Hank shook his head. "Is he siren?"

"Might be. It was hard to tell. He's old and powerful, and he knows a lot about First Ones." I explained our fight and how Leander had called back my power before it escaped enough to draw Sachâth, how he knew about First Ones and their Disciples. And the tablet. The fucking tablet. "And with it, went my chances of getting the cure for *ash*." Which, after everything, was a hard pill to swallow. I stared out the window for a long moment. "Leander knew about your family, the history, everything. Was he right about all that? About what the Circe did to them?"

Pain flashed through his eyes, pain and deep, deep guilt. I knew what he was thinking. If he'd never left the grid they'd all be alive. I thought about fate, and was on the verge of telling him that maybe he was meant to leave Fiallan, to become a different person, one worthy—because of what happened—to be given the Source Words.

"I'm sorry," I said. "About your family."

He was staring out the window again, his only response a curt nod. Hank had taken his revenge, and he'd blazed one hell of a bloody path to do it. I would've done the same. The Circe got off easy, all the lives they'd taken over the years, an entire family wiped out . . .

The taxi pulled up to the curb on Alabama Street to let Hank off. "Make the meeting with Leander, Charlie. I want to know what he knows. Sachâth is still out there. Neither one of us will be able to rest until that thing is dead. If we take the offensive and face it on our terms . . ."

Which was better than having an accidental power surge, or drawing it here in the heat of battle, or simply becoming divine enough until it sensed me all the time, in which case, I'd be on the run for eternity.

Sachâth *could* be killed or Sandra wouldn't have given me the prophecy. I—we—just had to put the pieces together to figure it out.

"I'll call you when I have a time and place."

Hank opened the door and got out, leaving me feeling a bit dumbfounded. He handed the driver a card, which was scanned through the machine in order to pay the fare, then gave him the address to my house.

I sat there, wondering if that was it. Now that we were back home, things had suddenly turned weird and awkward. I'm not sure what I expected, but even a *See ya later, thanks for the out-of-this-world sex and trying to save my ass* would've been better than . . . nothing.

I was so deep in thought that I didn't see Hank come around the front of the car and open my door. I nearly fell out of the car. He righted me and leaned in quickly, kissed my lips, withdrew just enough to look into my eyes, and said, "Put the jewels and the gown in a safe place. We'll be needing them later." He winked, shut my door and then banged on the top.

Before I had a chance to gather my wits and respond, the taxi was already pulling away from the curb.

The ride passed in a blur.

I used the spare key to let myself in the house. Emma was in school and my Tahoe was gone, which meant Rex had gone somewhere.

I set the letter on the bedside table, hung up the gown, hid the jewels in an empty shoe box in the closet, and then took a long shower. After rummaging for leftovers and filling my belly, I crawled into my bed and went to sleep.

Emma's sweet voice saying hello and her soft kiss on my cheek made me smile, but I didn't open my eyes right away. I'd slept damned good for once, thanks in part to Panopé healing my wounds. I'd vaguely acknowledged Emma and Rex coming home, heard the back door slam and the usual sounds of people in the house, but then must've drifted off again.

"I bet if you pinched her nose and covered her mouth, she'd wake up."

*Rex.*

"She's already awake, Rex." Emma's weight settled on my bed as I opened my eyes and stretched.

I pushed up to a sitting position and then froze, eyes widening in disbelief. "Rex!" He had pulled the chair from the small writing desk next to my bed, had his feet propped on the mattress, and was reading Sandra's letter.

I leaned forward and swiped at it, but he was too fast, moving it over his head and out of reach. "That is *mine*. Give it back before I hurt you."

One eyebrow lifted, then he handed it over. I snatched it and folded it back up, promising revenge with my look.

"So . . . what happened?" Emma asked. "Where's Hank?"

I proceeded to give the short, PG-13 version of what had gone down in Fiallan, then turned my attention to my daughter, intending on asking her about her week and school—the usual. "Are you wearing eyeliner?"

She sat back, tucking her foot beneath her thigh. "No." A beat passed. "Okay, yes, but just a little bit. You can barely tell."

"You let her go to school like this?"

Rex rolled his eyes, huffed, and then studied Em's face, shaking his head. "I don't see anything."

Emma, of course, grabbed on to that. "There. See, Mom. You can barely notice."

"No makeup," I told her, then glared at Rex. "How many fingers am I theoretically holding up?" I asked, meaning the middle finger.

"Funny. My eyesight is perfect. So what's with the letter?"

"Gee, I don't know . . . maybe that's because I haven't *read* it yet. You might've noticed it was *sealed*."

Rex shrugged. "Might've. So?"

Emma made a grab for it. "Let me read it."

I gave up, let it slip through my fingers, and fell back onto my pillows as Emma cleared her throat, intending to read it aloud. "Ohmigod, that is so freaky! She knew I'd read this to you! How cool is that? I just got goose bumps. Okay, starting over . . .

> *Since your daughter is reading this to you, I will behave. Charlie, I write this because my end has been revealed. I cannot see yours nor all the events that will lead me to mine—I only know that it will happen and I must follow the path Fate has laid out for me. I have, however, seen a glimpse of Death, and your future, when you drew it here last night to my club (thanks for listening by the way. You owe me three grand in damages).*
>
> *Sachâth will soon recognize you as divine, and, stating the obvious here: it will kill you unless you kill it first. It's*

*you or it, Charlie. Plain and simple, no?*

*Ask yourself why it has been so successful, why the Archons themselves feared it. Not even they had the power to end its existence. Therefore, neither do you. Though, in a roundabout way, you do. Makes you crazy, doesn't it? Welcome to my life.*

*Here's the thing. I see random bits and pieces. I don't see the complete picture. But (and I hate to say this) the things I have seen tell me that (gag) you and I bond, become (gag, again) friends, so I want to help you. Who knew, right? You will hurt for me, which is nice to know. I hurt now even though I don't understand all of it.*

*Just know that I will be with my sister Fates in the end, and the prophecies I will continue to give will be more powerful than ever (if such a thing is possible, because, hello, World's Best Oracle here).*

*And remember this: the Creator didn't account for everything.*

*Bye, Charlie. I don't get to say that in the end, so I'm saying it here.*

*~ Sandra.*

*P.S. I hope you find your siren.*

*P.P.S. On the three grand: I take cash, credit cards, and checks. Just give it to Tuni.*

I pressed my palms to my eyes, feeling a sting in my throat and behind my eyelids. My chest felt like it had been punched. I wanted to laugh and cry, and wished to God that Sandra was still around so I could shake her and hug her. Damned oracle.

After a heavy moment, Emma cleared her throat and said, "So you have to figure out how to kill this Death person. And what's an Archon?"

I sat up to find her sitting cross-legged, the letter in her lap, a thoughtful expression on her cute face, and a dimple in her cheek that told me she was biting the inside like I often did. I stayed quiet, not about to clue my kid into the fact that First Ones still existed, but I couldn't deny the threat that Sachâth posed.

"But you won't be able to," she continued, however, not waiting for me to answer. "But you kind of can."

"Frustrating, isn't it?" Rex told her. "Oracles are always like that. Take my advice, avoid them at all costs."

I told them about Sandra's prophecy. *Accept yourself to make the shadow whole . . . together, together . . . but not by your hand . . . and death will come to death . . .*

"So, if you accept yourself, you make the shadow whole . . ." Rex said, resting his chin on the teepee of his fingers. "Whole could mean physical. If it's physical, flesh and blood, it can be killed."

"And accepting yourself could just mean all your powers coming together or something," Em said. "And *not by your hand* . . . does that mean you use your power, Mom? Like from a distance? I don't get it."

I sighed. I'd already worked most of what they were saying out for myself. "I don't, either." And I needed to work it out because I sure as hell couldn't call Sachâth here to fight unless I knew how to defeat it.

"The oracle seems certain you become divine," Rex observed.

I'd definitely come into a strange sort of power in Fiallan; the fact that I could use my arm with the same effect as Ahkneri's sword; the fact that everything seemed to work together inside of me to make that happen. It hadn't been just one power, but all of them, everything inside of me, all the human and off-world genes coming together. And I was starting to suspect that I'd had a little help in that department from a certain earth sylph who had once told me I was fractured on the inside and offered to fix me. I'd temporarily been given the gift of Nwyvre, the Hidden Element, in order to save my sister Bryn, and now I was starting to believe it had brought peace to the warring powers inside of me, made me whole.

"How much homework do you have?" I asked Emma.

"A ton. Geometry and more Geometry, Astrology, and I have to study for a Crafting Vocab quiz tomorrow."

"You'd better get started, then," I said.

Since it was only four o'clock in the afternoon, and Sandra's letter burned in my brain, I decided to pay a visit to the one being I knew had some answers. "I need to make a quick stop at the Grove and grab another cell phone from the station." I already had a duplicate ID, badge, and weapons at the house, but the cell would have to be configured with my old number and contacts by the tech guy at the station. "How about I pick up a pizza on the way back and then I can help you study? Sound good?"

"Two pizzas," Rex said.

"One cheese," Emma said.

"One with everything. And get some of those breadsticks," Rex added. "And you've got yourself a deal."

I stuffed the letter back into the envelope and then held out my arms to Emma. "Hug."

After a long, tight hug, I kissed the top of Emma's head and smoothed the wispy hairs that had escaped her ponytail. "Missed you, kid."

"Missed you, too."

Rex cleared his throat. The lifted, expectant eyebrow and the exasperated look in his lavender eyes had me nudging his foot with mine. "I know," I said. "You missed me, too."

His eyes rolled to the ceiling, but his lips curved

into an attractive smile. He promptly removed his feet, stood, bent over, and kissed my forehead. "I did, actually." And then he walked from the room, calling out, "And don't forget the breadsticks, woman!"

Em laughed. "He's so weird."

# 18

"You can't hold your breath that long."

"That's bullshit and you know it. The lake's not that deep. And besides, all you have to do is blink me in. You're the Druid King, so I know you can do it."

Pendaran and I stood in his private quarters, away from the main temple and courtyard. The breeze over the lake stirred the white curtains that hung on either side of the large opening to Pen's private dock. He stood framed in the space while giving me his lame-ass excuses.

"You're being a bit overprotective, aren't you?" I asked. It was one thing to keep Ahkneri hidden and protected from the outside world—it was detrimental, in fact. But I wasn't just anyone. I had every right to see her if I wanted to, more right than him for sure.

Pen turned and glowered at me, and I had to grudgingly admit, he was intimidating. Maybe if I hadn't seen him turn into a dragon, things would be different, but once that image was seared into my mind, it was hard not to be a little leery of the guy.

"My borders are being crossed. My kin are at risk. Protective?" he asked mockingly. "Damned right I am. Why do you want to see her?"

"I just want to talk to her, to try and communicate. I have things I need to ask her, and she's the only one who can answer." If she chose to. "Look, I'm the one who wanted her protected in the first place. I'm lying to my boss and my superiors; I even lied to my own kid to keep her secret. Letting me in that cave won't change anything, but it might save my life, which I'm kind of partial to, so . . ."

He stared at the water, arms crossed over his chest, profile as stubborn as his body language. "I stay with you the entire time."

"Fine." Even though we'd been through battle together and had trusted each other, it didn't mean Pen trusted me with this. I supposed I couldn't blame him. Anything could happen in that cave. Hell, if Ahkneri decided she wanted to take a tour of Atlanta's hot spots, who was I to say she couldn't take over my mind and make me release her? There were things that could go wrong. Very wrong. Having the Druid King by my side was a bonus.

Pen faced me, placed his gigantic hands on my jacket-clad shoulders, and we were off.

"Don't move yet." His deep voice filled the darkness as my weight settled back into me. "The floor is rocky."

A light flared, followed by another. Sconces on the damp bedrock walls held dancing arcane light. It was green and dim, but enough to allow me to see.

The underwater cave was enormous, holding a huge air pocket deep beneath the lake. Water dripped in loud echoes. It wasn't cold like I'd expected, but warm and humid. Pen reached out and snagged my hand. "This way." He pulled me along like I was an errant child, still reluctant to have me in his private space.

The cave floor was uneven and filled with loose rocks. Even though I didn't like being led around, I was grateful for the strength of Pen's hand since it kept me from falling and twisting my ankle on more than one occasion.

Lights flared as we passed between rocks as high as my shoulder, finally coming to Ahkneri's resting place.

Pen stopped and released my hand.

I'd forgotten how stunning the sarcophagus was, how large and significant. The thing had been carved out of one enormous piece of agate, so smooth it gleamed in various colors of honey, flaxen, and cream. Not a single marking lined the body. Only the thick agate lid bore a line of script around its perimeter— the same type of script on my arm.

As beautiful as it appeared, I now understood it for what it really was: a prison.

"I'll wait over here." Pen's deep voice echoed in the cave as he picked his way over the rocks to a flat oval depression in the ground. I shouldn't have been unprepared when he shifted into his dragon form, but just seeing it took me by surprise.

The light bounced off his black scales as he circled and then lay down, giant jaw resting on his front legs, wings folded against his back. He was so large I could hear his breathing from where I stood and see the slits of his nostrils move in and out with each breath. His eyes blinked and then stared at me calmly, quietly, that weird abalone color filtering across the irises.

Ahkneri hung at the edges of my mind, always that welcome, that whisper of acknowledgment. I turned back to the sarcophagus. Now that I knew more of what she'd gone through thanks to Sandra and the dream I'd had in Fiallan, I wanted her to be free. She'd been totally shafted. All she'd wanted was to live her own life, and to suffer like this was unimaginable and unfair.

Would this be my eventual fate? The thought left me a bit sick to my stomach.

*I need to know, Ahkneri.* I placed my hand on the smooth agate and pleaded in my mind. *I need to know how to defeat Sachâth.* Part of me thought the obvious: if she knew, then she would've defeated it a long time ago. But then knowing and actually doing were two different things.

I felt her smile. Weird, that. *Please. Tell me.*

*I will show you instead.*

Immediately, I was taken out of time and reality. I wasn't sure if my body was still standing there in the cave or if I was really standing, in the physical sense, on the wide, level rock on a vast red plateau. But I sensed I was just a visitor, not part of the scene, not able to affect or alter anything around me.

Not that I could move if I tried. The scene playing on the plateau rooted me to the spot.

Ahkneri was there, dressed in some *badass* black armor and it wasn't the polished, gleaming type; it was dented, bloodied, and spiked. Her black hair was in two long braids; she had what looked like war paint on her face—stylized symbols slashed across one cheekbone and around the corner of one eye. She held Urzenemelech in her hand, and the blade glowed like my arm had glowed.

She and five others, four males and a female, all armored, all wielding swords, fought against what I knew had to be Sachâth, only it wasn't just shadow, it was like them, a physical body, but male and without the armor. The shadows were there, too, like an extension of its body, seeping from its skin like smoke, swirling around it, lashing out. The shadows *were* its armor and its weapons.

Red dust flew in the wind, grunts and steel echoed over the plateau. The fight was hard, nasty, and brutal.

It appeared as though they worked in three pairs. Each pair consisted of one without a helmet and one with. Ahkneri and a male. The other female and a male, and then the two males. The two females and male who fought without helmets were on point, and their partners worked in rotation with them, defending, giving them time to regroup and attack when necessary.

I was pretty sure since Ahkneri was without one, that the ones without helmets were First Ones, and the ones with were Disciples, and they were no less intimidating than the divine beings they protected.

The shadows flowing from Sachâth got a piece of the male First One, slicing through his arm, severing it. It fell, still gripping the sword. Before he could dodge, the shadows curled around him, enveloping him, and then like some fucking porcupine, shot him through with spiky shadows wherever there was a break or weakness in the armor. The First One's wings shot out—wings as white as snow—released in panic, fear, death, I didn't know, but a scream erupted in my head as light burst from the body. It happened so fast, like a vicious blur, and it was done. The First One was dead, dropped to the ground, discarded.

*Shit*. My heart pounded as his Disciple roared with fury, attacking with a passion and speed that was incredible to witness. He rolled, coming up with the First One's severed arm still gripping the sword. He shoved it into Sachâth's side. A spine-chilling screech filled the plateau as the creature stumbled back. I held my breath. It was wounded. It could be wounded.

A shadow lashed out and decapitated the Disciple.

The helmet rolled, skipping over rocks before coming to a stop several feet from the battle.

Ahkneri and the other female lunged at the wounded Sachâth, pressing the advantage. Ahkneri closed in and they fought with such pace, it was like watching a battle on fast forward. The two Disciples rotated in; Ahkneri's Disciple took over and was stabbed clean through the armpit as he lifted his sword arm. The shadow came out through his opposite shoulder blade. His sword clattered to the ground. The shadow withdrew and the Disciple crumpled to the red ground.

The other female First One rotated in and delivered a vengeful blow, her blade sinking straight into Sachâth's heart.

Ahkneri screamed, "No!"

I knew it was a killing blow.

Sachâth looked down in surprise and then its face became more animated, more humanlike. Emotion poured into its eyes as its shadows reached out and pulled the First One close. "Forgive me, sister," it said before darkness threaded its way from the wound, wrapped around her sword, covering her hand and then scurrying up her arm, covering her like a horde of insects.

The female's Disciple went berserk, hacking at Sachâth, attacking, trying to save her, but he was tossed like a rag doll. He landed forty feet away, the crash of his armor loud in the sudden quiet.

Ahkneri lowered her sword and began backing up.

*That is why we cannot kill it. Strike a deathblow, and you become Death. It's a fail-safe. To ensure there is only one outcome—the total annihilation of my kind. When the last one of us is dead, Sachâth will return to the Creator.*

Ahkneri's black wings shot out as she moved slowly away from Sachâth. Then she turned in my direction, and ran. Supernaturally fast. Arms pumping. Face determined and haunted. She took flight, shooting past me, the tip of her wing passing through my shoulder, heading for the Disciple who'd been thrown.

He was flat on his back, but jerked suddenly and woke swinging, as if from a nightmare, a broken cry on his lips. He struggled to his feet, jerked the helmet from his head, and flung it, roaring his pain to the sky. His golden hair was damp with sweat and blood, and his power and grief were so raw that his cry seemed to rip the air apart. And for a moment, I thought I was looking at Leander, but then Ahkneri's wings swept in, blocking him from view. She grabbed him and flew away.

The scene retreated as though I was being pulled away along with Ahkneri and the Disciple.

I returned to the cave, swaying slightly at the sudden disorientation, and having to grab on to the sarcophagus for support. Pen's dragon head lifted. He watched me with solemn eyes as I bent over and tried to get my wild pulse under control.

I felt like I'd been in battle myself for how shaken I was and how hard my heart pounded. Ahkneri had allowed me to see something of great significance. All of it brutal and unbelievable. All of it needing a moment to sink in, which I took.

*That was the last battle ever fought with Sachâth. You can kill the creature, Charlie, but you will take its place if you do. You will become Death. Sachâth can only be killed with a divine weapon. No one but us can wield them. And yet, you strike the blow, and you take its place. Another fail-safe.*

I thought for a long moment. *What about someone else, can someone other than a First One kill Sachâth?*

*As you saw, the Disciple delivered a blow with a divine sword that wounded the creature. Had he held the sword, however, it would've killed him. There were times in battle when Disciples attempted to slay the creature with our weapons . . . suicide, they knew, but just one moment was all we'd need, just one killing blow that did not come from our hand . . . and yet that blow never came. We tried everything, coordinated attacks, launching our weapons from afar, but our weapons are an extension of us. Struck by hand or afar, the killing blow still kills the weapon's owner and another Sachâth rises. If another were to use my sword and kill the creature, I'd still become Death, wherever I was.*

*What about using a sword from a First One already gone?* I asked. *Sachâth would die, and there'd be no First One to change into Death.*

*It was a thought that worked better in theory. No one can wield our swords, Charlie. And most, even if they could for a few minutes, did not have the strength to defeat Sachâth in that short period of time.*

*What about other races,* I went on, *their powers, can they harm it?*

*We fought Sachâth at a time when other races were in their infancy. There are primal powers perhaps strong enough, but Sachâth is . . . perfect.*

*Anything else you can tell me?*

*Sachâth will only attack one of my kind, unless it is provoked, then it will defend itself. But it is not programmed to seek out and kill others. Just us. That is all I know . . .*

"Thank you," I said, hand flat on the sarcophagus.

That incredible being I'd just seen fighting her heart out was lying beneath the lid. I shook my head. It wasn't right. Ahkneri was good, not some evil being cast to Earth like in our biblical stories.

*I have accepted my lot. You are . . . like us, but . . . different. You wear your weapon on the inside. You are the weapon. But you will still become Death should you strike the blow that ends the current Sachâth. Even now, your power calls to it. You grow stronger every day. Soon it will hunt; your power will be a beacon, a lure it cannot resist. If you run now . . .*

*I can't run.* I had a life. A family. A *child*. I couldn't leave her. Just the thought of it was like a kick in the gut. Leaving Emma and running was no different than if I died trying to defeat Sachâth. Either way I was out of her life for good. Because I sure as hell wasn't going to uproot her and drag her all over the world while Mommy slept in a fucking stone coffin.

*I, too, had a child, a family . . .*

*Well, it's not right. It's not fair,* I told Ahkneri sadly. *I have to face it, or sooner or later I'm dead anyway.* And

I'd do it on my terms, and hopefully with a little help from my friends.

The emotion I got from the ancient being was patient understanding. No doubt, she'd felt the same as I did at one time. She'd been there, tried that, and look where she ended up.

I straightened, not allowing myself to think like I was defeated before the battle had even begun. If Sandra thought there was a way, then I had to think the same.

And one thing I knew for sure—the oracle was *never* wrong.

I sat at Pen's kitchen table, nursing my beer as he grabbed his second one from the fridge and bit off the cap. He spit the cap into the nearby trash can, parked his hip on the edge of the counter, and then took a long, deep swig. Since he was no stranger to the truth about the First Ones, I confided in him about Sachâth, the details of my vision, and Alessandra's prophecy. He might have embraced some of our modern ways, but Pen was old. Rumor was he'd once been worshipped as a Celtic god. He was a Druid, too. And he was intimately acquainted with the arcane and with Nwyvre.

"Nwyvre is a primal power source," he said, picking up where our conversation left off. "The Creator didn't create Earth, or Elysia and Charbydon for that matter. They were already there; they exist outside of divine influence. The Creator simply made the First Ones and then seeded the worlds with their off-spring. The Adonai, the nobles, and humans all descended from the Creator's divine children, but the rest of us, we rose directly from our home; we evolved on our own, albeit much later. Interesting thing," he said, eyes going narrow and thoughtful, "you have the power of all three noble races within you, which makes you divine, but . . ."

"Yeah?" I prompted when he fell into silence.

Pen smiled wryly and pulled out a chair, flipped it around, and sat down. "Well, think of it this way . . . Even the noble races have evolved since they were first given life. They've acclimated and changed. The Adonai, for instance, they learned to utilize the power of Elysia with utter precision, they wield it, heal from it, draw it into themselves . . . You don't think that has changed them over the course of millennia? It has. You weren't given the genes of those early ones who seeded the worlds; you were given the genes from those who had evolved over thousands and thousands of years."

"True," I said. "It makes sense, but how is that going to help me?"

Pen shrugged. "Not only are you divine, but you have ties to each world. You don't rely solely on divine power. You've used Charbydon and Elysian power in the past, yes?"

I nodded.

He took another drink. "Sachâth's power is divine.

The Creator is also a primal power. How do you fight primal power?"

"With another primal power," I answered. "We fight Sachâth with Elysian or Charbydon. Or both."

Pen smiled. "Or we hit him with all three."

I knew there was a reason I liked the Druid. A very tiny spark of hope lit in my mind.

"I can pull insane amounts of Nwyvre through the henge, so I've got Earth covered. You come with Elysian and Charbydon power and we strike it with all we got . . ." He shrugged and drank. "Then we *might* have a shot."

"That's drawing the creature right into your territory, using the henge," I pointed out.

"If it only attacks other races when provoked, I don't see a problem. I'll make sure my Kinfolk won't attack. The bigger problem is getting a primal energy source, raw, arcane stuff, from both Elysia and Charbydon. Good luck with that."

"Thanks." I stood up and set my half empty beer on the counter before turning toward Pen and giving him a long, curious look. "Why would you help me? There's nothing in it for you."

He went still as he studied me and the hairs on the back of my neck lifted. Then the sensation was gone as quickly as it came. "If Sachâth is gone, Ahkneri will be safe."

Oh, I had a feeling I knew where he was going with this. Not good. Not good at all. "She can never rise, Pen. You know that. No one even knows how to awaken her, except maybe a Disciple. And the tablet about them was destroyed by the Circe. And even if she could rise, her existence would start a three-world war. You can't seriously be thinking this."

He drained the last of the beer, watching me as the liquid slid down his throat. He set the bottle on the table. "She rises. We reveal the sarcophagus. Let the jinn, the Sons of Dawn, and any other cult out there see that it was empty all along, then she can live in peace. That's all she ever wanted, Charlie."

"And her weapon? Her power. You can't hide that."

"Sure I can. I'm the Druid King." A small smile played on his lips. "Tell me you don't want to see her free, too."

"Of course I do," I answered immediately. "Christ, Pen . . . Let's just take this one step at a time, okay? We get rid of Sachâth and then we'll work out a plan. But we have to agree, have to cover all our bases, before we even seriously consider what you're thinking."

"Done."

That was too easy. "I want a *geis*. Your vow."

His expression went shrewd and that eerie color washed over his irises again. His chair screeched along the floor as he unfolded himself. He held out his left hand, palm up. "Place your palm flat over mine."

Having never actually demanded a binding vow like this, I was a little hesitant as I stepped forward and placed my palm over Pen's. A tingling energy wrapped around my hand and the winding tattoo that covered his left side moved, or at the very least shuddered, awakened . . . Along his wrist and hand, a shadow of it climbed over my skin like vines, threading together and making a knot over our hands. A bond. As it did this, Pen vowed that Ahkneri would not be awakened until we agreed upon terms.

And then he dropped his hand and it was done.

I rubbed my hand. "So what happens if you break the vow?"

"I can't even if I wanted to. I won't be able to move beyond an intention to break the vow, so it's a moot point." I slid my hand into my jacket. It felt prickly, like it had fallen asleep. "The henge is yours. You let me know when you figure things out."

"Thank you."

"Don't mention it. You'll be taking over Killian's case, now that you're back, I presume?" It was phrased as a question, but sounded more like a demand, a very subtle one, but still.

"Yeah, let me get Death off my back, and I'm all yours." Pen's eyebrow arched, a raven's wing that didn't seem to appreciate my sarcasm at all. "I'll get an update from Ashton and Liz, look over the labs and paperwork. I'll let you know the status as soon as I can."

# 19

I returned home with pizza and breadsticks, helped Emma with her vocabulary, and then settled in for the night. I'd never made it to the station, but I planned on being there first thing in the morning.

My dreams that night were a rehashing of Ahkneri's battle, Alessandra's eerie head spouting off prophecies, and random bits of me and Hank, his torture, and the fight against the Circe.

By the time I woke, I felt like I'd relived a couple lifetimes in just a few hours. I took a cool shower to wake me up, ate breakfast with Emma and Rex, and then dropped Em off at the League of Mages school before continuing to the station.

"Well done, Madigan." The chief clapped me on the shoulder as I entered our work space. He must've decided that wasn't enough because he pulled me into a bear hug. "Well done." He set me back, the look in his eyes warm and fatherly. Then he winked at me and went right back to work mode. "You're going to have one hell of a report to file, so better hop to it. And don't forget to file a report on the oracle as well. Sian will send a copy over to the folks in Ithonia. Glad to have you back."

"Has Hank been in yet?"

"He's over in legal giving a statement." The chief grabbed a file off his desk. "I'll be back after noon. Ashton's in the process of following up a lead, but he's got until the end of the week to get his reports and notes together on the Grove case, then it's back over to you and Hank."

"I'm sure he loved hearing that."

The chief gave a merciless shrug. "He knew all along he was just filling in. Good to have you back, Madigan."

"Thanks, Chief."

The chief barreled out of the office. Sian finished making coffee in the small kitchenette, and offered me a cup. "You should've seen his face when he found out you and Hank had come through the gate. He had to sit down, on the floor. I swear I thought he was going to have a heart attack. Teary-eyed and everything." She handed me a bag of bagels. "For you."

"Thanks, Sian. And thanks for . . . before . . ." When she'd tried to comfort me as Hank's supposed execution dropped me to my knees.

"No problem. I got you a copy of the latest report

from Liz. That hair you found by the lake came back as sidhé fae. I'm still searching the histories for that 'old school' group that showed up in the oracle's club. Might be the same guys . . . I mean, pretty coincidental, right?"

I sat down at my desk. "Could be." Probably was. This wasn't going to be a cut-and-dry case, and I had a feeling Killian's murder was just the beginning. As soon as I took care of my literal shadow of death, I'd be able to put my full attention to solving Killian's murder. For now I was content to let Ashton finish up with his lead. I didn't like him or his tactics, but he was a good investigator. "We'll see. Keep searching. Try searching the word *Disciple* and see if anything comes up, will you? And run the name Leander through the database. Let me know if you get a hit."

"Sure. That all?"

"No," I said, chewing my bottom lip. "Can you get a courier up here? I need to send a message to the mages' headquarters in Ithonia."

"I'll call downstairs and see if one's available now."

"Thanks." Edainnué Lightwater was an Elder in Ithonia's League of Mages. And I had her marker. If there was anyone who might know how to defeat Sachâth, it was her. And Leander. Leander knew way more than he let on . . .

After working all morning, I broke for lunch and headed into Underground to eat with my sister Bryn. We chose Abracus since it was right across the street from her shop. Using the same details as I'd given

Emma and Rex, I filled her in on the happenings in Fiallan, leaving out Panopé's "gift" to Hank and me, which I knew she'd love to hear *all* about, but I just didn't want to talk about it; it was too new and tenuous at this point, and honestly a little unreal.

Bryn made up for my surprising lack of appetite, eating her burger and fries, and then picking at mine. "I take it things are better," I said.

"As in?" she asked, mouth full.

"As in your health and relationship with Aaron."

She grunted and swallowed a drink of sweet tea. Emma and Bryn looked so much alike it was scary. Big brown eyes and wavy brown hair—though Bryn's coloring on both was lighter than Em's. They had the same full lips, slightly upturned noses, and that impish quality to their look. "*Ash* is still kicking my ass. But I'm managing. As for the warlock . . ." She rolled her eyes and snagged another fry. "Irritating. You'd think a guy like that with a couple hundred years of mage training and scholarly pursuits wouldn't be so . . . pigheaded and alpha all the time, you know?"

I laughed. "Shouldn't surprise you." With all the scholarly pursuits, Aaron was still a warlock—a warrior class of mage.

"It doesn't. It's just annoying. After everything, *now* he wants to take things slow when before he wouldn't leave me alone. And now, suddenly, I'm the one who wants everything right now and he doesn't."

"I think he's just worried about you. You've been through a lot. So has he."

"I know. But"—she pointed a fry at me—"what better reason to grasp love by the horns while you can, before something comes along and snatches it away from you?"

She did have a point and as she went on about her complex relationship with Aaron, I smiled. I hadn't seen Bryn this animated since before her exposure to *ash*. She still had shadows beneath her eyes, still had gray threaded through her aura, and I knew she suffered, but even with all that she seemed more like the little sister I knew and loved.

I'd held that stone tablet in my hands, the very thing that could've freed her from addiction, and then watched it shatter along with Ephyra. Gone.

But the cure still existed . . .

And if Leander had it, then I sure as hell was going to find a way to get it. Tablet or not.

After lunch, I walked back toward the plaza where Mercy Street joined with Helios Alley and Solomon Street. The scene—people shopping, goblins pushing their sale carts, patrons sipping coffee at the outdoor tables in front of the imp's bakery, the sound of the fountain and the traffic echoing from the city above—it was comforting. It was what I knew, what I loved, and I hoped to God my inter-dimensional travel days were over.

I hadn't told Bryn about Sachâth. Doing so would involve her in knowledge that was far too dangerous to have. And while I'd turned a corner when it came to including those I loved in details of my life, this wasn't something I would or could share. Pen, Hank, and I had made a promise when we hid Ahkneri in the lake. No one would know. No one.

For Bryn or Rex or Emma, even the chief and the ITF, to know that a First One existed, that a divine *weapon* existed, was knowledge that'd get them killed, used, targeted . . . And I couldn't reveal details about Sachâth without getting too close to the truth.

As I came to a stop in the middle of the plaza, I felt Hank before I saw him.

I turned slowly and watched the main stairs that led from Topside Atlanta down into Underground. First his combat boots stepped casually down the steps, then tan cargo pants, standard issue equipment belt with hip weapon, black tee . . .

His eyes were on me the second they came into view and it felt like the crowded plaza vanished. Wavy blond hair, sardonic tilt to his mouth, five o'clock shadow. I knew what those arms felt like, how the skin tasted, knew how it felt to suck on that slowly curving lower lip.

Partner. He was my partner. As in *work*. As in: how the hell was I supposed to separate the work from the relationship?

I let out a shaky breath as he strode toward me, all large and male and greedily taking up all the oxygen and space in the plaza. "Charlie," he said, purposefully making his voice lower and deeper than it already was.

"Hank," I countered, narrowing my eyes, but not being able to keep from smiling. Damn him.

"So, listen . . . I know it'll be tough, but try to keep your dirty thoughts to a minimum. Once we clock out, we'll go back to my place, and you can have your wicked, wanton way with me. Sound good?"

He was enjoying this way too much. But then, I guess, so was I. He waited a beat, and when no response came out of my idiot grinning mouth, he leaned in, kissed me, and walked around me, saying, "Awesome. It's a date."

*Nice, Charlie.* I rolled my eyes at myself, spun on my heel, and fell in step beside him. On one hand, I was glad he was trying to fall back into his old routine—the easygoing, likeable, flirtatious guy. On the other, I wondered how he really was and how he was dealing with the wounds on his mind and soul. I knew what it was like. To forge ahead, to pretend something didn't happen or just deal with it in the quiet of your own space, in your own time.

We entered Helios Alley—or as I often called it Elysian Territory—and headed down the middle of the street, avoiding the busier sidewalks. "How did it go at legal?"

"The usual barrage of boring, repetitive questions. The Feds are sending a group to Fiallan to help with the fallout. The king has abdicated the throne . . ." He slid a glance my way. "I hear the delegates told you I was executed."

"Yeah." Not a pleasant memory.

He bumped me with his shoulder. "Thanks for not believing them."

I bumped him back. "You're welcome."

Helios Alley dead-ended into the underground lobby of Helios Tower. After a quick walk through the tunnel, we emerged into the spacious lobby complete with restaurant and bar/lounge. We bypassed the receptionist's desk and took the elevator.

"This is giving me flashbacks," Hank muttered.

"Tell me about it. At least we're only going to the fourth floor this time." Instead of the rooftop, or the forty-sixth floor from whence we took our tumble . . . I shuddered with the memory.

The lower floors of the tower were devoted to businesses. The address that had been on Leander's card had said *4th Floor, Suite 107*. No name. Nothing else but a phone number. The plaque indicating Suite 107 was also otherwise blank.

I opened the door to find a typical waiting room and a desk behind which sat a thin middle-aged woman whose fingers tapped efficiently on a keyboard. She stopped typing, looked up, but didn't say a word in greeting. How lovely.

"We're here to see Leander," I said.

She peered at me, then Hank over the rim of her glasses. "Who may I ask is inquiring?"

"Detectives Madigan and Williams," I answered.

"One moment, please."

As she left the room, I glanced around the small front office, noting that it looked like my accountant's office, and not what I expected from the mysterious Leander.

"Right this way," the receptionist said, returning to lead us down a long hallway to an end door, which she held open and then closed behind us.

The room was the size of my entire downstairs cottage in Candler Park. Two gigantic windows offered views of the city. The chair behind the massive desk was empty and it looked as though neither one had ever been used much. To the left were two couches with a coffee table between them and beyond that an entire wall of books from floor to ceiling.

Leander, however, was to the far right with his back to us, playing a pinball machine.

Hank gave me a look that said, *You're shittin' me. This is the guy?*

Oh yeah, this was the guy. There was no mistaking the power in the room. We walked over. The words *Bally's Wizard!* were painted across the back glass along with some curvy, barely clad women, and if I wasn't mistaken a guy that looked like the Who's Roger Daltrey in the middle wearing a *Pinball Wizard* T-shirt.

From the less than impressive score, either Leander had just started playing or he sucked at pinball. I was guessing sucked, since he lost the ball seconds later.

Leander barely acknowledged me. His gaze went straight to Hank. They stood several feet apart, about the same height and weight, both broad shouldered, both powerful, and easy on the eyes. "So you brought back the last son of Elekti-Kairos," he said to me while studying Hank.

"Actually, he kind of brought *me* back," I said, giving props where they were due.

Hank stared so intently at Leander that my hand moved to rest on the grip of my firearm. The energy in the room shot up and the hairs on the back of my neck rose.

Leander folded his arms over his chest. "Ignoring it won't make it go away, siren."

"So what does, then?"

"Nothing, really. Time. Distraction. Women. Killing things . . . they just make you forget for a little while."

"What are you?" Hank asked.

Leander cocked a smug eyebrow and then finally turned his attention to me. "Where's the tablet?"

"Destroyed."

He leaned back against the pinball machine, his casual stance deceptive because I could feel the surge of anger that ballooned around him. "Then you waste my time."

"I'm going to face Sachâth," I said, surprising both Leander and Hank.

Leander recovered first and snorted. "Didn't figure you for a total head case."

Hank was watching me, his eyes narrowed, his mind working. "What makes you think you can defeat it?" He knew I'd never face Sachâth unless I felt I had a chance.

"Yes, do tell," Leander added, amused.

"Since you know about Ahkneri's existence . . ." I said to Leander. "She gave me a vision. She showed me the last battle she fought with Sachâth." Leander straightened and the quiet intensity that stole over him made me stutter.

I forged on, though, and told them about the vision, what Ahkneri had told me about the nature of Sachâth, and of my talk with Pendaran. Leander looked a little pale, and strode over to a cabinet and poured himself a drink. He tossed it back in one gulp and then turned to us, cradling the empty glass in his large hand. "So you think all you have to do is pull together three primal energy sources and that will be the end of the Creator's assassin."

"Do you have a better idea?" I shot back.

But Hank was watching Leander. "Has that ever been tried?"

"Not to my knowledge," Leander admitted. "Sachâth was always engaged by First Ones and their Disciples. Every weapon conceivable was tried, to my knowledge," he felt the need to add again.

"The indigenous people of Elysia and Charbydon developed outside of the Creator's influence," I said. "They sprung from the primal deities and energies that emerged in those worlds' infancy. Like the sirens, fae, and nymphs," I said. "And the jinn and the ghouls . . ."

"So you want to hit Sachâth with powers that aren't connected with the Creator," Hank said.

"Right. I just need to figure out how to bring them together. Pen can direct the Earth's arcane energy . . ." I looked at Leander. "I just need a means to use Elysia's and Charbydon's. I don't know what you are, Leander, but you must have some idea of how I can do this."

He eyed me for a long time. "Did you read the tablet?"

I blinked at his change of direction. "Um . . . yeah. I read it."

"Out loud?"

"Yes," I said slowly.

"In the ancient tongue?"

"I believe so. Why?"

He walked to another wall of cabinet and bookshelf combinations, and pulled out a drawer. Inside he retrieved a metal cylinder and then walked back to me. "Here."

I took it. It was cold. "What is it?"

"Your antidote."

My hand tightened around the metal, and my heart lurched inside of my chest. "What do you mean? This"—I shook it at him—"is the cure to *ash*?"

"Yes. But maybe you shouldn't shake it like that."

I froze. "But why?" And I didn't mean the shaking.

"Because, *Detective*, the entire point of retrieving that tablet was to read it, out loud, and in the language of the First Ones. Since you have done that, I'm upholding the bargain."

Wariness flooded down my back, setting off every warning bell I had. "What the hell did I read, Leander?" But based on what he told me before about the tablet, I had a good idea. "I woke a Disciple."

He grinned. It wasn't happy or smug or even satisfied. It was feral.

"Tell me something, Leander," I said. "Where did the Disciples come from?"

"They were among the first generations born to the First Ones when they seeded the worlds. The first Adonai, the first humans . . . There were none more powerful than them save the First Ones. They offered their swords and their lives. Some guarded mothers and fathers, some guarded lovers, husbands, wives . . ."

And then I took a chance. "I saw you in the vision."

There was no reaction at all in those golden eyes, almost like he'd been waiting for me to say it. "You saw what you wanted to see."

"I know what I saw."

His voice was soft, but lethal. "No, you saw your precious *Ahkneri* turn her back on her own Disciple to save another. That is what you saw." He moved back to the pinball machine. "As for Sachâth . . . If your plan will work"—he shrugged—"who knows. But I will lend my aid at the time and place. Just call my secretary. Now if you'll excuse me, I'm extremely busy running my empire."

He turned back to the pinball machine, pulled the lever, and set the ball free.

Hank wasn't happy with me. I could tell. It might've been the heat radiating off his hand when he grabbed mine and pulled me to a private spot in the lobby. Or it might've been the pissed off gleam in his eyes, or the plowing of his fingers through his hair and then the exasperated way he parked two fingers on his hip, dropped them, and paced before me.

"When did you plan on telling me about this *idea*?"

"Today."

"Christ, Charlie!" he hissed and dragged me over to some tall palm trees in pots. "You can't seriously think . . ."

"You're the one who said in the cab we had to get rid of it!"

That seemed to take some steam out of him. "I know what I said." He stared up at the ceiling, blew out a deep sigh, and then faced me again. "We have one shot. One. And that's it."

"Well, no pressure or anything," I said, knowing exactly the risk involved. "And what the hell were you and Leander talking about anyway?"

He gaped for a minute, his focus still on Sachâth. "The NecroNaMoria." Completely deflated, he slumped into a nearby chair. I did the same in an adjoining one. "Whoever he is, it happened to him. Even if he hadn't said anything I knew . . ."

"What do you mean, you knew?"

Hank shook his head as though he was confused by it all. "I don't know if I can even put it into words. It's a sense of him being . . . not whole . . ." He let out a heavy breath, and gave up. Obviously not really something he wanted to think about.

I let that simmer for a moment, honestly not knowing how to respond, and disconcerted by the notion that if Leander exhibited a sense of not being whole, then Hank most likely did, too. I stared at Hank, this big, capable guy, sprawled on the chair, his head back against the cushion, who was still cracking stupid jokes and trying to fall back into the person he was before the Circe got ahold of him, and knew he was struggling. On the inside. Where no one could see. Where he wouldn't *let* anyone see.

"You get a feel for what he is?" I finally asked.

He lifted his head off the back of the chair and scrubbed a hand down his face, leaning forward in the chair, knees apart, hanging his forearms over them. "He's not siren. I don't know what he is, Charlie. You really think he's a Disciple?"

"I don't know. I was hoping to get more of a reaction out of him."

"Was he in the vision or were you just bluffing?"

"I don't know. I thought . . . if not a Disciple then what is he?"

"He didn't deny it."

"No . . ."

Hank opened his hand, staring down at his palm for a long moment. "Well, I know how to solve the Elysian part of your problem. Straight from the deity herself." He lifted his head and held out his branded palm. "Primal Source Words."

Since we were comparing weapons . . . I lifted my arm, the one with the symbols, and smiled weakly. I hadn't told him everything. "Ancient divine weapon."

His crooked smile threw me off-balance. "Some arm you got there, kiddo." At my confusion, he said, "I saw you use it. In the cave. When Arethusa died."

Oh. Right. "Yeah, well, I was a little distracted."

"You and me both."

"So now what?"

"Well, now we work on the third power problem."

And what was likely to be the impossible one. "Charbydon."

# 20

The cure for *ash* had been passed along to Titus Mott. It would need to be studied; its properties identified, then re-created and put through a series of tests before using it on live subjects. For now, we were keeping it under wraps—no need to get anyone's hopes up if it didn't work. But I was pretty sure that whatever Titus discovered in that cylinder would be the key to *ash*'s demise.

I'd sent out the courier the day before and had just gotten a reply. Lightwater said no. Apparently a stickler for details, she required her two days with me *before* giving me her marker. That had been the deal struck, and that's the way it would stay. I wanted to send another courier saying that if I *died* then she'd never get her two days, but decided it was pointless. Lightwater wasn't a fool; she knew exactly the kind of gun I was under. And she'd had the nerve to write *Good luck*.

I couldn't exactly go into Ithonia and give Lightwater her two damned days first. She wanted to study me, and my power. No way in hell I was going to chance Sachâth coming again. The next time it did, I was sure it would be my last.

And I'd yet to go to Hank's apartment to have my wicked, wanton way with him, and was pretty sure this contributed to my bad mood. Last night, he'd come back to my house and eaten dinner with me, Emma, and Rex. And since I hadn't told Emma anything about a relationship existing between Hank and me, I wasn't going to go home with him after. We ended up back at the station to work late with Sian, researching the sidhé fae, every myth and legend I could get my hands on concerning the First Ones and their Disciples, and the ITF database for Charbydons in the city (and beyond) who were old enough and powerful enough to beg, blackmail, or threaten into helping me.

Lost cause, really.

I'd made enemies of the two most powerful Charbydons in the city: Grigori Tennin and the Master Crafter of Atlanta, the ghoul, Nuallan Gow. Hank was willing to put his life on the line to fight Sachâth, and Pen had an ulterior motive he thought was worth the risk, but there was no Charbydon who'd be willing to do anything of the sort. In fact, they'd stand on the sidelines cheering Sachâth for the win.

The following morning, I was tired and cranky as I sat at the kitchen table eating a bowl of cereal, not looking forward to starting yet another day of endless frustration and roadblocks. Soon Sachâth would come whether I used my power or not. I had to be prepared, had to face it on my own terms. I had to win.

*The Creator didn't account for everything.*

I kept coming back to those words Sandra wrote in her letter. I felt certain she was telling me Sachâth wasn't perfect. There was a flaw in the First One assassin, the flaw being, in my opinion, that it was only created to kill First Ones. Not other beings. Sure, the fail-safes were there, but had those other races been taken into account? They were only in their infancy, not even a blip on the radar during the time of the First Ones. Had the Creator taken into account that ages later those "blips" would become intelligent and powerful?

I was sure I was on the right track, but I hit a wall when it came to the Charbydon issue.

Emma flounced down the stairs, dropped her backpack in the middle of the kitchen floor, grabbed a bowl and spoon, and then slid into a chair at the table. She grabbed the cereal and milk from the middle of the table and poured. After her first bite, she said, "So?"

"So what?"

"Mom." The expectant look she gave me was wan and no-nonsense, and very much like . . . me. "The problem. What is it, what's bugging you? We only have fifteen minutes, so be quick."

I returned her look, shaking my head, and deciding to play along. "Okay. Fine. Say you had a project where you had to draw on power. Not just any power, but the arcane energy from each world, really primal stuff. So three different sources. And you have Earth and Elysia covered, but not Charbydon."

She chewed thoughtfully for less than ten seconds before she said, "Simple."

I smiled. "Oh, is it?"

"Yeah." She flipped her spoon until it was pointing to the ceiling. "You just take it from the darkness overhead. It's all raw energy from Charbydon anyway."

And just like that my twelve-year-old kid floored me. *Floored.* I dropped my spoon, clattering milk and cereal all over the table. My mouth hung open and she just looked at me, then around the room. "What?" she asked, cheeks full of cereal.

"Nothing. Nothing." I grabbed the spoon and bowl, standing up, shaking. "You're just . . . that's just . . . genius. And right. It's right."

Her mouth split into a smile, and she continued chewing cheerfully, completely in bliss at being right. After she swallowed, she said in a very aristocratic tone, "I shall mark this day down in the annals of the Madigan Family Saga. The day Emma Riley Garrity, the *Genius,* was right. Right, I tell you! Right, I say! Right, right, right!" She punched her spoon into the air with each word.

Rex shuffled into the kitchen, all sleepy and grumbly. "Right. Whatever. Coffee. Emma. Stop being happy. It's too early for happy."

She laughed and resumed shoveling cereal into her mouth as I stood at the sink, rinsing my bowl out, amazed and embarrassed that I'd been so intent on the Charbydon races that I'd missed the obvious hovering right over my head.

And I didn't need a Charbydon to use the darkness, just like Pen didn't need to be human to draw out Earth's energy. All one needed was strength, knowledge, and a shitload of power.

"Rex," I said, turning to eye him. "I don't suppose you know any jinn rituals for calling down or commanding the darkness, do you?"

He shut the fridge and gave me the blandest expression, like I was wasting breath even asking him such a ridiculous question. One that didn't even warrant an answer.

Well, I had to give it a shot. But I was already well on my way to solving the problem because I knew another who had manipulated the darkness. Llyran, the level-ten felon who had stolen a tome from the Adonai's Hall of Records, one that told him exactly how to command the darkness.

And guess who had that book? The Druid King.

I wiped the table, kissed Emma on the cheek. "Hurry up, we need to get going."


After dropping Emma off at school, I placed a call to Hank, filling him in on Emma's brilliance, then to Pen to let him know we were on our way.

As I parked by the curb near the 10th Street entrance of the Grove, Hank ducked out of his car and my belly went light. I ignored the feeling, turned off the engine, and got out.

Hank approached as I shoved one side of my hair behind my ear and locked my vehicle. I slipped my keys into my pocket. My mark grew warmer. The darkness overhead made me tingle. And my heart rate rose at the idea of facing Sachâth again. *Ugh. Talk about edgy.* And it was only going to get worse.

"Morning," Hank's rich voice broke the quiet.

I drew in a deep, steadying breath and turned. "Morning." I continued, stepping past him and onto the sidewalk. "Sure you're ready for this?"

His answer was a casual shrug as he fell in step beside me. "You call Leander yet?"

I stopped. Hank walked a few more steps before turning around with an eyebrow lifted in question. "Hank, are you really sure about this? Sachâth might be designed to kill First Ones, but it'll attack anything if provoked." And that meant Hank and Pen were as much a target as I'd be.

He took three long strides, coming to stand directly in front of me, so that I had to lift my chin to look him in the eye. "Were you sure when you left the city to find me?" Of course I was. I didn't even need to think about it. I nodded. "It's the same thing, Charlie. We defeated my demons, now we defeat yours." He tossed a look over his shoulder toward the gate. "Come on."

We fell in step again. Hank asked again if I'd called Leander. "Not yet. I want to make sure I can read the tome and do what Llyran did. If I can, then we're all set and should do this as soon as possible. Pen's meeting us at the henge."

Sometimes, when it was sunny beyond the darkness, a little light would filter through, leaving the daytime looking like a dark, dark thunderstorm was approaching, but this morning it must've been cloudy and overcast because it was black as night outside.

The Grove had become a creepy place since the darkness had parked itself over the city, but now—knowing what I needed to do—it looked downright scary. The ever-present flashes of green snaked through the swirling mass overhead, and the city lights beyond the park bathed Oak Hill in light.

We veered off the main path and walked up the grassy hill to an exact replica of what Stonehenge looked like when it was completed in ancient times. The monoliths were colossal and seemed to grow higher as we went up the hill; they dwarfed us and everything around us.

Pen stood in the center of the henge, the tome spread out on the altar stone in front of him. As I stepped into the circle, a slight vibration of energy went through me. I came up next to the Druid and stared down at the ancient tome, one of the histories of Elysia.

The writing on the pages was a blending of early Elysian, a bridge between the language of the First Ones and the language of the Adonai, which then evolved into the modern Elysian language used by most of the races of that world today. In other words, a bitch to read. There weren't many people who could.

But I tried to remain optimistic. Llyran had figured it out. And Pen had been in possession of the tome since the battle on Helios Tower. He'd been studying it, trying to decipher the language and the commands Llyran had used to control the darkness.

"Here," Pen said, passing me an amulet. "I've been wearing this to aid in the translation. It should work for you, too. Try it."

I placed the amulet over my head, let it rest against my skin, and felt its heat snake into my body. It took a minute, but eventually, the words on the tome took shape, some of which I could understand, some of which I couldn't. "It's not working all the way."

Damn it. This *had* to work. Why wasn't it working?

"You read the stone tablet in Fiallan, right?" Hank reminded me. "How did you manage that, how did you understand the words?"

"I only read it; I never understood the words. I don't know . . . this is different writing, though, so maybe . . . Before I used my power. Not anything big, but just . . . engaged it, I guess you could say."

"Try using your power with the amulet," Pen said.

Hank leaned closer to me, our shoulders touching. "Just be careful. Don't draw too much. We're not ready for war just yet."

I wasn't ready for war at all.

I centered myself, drew in a deep, even breath, and

closed my eyes, imagining a pinprick of light appearing in my core that worked like a magnet, pulling power from my cells and creating a small well of energy swirling inside me.

Then I opened my eyes. Words reshaped themselves through my vision much quicker than I expected and I understood some of what I saw. "It's working," I whispered.

I began flipping carefully through the old pages, until I found what I was looking for and what I knew now were the same words Llyran had read to manipulate the darkness.

If only I could test it first . . .

I released the energy, careful to bank it within my core rather than let it go outside of myself where Sachâth lived. "I need to call Leander." I slid a glance at the two powerful beings staring down at me from lofty heights. "Are we ready to do this?"

They both nodded.

Goose bumps spread over my skin. "Sachâth won't sense Ahkneri being this close?" I asked Pen.

"The agate has masked her power for thousands of years. There is a reason she chose that sarcophagus. The water adds a layer of insulation as well." He crossed his arms over his chest and parked a weighty stare on me. "So what's the plan, Detective?"

Thirty minutes and about a hundred *I can't believe I'm doing this* mantras later, I stood in front of Hank.

Leander and Pen were over by the altar, arms folded over their chests, feet planted, eyeing each other suspiciously and curiously. They'd been at it for at least three minutes.

"All set, kiddo?" Hank asked, flicking the ends of my hair and smiling a crooked smile.

"I'm pretty fucking scared right now, Hank." A gazillion second thoughts ran through my head, along with every single thing that could go wrong. And I tried like mad *not* to imagine someone walking up to my front door, telling my kid I'd failed. I was gone. But the thought remained a shadow in the back of my mind.

*Shit, shit, shit.*

"It's a good plan, Charlie. The oracle is never wrong. She wouldn't have said those things if there wasn't a way to kill it. She wouldn't have written you that letter and led you down this path. We'll win because we were meant to win."

I frowned up at him, wondering if he really believed that or he was just saying it to boost my confidence. He cupped my face in his big hands, leaned down slowly, and kissed me gently. I grabbed his jacket and pulled him closer, trying to brand the feeling onto my soul. In case I didn't make it, in case the only thing left of me was energy and memories.

Hank drew me into a hug, just holding me as tight as he could, and I knew he was doing the same as I was, committing me to memory. Just in case.

We stepped back at the same time. "Thank you."

If I didn't get to say it after, I was saying it now, so he knew how much this meant to me, this . . . standing by my side.

I took my place at the altar where I could read from the book. Pen walked to the largest trilithon, the center stone set in a horseshoe ring of five that stood within the circle. It was directly across from the altar stone, making Pen and me face-to-face over the distance. Hank and Leander took up places about ten feet away from each end of the altar stone, facing toward it.

*Here we go.*

Pen began first, feet braced apart, clasping his hands together in front of him and bowing his head as though at church. It was such a familiar stance; it took me by surprise. And then the familiarity ended. The intensity of the henge rose until pain flowed through my eardrums. It was like standing inside a heartbeat—Earth's, to be exact. The center trilithon behind him began to glow and soon every monolith and capstone had taken on a soft gray light.

When the Druid lifted his head and opened his eyes, they were the same color as the stones. *And that's why he's called the Druid King,* my inner voice said in awe.

Next came Hank. I glanced over, heart pounding now. His eyes connected with mine. He closed his fist, and the shimmering golden light began like it had before. The lopsided grin he shot me said, *Yeah, I know it's cool.* I smiled. Show-off. His grin widened. His hand brightened. Light flooded through his veins, a beautiful web of primal golden power.

I turned to Leander, not really knowing what the hell he was going to do or what power he planned on using. Or, hell, maybe he'd just come to watch. He just stood there, arms folded, and cocked an unimpressed eyebrow at me. Whatever. Guess it was my turn.

*Dear Lord, please get me through this.*

According to the tome, once I read the words, I need do nothing more than use my intention to command the darkness. I drew on my power like I'd done before. The words took shape and I opened myself up, allowing my power to grow and brighten and consume me. Hot and cold stung my insides as everything came together, and then hummed with crystal clarity and unity.

I vibrated with energy. The symbols on my arm began their strange bluish glow. *Accept yourself. Make yourself whole. Make the shadow whole.* I was Charbydon, Elysian, Human, Divine. Not one or two, but all. It was time to accept every part of me and let go of the past and the fears, to stop clinging to my humanity and the shadows of my former self. The barriers I'd built had to come down. *This is who I am now. I accept it. I welcome it. I seize it by the fucking balls and bend it to my will.*

I felt the break, the snap of final resistance giving way. I burned, but the burn felt good, strangely . . . right.

*I know who I am now.*

When I opened my mouth to issue my commands, there was enough force behind them that Sachâth would notice.

I tilted my head back, shouting the words into the sky. With intent, I commanded the darkness to move, to swirl like a hurricane. Bottle green flashes snaked like lightning through the undulating gray as its motion began to realign, slow and slumberous, a giant waking. I'd been inside that mass, courtesy of Llyran, and knew millions of tiny particles of raw energy were there for the taking.

Leander finally looked suitably impressed. But then his attention snapped off to the left. Fuck. Incoming. The sonic boom rent the air and shook the ground. Adrenaline pumped through my veins swift and strong.

I held on to the altar. Death was here.

# 21

A jagged shroud of gray hovered over the henge and then floated down, coming together into form as it landed on solid feet. A solid being. Like I'd seen in Ahkneri's dream. I swallowed, using my intent to summon the darkness, to draw it together and build its energy, bringing those tiny sandlike particles together over the henge.

*Make the shadow whole.*

*Together, together. But not by your hand.*

It stood between me and Pen, blocking the Druid King from my sight. The altar I stood behind created a barrier, but that was just an illusion in my head—nothing was going to keep Sachâth from advancing, altar or not.

No longer needing the book, I closed it slowly. All I had to use now was my focus and intention. I backed away from the altar. It advanced. My hair stirred. I wanted to look up, but didn't. I shoved away the images from the vision and pulled the darkness down, imagining it as a sliver, a thread pulled from the swirling mass above.

Sachâth spoke and the force, the power behind it, sent me back two steps. Oh, yeah, it was definitely going to strike. There was no confusion, no curiosity, or frustration in its ancient tone this time.

I backed away as it strode forward. It jumped onto the altar and when it did, I yelled, "Now!"

With everything I had, every bit of will I possessed, I commanded the darkness into Sachâth, imagining it shooting forward like a rocket, the mass above forcing it down, sending all those particles of energy into the blow. At the same time, Pen stepped back and the trilithon swallowed him whole; the only thing I could see was his outline, which brightened, and then the staggering power of Mother Earth shot out from him/the stone and hit Sachâth from behind as the darkness hit its chest.

An eerie scream popped my ears.

It floated up and onto the altar, intending to step down and continue on its driven path to assassinate me. But it was hit by an arc of brilliant gold. Sachâth's shadows wreathed like snakes around its body. The female face elongated, eyes going hollow, mouth turning black, then gray, then translucent.

My arm went hot. My power wanted out. It pushed at me, begging, needing to fight. It craved battle on a level that felt inherent. *No.* I couldn't strike the blow or I'd *become* Sachâth. Didn't matter that I had no weapon; my arm *was* the weapon.

The three primal powers snaked over Sachâth, battering against the Creator's divine power. The creature writhed and screamed, but it wasn't dying.

Panic cracked my focus. I glanced at Leander. Or where he'd once stood.

Leander was gone.

*What the fuck?*

My heart hammered until it was all I heard. Power pulsed through me. I had to regain focus. Calm down. I looked up at the darkness, struck by how angry and alive it seemed, how a huge arm of it had reached down and curled around Sachâth, pushing at it, trying to get inside. *More. Fill it up. Tear it apart.*

Hank's power glowed from the center of Sachâth's chest, like a bright flame trying to eat its way inside, trying to destroy. And yet it was getting nowhere.

My arm lifted on instinct. I forced it back down. Goddammit. But I remembered. I could wound it, take out its legs, and weaken it. I renewed my command on the darkness and then zeroed in on the creature. *Yes, strike,* my power urged, compelling me, building until my arm went completely numb. I lifted my hand and blasted the fucker.

It hit Sachâth in the ankles and split the altar stone with a booming crack. The creature buckled and fell in a shower of divine light. Its screams filled my head. Oh yeah, it was wounded.

As if sensing weakness, Pen, now in dragon form, shot from the blinding light of the stone. His large black body came at Sachâth talons first, his muscled legs outstretched, talons curved like razor-sharp scythes. He slammed into the creature, claws sinking deep into the chest. The force sent them tumbling. It was quick and vicious. Sachâth's shadows snapped and stabbed and constricted. Pen bit and ravaged with fangs and talons. Hank surged forward as Sachâth righted itself, floating above the ground. Pen went tumbling across the grass and struck one of the outer monoliths. The glow in the center trilithon went weaker, but power surged through the other stones and brightened where Pen had landed, filling him up again. The dragon's eyes popped open. He righted himself, crouched, and let out an angry roar.

Shadows sliced and jabbed around Hank, but he was preternaturally quick. He would've made an awesome Disciple, I thought in a weird moment of observation. And then Pen was back in the fray, and the siren and the dragon faced off against Death as I kept my focus on the darkness.

If I could wound it again . . .

But then in a burst of clarity, I had another idea. I sent an order to the darkness. I'd strike a nonlethal blow, and the darkness would attach itself, ride with my power straight into Sachâth's body. Hank's power was already trying to fulfill its destructive purpose. With the Charbydon energy also inside . . . They'd blow Sachâth sky high. Hopefully.

A shadow pierced Hank's thigh, through the front and straight out the back. He faltered, going down on one knee as another sliver rose up to take his head. Pen struck, using his tail to knock Hank out of the way. The shadow redirected, slicing through Pen's wing. The roar that followed . . . I blanched, knowing Pen was seriously wounded.

Sweat rolled down my back as I gave everything I had to growing the divine power inside me and keeping the darkness attacking Sachâth. Hank forced himself up, but Sachâth was quick. It used its shadows like thin razor-sharp slivers and pierced Hank's body in multiple places, pinning him into the grass.

*No!*

In instant reaction, I threw everything I had at the creature. Sachâth's head came up as my power slammed into its shoulder. A tendril of darkness shot through with my power, entering Sachâth's wound like a rocket.

Enraged, Sachâth released Hank and advanced, determined to kill me. It stumbled, but kept moving. It was being eaten from the inside out and yet it fought; its power staggering.

Well, fuck it. I was enraged, too.

It screamed at me and I screamed back, moving toward it. But arms enveloped me and lifted me off my feet. "No, Charlie. Don't." Leander.

"Get off me, you coward!"

"Coward." He laughed. "I'd like nothing better than to fight, but this kill belongs to another." He held me so tightly I couldn't breathe. "Just watch."

Sachâth's steps slowed. It turned its head away from me as though sensing something. Leander released me. And I swear to fucking God a knight walked into the circle. No, not a knight. A Disciple. "We must move quickly," Leander said.

The Disciple intercepted Sachâth, and what I'd seen in my vision was ten times more stunning in reality. The speed and precision was . . . unbelievable. "Charlie!" Leander hissed.

I turned as Leander shoved the lid off a long agate box. Power swamped me like a wave and continued on through the circle, dissipating as it went. A quick glance told me that Sachâth felt it, too. It started for us, but the Disciple intercepted again.

Leander bent down and pulled a divine sword from the box. He was *touching* a divine sword, hand wrapped around the hilt, the blade pointing down. And he wasn't dying. I didn't have much time to digest that when he started for me, tossing me the blade. Heart in my throat, I caught it on instinct. Heat seared my skin and shot through my arm, my symbols flaring bright, so bright they were no longer blue but white. My power ignited, wrapping around the weapon, joining.

Leander grabbed me by both shoulders and turned me toward the battle. "Sachâth is wounded. Get close. As soon as it falters, give the sword to the Disciple, he'll know what to do."

Hank was back up fighting, but he was wounded

and his energy would soon wane. He'd used the Destruction Source Word. He wouldn't last long before he was completely depleted.

"Do it. Or we all die."

With each step, calm settled over me. Sachâth's head whipped up. It was eager to meet me, to get the job done. I was its target, not the Disciple.

Sachâth sent Hank flying. He crashed into one of the trilithons. The Disciple's head turned toward me, a golden flash in his eyes barely visible from the slit in his visor.

As I strode, I gathered momentum, using it to lift the heavy sword off the ground and on my last step, I swung with all my might.

Shadows blocked my strike. A sliver snaked out and pierced my side. The Disciple pressed. *Just wound it, get it on the ground.* I did my best, giving in to the strange sense of urging from my power. To fight. To move. Block. And strike. Like it knew how to dance this dance.

Shadows pierced me as I spun; one jabbed into my hip, the other into my shoulder. I screamed and swung out in a wide arc, slicing through its torso, and kept going until I was back around again, facing it and about to shove the sword into its gut, when the Disciple's armored hand clamped down on my wrist.

His eyes met mine through the visor. Hard. Unreadable. And yet calm, like he had long ago accepted his fate. In one smooth motion, he grabbed the sword.

He couldn't grab the sword or he'd die. *What the hell's he doing?* But I already knew. He'd hold it long enough.

He shoved me back as a shadow pierced through his neck and came out the other side. The hand that held the sword began to burn, the armor turning red and hot. A deep bellow echoed from him as he hefted the sword, and spun, shoving the sword into Sachâth's heart.

I fell to my knees, cushioned by the soft grass, and grabbed my side. But it was my hip that made my stomach turn; the shadow had hit bone . . .

Sachâth didn't scream. In fact, it went eerily silent. Its writhing, deadly shadows stilled. The Disciple didn't let go of the sword. *Let go.*

Together, the Disciple and Death fell backward. Sachâth landed on its back, the shadows evaporating, leaving behind the First One, the female I'd seen in Ahkneri's vision—the one who had killed the Sachâth before her. The Disciple landed partway on top of her. His hand was already gone, along with half of his forearm, the divine power eating away at him. Despite the pain I knew he felt, he rose up and ripped his helmet off with his other hand.

Golden hair, long to his shoulders. He turned, nodded gravely to a point over my shoulder. Leander stood there, his face stony as he nodded back. He radiated power, emotion, even though there was none to be seen on his face.

The Disciple turned back to the First One. No one

had to tell me. I knew now that he was her Disciple. That he'd been the one taken to safety by Ahkneri when the First One killed Sachâth. And now he had his revenge.

He touched her face as she blinked up at him. His shoulder was gone now, eaten up by divine flame, and yet he didn't cry out, determined to see her, to make her see him. Jesus. My throat thickened.

She lifted her hand, smiled, and cupped his cheek, and then the fire consumed his neck and head, and he was gone as her hand flopped to the ground and her head fell to the side.

Time seemed to pause for that one unbelievable moment. And then her body jerked, arcing as power shot from her, screaming out and exploding. It hit me before I could blink.

I came awake to a blurry vision looming above me. My throat was so dry it was hard to work my mouth, to speak. A hand smacked my cheek, none too gently.

Leander's face came into focus.

He moved away and I watched as he retrieved the sword lying by the broken altar stone and took it back to the agate box. With extreme effort, I rolled to my side, took a breather, and then sat up, my back against a chunk of broken stone. Hank. Where was Hank?

I found him not far from me on his back. He groaned and let out a soft curse.

Leander knelt down and slid the lid into place. As soon as he did, a vacuum of . . . normalcy fell over the henge.

Done.

Sachâth was gone. A disbelieving laugh bubbled out of me.

Leander hefted the box, which had to weigh a couple hundred pounds, onto his shoulder, balancing it with one hand. He approached, stopping at my feet. "Nice work, Detective. You and your friends have done what the Archons could not."

"How?" How was it even possible that we had done it, and they—some of the most powerful beings ever created—hadn't?

"Because they never had that kind of backup before. There were no Druid Kings, no henges, no powerful sirens back then who could wound Sachâth or hold it off long enough to allow a Disciple to strike a suicide blow. You don't think they tried?" He shrugged and said simply, "We had to wait until such a time came . . ."

"We?"

He waved the question away. "We. The world. All of us with a stake in the future. But this day, this day we won, and my brother had his revenge."

"Your brother. He was your brother."

Leander paused. "Brother. Son. Father. Don't seek to know my world, Charlie Madigan. You won't like what you find."

"His revenge cost him his life."

"His revenge set Asaria free."

"He loved her."

Leander shrugged. "That, too. You woke him by reading the tablet. Your power led him here to take his revenge. It was his to take, not mine."

"What are you, Leander? Disciple or First One?"

His mouth dipped down. "We'll have to work on your listening skills."

"You touched the sword."

"I did. Try not to let it keep you up at night."

Hank's groan drew our attention as he pulled himself to a sitting position, plowed his fingers through his hair, and then surveyed the scene. "We actually pulled it off," he said, amazed.

"You and your siren will be seeing more of me," Leander said to me. "Plenty of time to beat your brains out over who and what I am. Remember what I told you in Fiallan, Charlie? The shit storm is coming. And suddenly here I am with a divine being and the only siren in existence who can wield two of the most powerful Source Words ever created. The question is, what I am going to do with you?" He regarded us with cunning in his golden eyes. "I'll be in touch."

He walked away.

"I'm not the only divine being around, you know," I called after him. "And Sachâth is gone . . ."

Leander spun around, his face dark. "You'd better pray Ahkneri never rises, for if she does I will end her once and for all."

With that he turned and strode out of the fallen henge.

Too exhausted to think about Leander's words, I let my head fall against the rock behind me and closed my eyes. After a time had passed, I rolled from a sitting position to my front and belly crawled slowly over the grass to where Hank sat, one leg out, one drawn up with his arms resting over his knee. His head hung low. His side was bleeding badly and his thigh was drenched in blood.

I collapsed next to him, struggling to catch my breath before rolling onto my back and scooting up to sit. Several nymphs stood outside the henge, all with pale, stunned faces. And that's when it registered. "Holy cow." The henge was down. Every stone but one had fallen outward, blown out by the force of Sachâth's death.

The only stone that remained standing was the middle trilithon. And it still glowed a faint, strange gray . . . For a moment it seemed to brighten and then dim as a shadow filled it and Pen stepped out.

He strode over until his foot was inches from mine and glared down at us. "I thought you were wounded," I said.

He rolled his eyes, then one eyebrow arched. "Druid King."

I laughed through the pain. Arrogant bastard. "Sorry about your henge," I said, glancing around.

"They can be raised." He stared at the broken altar stone, then at me. He held out his hand, and for a moment I thought he was offering to help me up, but he said, "My amulet."

Hank reached over, lifted it from my neck, and tossed it to Pen. "I'm keeping the tome," Pen told us. "You have one more week to figure out who murdered Killian. I'm tired of waiting." With that he strode out of the circle and the nymphs turned and followed him.

Hank looked at the trilithon in envy, and I knew he was thinking about how easily Pen had healed. "Guess it's good to be king, huh?" he said, gruffly.

"Yeah. No doubt." I stared up at what little darkness remained. Powerful stuff, that. "You going to crash like you did last time?" I asked Hank. Using power words sapped sirens of strength and energy, causing them to fall into sleep, a deep sleep while their bodies recuperated from the intensive drain.

The limp hand hanging over his knee turned, so that the brand on his palm was visible. He stared at it a long time.

"Probably," he answered. "Last time I used one of the Source Words, Panopé gave me back all the energy it took to use it, or at least I think she did. But using it feels different than the normal words we use."

"Different how?"

He scrubbed a hand down his face, and then stared off into nothing. "I don't know. More natural, easier in some ways . . . It's part of me like my regular power never was."

"Well," I said thoughtfully, "Source Words are

supposed to be innate to specific sirens, so maybe that's why. It's part of your makeup, your niche. Destruction and Creation are your things. Which"—I slid him a pained smile—"is hot, by the way. I think you should create me a vacation."

Hank chuckled. "I'll work on it. That whole *divine being* thing is pretty hot, too. And you with a sword?" He rubbed his chest and grinned. "Sexy as hell."

I rolled my eyes. But talking like this helped distract from the pain, made it bearable.

"You gonna be okay while I'm out?" he asked.

I was about to answer him, but then it struck me and struck me hard. What we'd done . . . "We did it, Hank. It's over."

He smiled down at me, the crooked smile of his that made my chest feel light, yet tight at the same time. Then he leaned over and kissed my forehead. "We sure did, angel face."

I laughed, wincing as the movement jarred my side. "Ha. I draw the line at any and all divinity jokes."

"Aw, c'mon. I was just getting started."

"You know what else?" I said, filled with happiness. "What?"

"I can bring back the sun."

# 22

"If you want to live long enough to see the light of day, then you'd better unhand the snickerdoodles." Rex glared at me.

I grinned with my mouth full, chewing—and savoring every bite of—the snickerdoodles Rex had made for our picnic at Stone Mountain. I swallowed. "Since I happen to be the one bringing the light, I think I'll live."

The happiness and sense of wholeness I felt was still a bit of a novelty. Hank was back. Sachâth was dead. The darkness overhead was about to be lifted. And I'd come into my divine powers. They weren't exactly the same as the First Ones', but they were close enough, and I was more certain than ever I had the sylphs to thank for bringing my powers together and making the transition easier. That day I'd been buried under the ground, embraced by the earth, I knew *something* had happened . . .

Rex spread out the second picnic blanket on a flat area of granite while Hank played Frisbee with Emma, Brim, and Amanda. Apparently, all Hank had needed was three days of rest and he was back to his old, insanely beautiful self. Though if he didn't stop making "halo" and "angel" jokes, I was going to hurt him. But he was mine—another novelty I was still getting used to. He wanted a relationship, no matter how fast or slow I wanted to take it. He was here for the long haul; I knew that without him ever having to say a word.

Aaron and Bryn sat on the other blanket talking with Marti and Titus, who were now officially a couple. Titus was still in the process of identifying the properties of the liquid found in Leander's cylinder. His goal was to reproduce it and then put it through a series of tests before trying it on the *ash* addicts. It was a slow process since the substance was off-world and unknown to our scientists. But if all went well, then maybe, just maybe, we might have a viable cure in the days or weeks to come.

While Rex wasn't looking, I stole another snickerdoodle and popped it into my mouth as Liz, Sian, and the chief emerged from the trail and out onto the massive rocky landscape of the mountain. Since the darkness had spread itself over the city, the Summit Skyride, which offered a cable car ride to the top of Stone Mountain, had cut their hours of operation in half. Still, people liked to come up here to get a closer look at the darkness or to see the city lights of Atlanta in the distance.

I gave them a wave, thinking for the hundredth time how I could strangle Rex for telling everyone what I was about to do and then turning it into a family outing. I'd wanted to come to Stone Mountain because it was high, about eight hundred feet or so, and got me close to the darkness without, say, standing on top of a skyscraper—been there, done that, and wasn't doing it again. The massive exposed piece of granite was a prime spot to watch today's success or failure.

I still had control of the darkness. It was mine until I released it. I stood, wiped my hands on my jeans, and got ready to start the show. Hank came up behind me. "You ready to do this thing, angel cake?"

I turned and glared up at him. But it didn't last long because the blinding, bad-boy grin he gave me struck me like a gale-force wind. His irises shifted into topaz blue. He leaned down close, his nose nearly brushing mine. "Tonight. My place. Bring the damned jewels."

The breath left me. It took me a moment to find my voice, one that meant to say something insanely witty, but all I said was, "What about the gown?"

His grin grew deeper. His mouth brushed past my cheek to my ear, and he dropped his voice down to a level of potent, blatant lust. "You won't be needing the gown."

I blinked as a wave of heat shuddered down my body. He slipped his hand in mine. So maybe the relationship part would progress slowly, but the intimate part was already blazing a trail across the sky. And I wasn't complaining.

We stood at an area of the rock where it began to slope gently downward. Emma held my left hand, Hank held my right. Rex stood next to Emma with his arm around her shoulder, Brim standing between them. The others had gathered around us. I felt Bryn behind me, squeezing my shoulder.

It was now or never.

I gazed at the massive, tumbling waves of darkness, suddenly sad to see it go, which was weird enough for me to not delve into. Atlanta needed the sun back. The plants and animals, the people, needed the light. Hank and Emma squeezed my hand at the same time.

I grinned down at my daughter as she smiled up at me with a look of such belief and happiness.

*Deep breath. Focus with intention. Command the darkness back to Charbydon.*

Goose bumps lifted the tiny hairs on my arms. The tingling feeling traveled, engulfing me. The once forty miles of darkness was now less than half its size, thanks to events at the henge. Still large by all accounts, though, so it was a slow start as the behemoth began to swirl in one direction.

As it moved it eventually began to thin, the outer edges of it thinning first and finally disappearing until it grew smaller and smaller and smaller, revealing blue sky until there was just a shadow left over the sun.

I held my breath, heart pounding.

And then . . . sunlight. Gorgeous, warm sunlight burst through the last of the shadows and blinded us.

*He strode down the path leading to the Druid's temple in the Grove. The sun had already set, making the way dark and familiar—the usual. Ahead of him Charlie and Rex walked side by side. He could hear the soft murmurs of their voices as they drifted back to him. They didn't know he was behind them yet, but the closer he came, Charlie would know, would feel her mark warm. He was late, had meant to meet them at the gate. More evidence had been discovered along the lake and they needed Rex to take a look.*

*He was too far away to see Charlie clearly, but he saw enough. Dressed for work in cargos, light leather jacket, no doubt armed to the teeth . . . God, she was tough. And beautiful. And so fucking fragile of heart it made his chest hurt. The way she'd surprised him last night . . . He hadn't thought she'd actually show up. With the jewels. He loved those damned jewels.*

*He'd felt her shyness, though she'd die before admitting it. He'd felt her fear, too. Fear of getting her heart broken again. If only she knew the lengths he'd go to see that never happened . . .*

*She'd stood on his doorstep, a sparkling anklet dangling from her raised finger, those bow-shaped lips twisted into a brazen smile. And he'd been lost. Sucker punched.*

*Charlie. Bare skin. Jewels. Cavewoman talk.*

*His pulse leapt at the memory. Blood diverted. Down boy.*

*He was walking alone, in the dark, smiling like a goddamned idiot. And it felt good.*

*Last night, he slept without dreams, without nightmares and reminders, and this morning, he woke with . . . hope.*

*Ashton Perry, ITF detective and champion dickhead, headed down the path toward Charlie and Rex. Hank could feel the guy's rage even from this distance. Charlie liked to fight her own battles, but this was one he'd love to fight for her, to end the racist comments and sneers. The bastard needed to get a fucking life and move on. The case had been officially moved back to their department and, as expected, "Asston" had had a hissy fit. He was probably here to brownnose the Druid and convince Pen that he was better off with Asston on the case.*

*Hank's long stride covered ground and he'd gotten close enough to hear the exchange as Asston approached Charlie with his hands clenched at his sides—no doubt Pen had sent him packing, which would explain the higher than usual anger. "Druid's a fucking dick, so I'm sure you two have lots in common, Madigan."*

*"Bite me, Asston," Charlie shot back.*

*"They couldn't pay me enough to get that close to you."* *Asston slammed his shoulder against Charlie's as he passed. Hank's fists clenched tightly. "Where's your partner? Siren orgy at the Bath House?" he called over his shoulder.*

*Charlie turned. "Why? Jealous?"*

*"Yeah, right. How's it been, Madigan, slumming with an off-worlder?" Asston laughed and then turned back*

*toward the path where his face plowed into the wall that was Hank's fist.*

*Asston spun, already unconscious before he hit the ground.*

*Sweet fucking satisfaction flowed through Hank's body as he gazed unmercifully down and then stepped over the unconscious asshole on the ground.*

*"Nicely done," Rex said as Hank approached.*

*"Felt good, too," he replied in a deep timbre that he knew would get under Charlie's skin. He stopped in front of her. She gazed up at him with humor glinting in her eyes and he couldn't help himself. "So, how's it been?" His grin went lopsided. "Slumming with an off-worlder?"*

*She tried to hide her smile, and again there was that punch to the gut. "I wouldn't know," she lied for Rex's benefit.*

*He dipped his face close to her ear. "Want to find out?"*

*"Oh, geez! Get a room!" Rex cried, slapping his hands over his ears.*

*Charlie's laughter filled the Grove, sinking into his being and filling it with that sense of hope again. He thought suddenly of Fiallan, where he could be king, could rule and demand satisfaction for the wrongs done to him . . .*

*He shoved his hands in his pockets. To hell with being king. He was right where he wanted to be.*

# Acknowledgments

Deepest thanks and warmest regards to my readers for their continued support and kindness, to my family for putting up with the Deadline Crazies, and to my friends for sticking by me and remembering who I am after the writing-inspired hibernation/absences.

Much thanks to Megan McKeever for the excellent edit and to Miriam Kriss for keeping the business wheels turning.

But most of all, to my editor, Ed Schlesinger, who gets my work, trusts in my storytelling, and helps me make sense of it all when I can't, and who gave me the gift of time—a *lot* of time. Thank you!

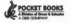